Andre Nguyen Van Chau  and spirituality of one of the gre dinal Van Thuan was not only a of Cardinals, but he remains a vi the Church because of the way h Crucified Christ.

He is an icon of the Vietnamese Catholic Church: Francis Xavier Nguyen Van Thuan. The lines of his story tell of a country and a people torn by the horror of violence and war brought on by their struggle for independence. His is an unapologetically political spirituality that is cultivated, nurtured, and sustained by the riches of the Catholic tradition. Written at the late Cardinal's own request, this biography charts the footsteps of a man who walked the long road of hope, urging us on to hope amidst the darkness of our own time and place.

Van Thuan survived a nightmare in human history and transformed it into a dream for a future of the Church and of humanity. A story unbelievably complex, a message incredibly simple: hope alive in one person can reform the world. A book for anyone who needs to keep their courage alive...

The power of simplicity is witnessed both in the life of this holy man and in its narrative. Written in a straightforward, unadorned style, which only serves to underscore and complement the intensity of Cardinal Van Thuan's message, *The Miracle of Hope* takes us on an inspirational journey, accompanied by both detailed descriptions of the natural beauty that blessed his beloved, strife-torn homeland of Vietnam, and the extraordinary spiritual beauty that radiated from within his soul. Thuan's motto, "Do not turn spiritual values into material possessions," is one we would do well to heed, and the triumph of his hope, despite the numerous trials he was asked to endure, is the miracle Cardinal Van Thuan has passed on to humankind.

Cardinal Van Thuan's greatest heritage is the Gospel in the purity of its message: a message of love and of reconciliation. Even to his last breath, he breathed this Gospel, which was the tranquil force of his entire life.

—*His Eminence*
Cardinal Roger Etchegaray
President Emeritus
Pontifical Council for Justice and Peace

I have been deeply moved by the example and writings of Cardinal Van Thuan. Any reader with Christian values will find in his biography and writings a new insight into Christian faith, hope, and charity. Having met the Cardinal on the day of his elevation to the cardinalate, I knew I was meeting someone very special. There was a certain inner light that touched everyone who spoke to him that day. I have only experienced this one time before—when I met Mother Teresa.

—*Rev. Benedict Groeschel,* CFR
Author, *Arise from Darkness*

An outstanding biography of a "prisoner and prophet," *The Miracle of Hope* captures the culture of social awareness and information media that inspired Cardinal Van Thuan from the beginning of his life. His well-honed skill at discerning the difference between truth and falsehood in national and world affairs was due, in great part, to his mother. Cardinal Van Thuan is a prophet for Gospel justice and peace. His story is a biography for our times.

—*Sr. Rose Pacatte,* FSP
Author, *Lights, Camera...Faith!*

Reading these pages is like making a retreat with a saint. Cardinal Van Thuan personifies the title of his book, *The Road of Hope,* written on scraps of paper, smuggled out of prison, and based wholly on Gospel passages he himself had lived. From 13 years of torture and imprisonment, 9 of them in solitary confinement, he emerges full of hope in God. From the horror of war in his native Vietnam he knows war's waste of human potential and becomes an anti-war activist devoted to the dignity of the human person. From his extraordinary life and convictions we take hope for our own time and the knowledge that in the end, only holiness matters.

—*Rev. Murray Bodo,* OFM
Author, *Poetry as Prayer: Denise Levertov*

Cardinal Nguyen Van Thuan, whom my family and I are blessed to have known personally, is now being venerated the world over as a "martyr"—that is, witness—of the Christian faith. Until now, little has been known about him in the English-speaking world except that he was President of the Pontifical Council of Justice and Peace, and through the translation of some of his books. We are grateful that now an authoritative biography is available for English readers. It is my fervent hope that through *The Miracle of Hope,* people of all faiths will be spiritually enriched by Cardinal Thuan's message, and in particular by his living testimony to the possibility that suffering can be a source of intimate union with God and loving solidarity with one's fellow human beings.

—*Dr. Peter C. Phan*
Professor, Chair of Catholic Social Thought
Georgetown University

I am as moved in reading these stories now as I was when I first heard them, during my personal encounters with Francis Xavier Nguyen Van Thuan, which began about a year after his exile from his beloved homeland. The gentleness of this saintly figure will remain with me as long as I live. This stirring and finely written account of a man who came from a dynasty of martyrs will bring the reader into the heart of a meek soul whose strength enabled him to endure much, because he loved much. This is an ideal book to take on a retreat.

—*Rev. Robert A. Sirico*
President, The Acton Institute

THE
MIRACLE
of HOPE

Francis Xavier
Nguyen Van Thuan

Political Prisoner,
Prophet of Peace

By Andre N. Van Chau

Pauline
BOOKS & MEDIA
BOSTON

Library of Congress Cataloging-in-Publication Data

Van Chau, Andre N.
  The miracle of hope : Francis Xavier Nguyen Van Thuan, political prisoner, prophet of peace; / by Andre N. Van Chau.
      p. cm.
  ISBN 0-8198-4822-0 (pbk.)
  1. Nguyen, Francis Xavier Van Thuan, 1928–2002. 2. Political prisoners—Vietnam—Biography. 3. Cardinals—Biography. I. Title.
  BX4705.N53 V36 2003
  282'.092—dc21

                          2002015652

The Scripture quotations contained herein are from the *New Revised Standard Version Bible. Catholic Edition,* copyright © 1993 and 1989 by the Division of Christian Education of the National Council of the Churches of Christ in the U.S.A. Used by permission. All rights reserved.

Printed and published in the U.S.A. by Pauline Books & Media, 50 Saint Pauls Avenue, Boston, MA 02130-3491.

www.pauline.org

Pauline Books & Media is the publishing house of the Daughters of St. Paul, an international congregation of women religious serving the Church with the communications media.

1 2 3 4 5 6 7 8 9   11 10 09 08 07 06 05 04 03

*This book is dedicated to Sagrario, my wife,
and to my children, Andrew, Boi-Lan, Michael,
and Francis-Xavier, who have had an unshakable faith
in Cardinal Francis Xavier Nguyen Van Thuan*

*It is also dedicated to
Cardinal Nguyen Van Thuan's parents,
his brothers and sisters, and to all those
who have believed in him and drawn strength from
his presence and his words.*

Vietnam.

A country of breathtaking beauty and unrelenting tyranny, of tropical heat and passionate ideals, of powerful memories and recurring nightmares. Even today, a country little known and even less understood.

And woven into this country's history: the Ngo Dinh family, descended from Christian patriots, destined to play a part in the glory and tragedy of a beloved country in the middle of the twentieth century. Cardinal Thuan knew the weight of belonging to such a family. His dedication to peace, mercy, justice, and compassion came from a spirituality burnished by political association.

Despite the ambiguity and intrigue, the whispers of plots and of coups that surrounded his family, Thuan loved and embraced his mother and father, aunts and uncles, brothers and sisters and cousins as just that—family. Thuan saw his family as men and women who paid a high price for faithfulness to what they believed was true.

Here they are seen through Thuan's eyes—for this is his story.

CONTENTS

PART THREE

THE STORMY YEARS

PART FOUR

THE TRIUMPH OF HOPE

ACKNOWLEDGMENTS

THE AUTHOR WISHES TO ACKNOWLEDGE that he received many of the photographs included in this volume from Cardinal Thuan himself, and from Cardinal Thuan's brother, Nguyen Linh Tuyen. He would like to thank Cardinal Thuan's sisters, Thu Hong, Ham Tieu, and Anh Tuyet, for the photographs they contributed.

The author also wishes to acknowledge everyone at Pauline Books & Media for their collaboration on this project, especially Linda Salvatore Boccia, FSP, Helen Rita Lane, FSP, and Madonna Therese Ratliff, FSP.

Pauline Books & Media would like to thank Lt. Col. Richard J. Alger, USMC (Ret.), who served as a commander in Vietnam, for reviewing the text.

PROLOGUE

God made human beings straightforward,
but they have devised many schemes.

Ecclesiastes 7:29

Abraham set out with the hope to find the Promised
Land. Moses set out with the hope to free his people from
slavery. Jesus himself set out: he came down from heaven
with the hope to save mankind.

The Road to Hope,
F. X. Nguyen Van Thuan

GENTLE AND SMILING, Cardinal Francis Xavier Nguyen Van Thuan would always advance toward his visitors with both hands extended in welcome. They soon noticed that he smiled more often out of his shyness than from mirth. Yet, even when not smiling, his countenance conveyed a warmth and reassurance. People felt comfortable in his presence; they felt at home with him.

He spoke slowly, choosing his words with absolute precision. His voice was soft and his speech eloquent in its simplicity. It was obvious that his simple ideas came from a great interior depth, and for those who heard him speak, his words became an invitation to soul-searching reflection.

Cardinal Thuan never changed his manner whether he spoke to a large audience, a small group, or to one person. He began with things familiar and gradually turned them into something startlingly new. He could quickly endow the seemingly trivial, the commonplace, and things usually taken for granted with new meaning so that they became attractive subjects for contemplation and beckoned the imagination.

Those who came to know him soon realized that they would have to abandon their entrenched views and comfort zones if they wished to follow him on the same intellectual and spiritual adventure he had experienced, and enter the fresh reality his words had thrust upon them.

Indeed, those who met Cardinal Thuan very often came away richer not merely in ideas, but in entirely new perspectives. Cardinal Francis Xavier Nguyen Van Thuan seemed always ready to offer the marvelous gift of his refreshing insight to everyone he met.

For the Jubilee Year 2000, Pope John Paul II invited the then-Archbishop Thuan to preach the annual Lenten spiritual exercises for him and the Vatican curia. The archbishop responded to this personal request with great humility and enthusiasm.

On the first day of the retreat, he startled his audience, telling them that he loved Jesus because of his "defects," and then proceeded to enumerate them. Instead of rebuking the archbishop for his unusual meditations, Pope John Paul II and the curia were enthralled. In fact, upon the pope's recommendation, the sermons were soon published in several languages. *Testimony of Hope,* as this series of sermons came to be known, reveals Thuan's humility and simplicity and illustrates how he touched people's hearts by allowing them to see familiar realities in a new light.

Cardinal Thuan was also a good listener. When speaking with him, one had the impression that he did not listen merely with his ears. It seemed his whole being was open to receive whatever someone might say, to hear and understand even a person's silence.

His door was permanently open to everyone. Though he was extremely attached to his family and friends, they never monopolized his attention. In fact, he tended to show some restlessness whenever too long in the company of friends, as if he were reminding himself that he could not give his life and time to only a select few.

I knew Francis Xavier Nguyen Van Thuan from the time he was eighteen. Our grandfathers had worked together on the construction of a church and our families have remained friendly since then. Later, Thuan and I attended seminary at An Ninh during the same years, although Thuan was four years my senior.

What struck me most whenever I saw Thuan was his great courtesy. He showed respect to all who crossed the path of his life, including those who betrayed, persecuted, or tortured him. Despite the depth of his thought, he remained as simple as a child. He accepted his vulnerability as the natural price for his sincerity and openness—characteristics certainly difficult for him to maintain, considering the harm people have done him and his family.

His life story is fascinating, yet the dramatic and often tragic events that fashioned him were dwarfed by the magnificent spirituality they fostered within him. And those who might feel tempted to see his life as a succession of dramatic moments apart from his faith in God miss the essential point. The dramas and tragedies that wove the rich fabric of his life definitely affected him in one way or another, but Thuan became the man of God he was because of and despite them.

To write about Thuan is no easy task, and the main difficulty lies in understanding his spirituality in order to convey it effectively. To my knowledge, few biographers attempt to write about a person's spirituality, for even the most naïve realize that such an undertaking is as daunting as the literary critic who tries to exhaust the beauty of a poem; a theologian who tries to describe faith; a Buddhist thinker who endeavors to express his or her vision of Nirvana. They would be better off trying to empty the ocean with their cupped hands. This is because spirituality is something experienced, not described. And yet, writing about Thuan without touching upon his spirituality would be to tell a meaningless story, it would be as if one took God out of his life—an impossibility.

To really come to know and understand Thuan, one should carefully read two of his books: *The Road of Hope,* written in 1975 while he was in prison, and *Five Loaves and Two Fish,* which was published in 1998. Both books trace the journey of his soul and allow the reader a glimpse into the vast expanse of the life of a beleaguered and suffering man who clung to hope and who, paradoxically, embraced life with intense joy at precisely those moments when it seemed an unbearable burden.

Some years ago, after I completed a biography of his mother, Thuan asked me to write about his life and spirituality. For the longest time, I tried to exempt myself, invoking various reasons and excuses on different occasions. Perhaps I was unconsciously afraid of my inability to adequately describe his spirituality. But in the summer of 1999, as we sat on a beach near Rome, Thuan and I spoke far into the night about his life and his thoughts. He asked me again to consider writing his biography. Although it took a long time before I had the courage to accept the task, I have finally written here of Thuan and his spiritual journey. I hope that those who read this book will learn as much from it as I have from writing it.

AUTHOR'S NOTE

CARDINAL FRANCIS XAVIER NGUYEN VAN THUAN passed away on September 16, 2002, a few months after the completion of this biography. In reviewing its content, I see no reason to expand or shorten the story told. The miracle of hope that was his life led him into eternity, serene and obedient to God's will.

Twice during his terminal illness, he asked me to come to see him at Casa di Cura Pius XI in Rome. In July, we spoke at length about this work and its upcoming publication. In September, when I returned, he was too weak to speak. Even then, I could read in his eyes his wish to see his spirituality live on. I hope that this biography will contribute in a humble way to the understanding of Francis Xavier Nguyen Van Thuan's vibrant message of hope and unity.

PART ONE

A CRUEL
AND
ENCHANTING
WORLD

I myself will take a sprig
  from the lofty top of a cedar...
I myself will plant it
  on a high and lofty mountain.

EZEKIEL 17:22

Vietnam is your fatherland,
  a country loved by its children for so many
  centuries.
It gives you pride; it gives you joy;
  love its mountains, love its rivers....

The Road of Hope,
F. X. NGUYEN VAN THUAN

CHAPTER ONE

The Seeds of Faith

Their inheritance [will remain] with
their children's children.
Their descendants stand by the covenants;
their children also, for their sake.

Sirach 44:11–12

Contemplating, from my childhood,
these shining examples,
I conceived a dream.

Five Loaves and Two Fish,
F. X. Nguyen Van Thuan

FRANCIS XAVIER NGUYEN VAN THUAN was born on April 17, 1928 in the central part of Vietnam, in Phu Cam parish, a suburb of Hue. Hue had long been the capital city of "Imperial Vietnam." By 1928, however, it was not without some irony that Vietnamese continued to call their ruler "emperor" and the country he ruled an "empire."

For almost a thousand years, until the early tenth century, the Viet people had lived under Chinese domination. But in A.D. 936, with the beginning of the Vietnamese dynasties, a long line of Vietnamese sovereigns from eight different dynasties succeeded in fighting off Chinese and Mongol invasions. Except for a brief period from A.D. 1414 to A.D. 1427, the Vietnamese managed to preserve national independence until the mid-nineteenth century, and to expand their territory south, away from China in an en masse "March to the South" or *Nam Tien.*

Despite Vietnam's self-governance, the Chinese to the north continued to "bestow" the title *An Nam Quoc Vuong* (King of the Pacified South) upon the Vietnamese rulers. The sovereigns, however, took for themselves the title of emperor when the Chinese Emperor was not looking. Beginning with the Nguyen dynasty, founded in 1802 by Nguyen Anh (Emperor Gia Long), the country was called *Dai Nam,* rendered "Greater Vietnam," or more simply, "Vietnam." But both the ruler's title and the country's name were somewhat ridiculous by the time Thuan was born, since Vietnamese rulers were mere figureheads of the French colonial administrators, who had taken the country's reins in the second half of the nineteenth century.

Although crowned the country's ruler in 1926, Emperor Bao Dai went to study in Paris as a ward of France. He returned to Vietnam in 1932 to rule only the small, central portion of the country. The southern provinces of the country had become known as *Cochinchina* and formed a separate French colony; the Northern provinces, known as *Tonkin,* were nominally under the emperor's rule, although actually administered by French colonial officials.

This three-part division of Vietnam by the French, whose conquest began in 1858 and ended in 1885, demonstrated their strict political motto: "divide and conquer." They had dismembered Vietnam and left the Nguyen emperors with little more than symbolic power over the central third of the traditional Viet territory. By the twentieth century, the emperor of Vietnam was no more powerful than the neighboring rulers of the French colonies of Cambodia or Laos—kingdoms that together with the three parts of former *Dai Nam* made up French Indochina.

◆◆◆◆◆◆

To truly understand Thuan, one must keep in mind the profound attachment he felt for his birthplace. Hue was known as the Divine Capital, the seat of the emperor whom the people called the Son of Heaven and considered a god. Vietnam's capital had changed many times under the various kings and emperors of successive dynasties, yet none of these ancient cities, including the northern city of Hanoi, preserved as much of their past glory as Hue—the only city in Vietnam whose impressive, centuries-old monuments have not been irreparably damaged.

From the heights of Hue's Phu Cam suburb, one could see the outline of the walls of the Citadel of Hue, and the city's Flag Monument. By ascending the pine-covered Ngu Binh Mountain, a half mile southwest of Phu Cam, one had a panoramic view of the Perfume River, which flowed through the center of Hue, and of the European City on the river's right bank and the Imperial City on its left. From that height, at the top of the mountain, the upper parts of various buildings of Hue's Imperial Palace could be seen emerging from behind a second set of defensive walls and moats. A string of imperial tombs dotted the banks of the Perfume River further south, the farthest away being the tomb of the first Nguyen emperor, Gia Long.

For the natives of Hue, these palaces, monuments, pagodas, and temples added to their city's natural beauty. Hueans believed that they were born to be poets and artists, and the environment was truly conducive to poetic and artistic aspirations. This native environment exerted a great influence on Thuan, who loved nature, the arts, poetry, and whose refined taste was born of the very air he breathed and water he drank in Hue.

Thuan's first love was not exclusive, however. Thuan grew to love intensely all the provinces of Central Vietnam, the rugged land where a resilient and passionate people lived, and later, as he traveled through it, all of his country.

When Thuan was born in 1928, Phu Cam was a sparsely populated community with fewer than a hundred houses surrounded by vast gardens and orchards. Its only distinction was that almost all of its residents were Catholics—a miracle since only forty years earlier Catholics were still being persecuted throughout the empire.

For over two centuries, from 1644 to 1888, Vietnamese kings and emperors, ruling princes and their mandarins (who were officials of the imperial administration), as well as misguided scholars (the *van than*), had lashed out at Catholics. They carried out persecutions sometimes lasting a few years, occasionally for decades, but always fueled by a fear and hatred of the little-understood new religion introduced to Vietnam by sixteenth-century European missionaries. These persecutions, however, were not religiously but politically motivated, for the rulers and the mandarins foresaw that the new Catholic religion would bring cultural, social, and political changes, which would eventually threaten the established order.

Within these official periods of persecution, bloodthirsty mobs, encouraged by the silent consent or whispered prompting of the Vietnamese Imperial Court and mandarins, went on rampages against Christian communities. Thus, Christians were arrested, imprisoned, tortured, and executed by authorities, as well as humiliated, terrorized, and massacred by frenzied mobs.

For 244 years, these persecutions raged, subsided, and then raged again, resulting in a total of 150,000 martyrs: bishops, priests, religious, and lay men and women. More than 3,000 Catholic churches were burned to the ground, entire Christian communities slaughtered, and their homes plundered and torched.

Yet, after the most violent and vicious persecutions under the Emperors Minh Mang (1820–1841) and Tu Duc (1847–1883), Phu Cam parish still stood proudly on the southern hills of the capital city and testified to the resilience of Vietnamese Catholics. For Thuan and his parents, the survival of the parish also testified to the power of their crucified and risen Lord.

———◆◆◆———

THE YEAR 1885, WITH THE FRENCH MILITARY conquest of Vietnam, proved a fateful and disastrous one for both Vietnam and Vietnamese Christians. The French conquest, begun in 1858 with the excuse of intervening in the persecutions, had met with stiff, but ineffective resistance. Though the Vietnamese army fought valiantly, they were no match for France's "modern" rifles and cannons; one province after another fell to the French advance. The Vietnamese signed treaty after disastrous treaty, which only served to sanction the *fait accompli* and expand the French hold on the remaining territory.

By 1885 North and South Vietnam were firmly in the hands of the French, although the Vietnamese Imperial Court was permitted tenuous control over North Vietnam. The provinces of Central Vietnam were given the status of a protectorate, which meant that the Vietnamese emperor and his mandarins had power there, although it was extremely limited, and the French continued to gradually reduce the remnants of the emperor's authority. The emperor still possessed the semblance of a treasury, absolute power within the walls of his palace in Hue, and a small army—weak as it was.

On July 4, 1885, in the face of the arrogance of new demands made by the French, the two regents of the child Emperor Ham Nghi ordered the imperial army to launch an all-out attack on the French garrisons in Hue. It was an unfortunate decision. The poorly planned attack was doomed to fail from the start. The antiquated "gun gods" of the Vietnamese roared throughout the night, with most of the cannonballs flying into the Perfume River. Damage to the French garrisons was negligible. At daybreak, the outcome of the battle was immediately clear even to the most hardheaded of mandarins. Then the French launched a counter attack. The young emperor was hurriedly escorted out of Hue and taken on an exhausting march to the surrounding mountain strongholds. He was finally captured and exiled in 1888.

The mandarins who had accompanied the emperor into the mountains appealed to the village people to fight the French. Overnight, armed bands sprang up all over the country and formed a somewhat cohesive network of resistance against the French. At the same time, the mandarins spread rumors, blaming the recent defeat of the Vietnamese imperial army on Christians. The *van than* joined in, accusing the Christians of being traitors of the nation; they were the country's "inner enemies" who had to be exterminated. From 1885 to 1888, the *van than* militia killed tens of thousands of Catholics.

One night in the autumn of 1885, the people in the village of Dai Phong heard rumors that a *van than* raid had been planned against the Catholics in their village. Having no time to arm themselves to fight or to take flight, they rushed to the small thatch-roofed church, all the while knowing that they would probably not escape death. Among the Christians gathered in the church that night was most of the family of Ngo Dinh Kha, Thuan's future grandfather.

As the people prayed, encouraged by their pastor, an armed mob encircled the church. Suddenly flaming torches were thrown onto the roof of the building that quickly caught fire and spread to the mud and bamboo walls. Inside, the chanting of prayers could no longer be heard above the screams of children. Parents frantically tried to save their children by throwing them out of the windows. Most of these unfortunate children were immediately caught by members of the militia and thrown back into the inferno. But some, thanks to the darkness of the night and the billowing screen of smoke, did escape.

One who escaped in this way was Kha's younger cousin, ten-year-old Lien. "Aunt Lien," as Kha's cousin was later known, moved to Phu Cam and lived there until her death in 1938. Children and adults would often come to hear her tell, in simple words, her account of what happened on that terrible night in Dai Phong.

Another who escaped was Kha's mother, who had been away from the village. Fortunately, Kha had also been away, studying at the seminary in Penang, Malaya (now Malaysia). Due to difficulties in communication, he learned only several months after the tragedy that almost his entire family had been wiped out.

Kha's teachers at the seminary encouraged him to return home to marry and carry on the family name. While the idea of perpetuating a family's name was certainly a more traditional Confucian duty than a Christian concept, Kha's teachers understood its importance. Kha accepted this advice and headed home. He knew that he would have to provide for his ailing mother, now left without any resources.

Much later Ngo Dinh Kha would play an active role in the Imperial Court as a close advisor of Emperor Thanh Thai. He carried out several major functions during his service to the court: he was the Grand Chamberlain (*Thi Ve Dai Than*) to the emperor, and as such, also the Palace Marshal in charge of protocol, and the Commander of the Imperial Guards. In 1902, the Emperor granted Ngo Dinh Kha the title of Great Scholar Assistant to the Throne (*Hiep Ta*

Dai Hoc Si), actually placing him in the ranks of the court's permanent ministers. Kha also held the title of Imperial Tutor *(Phu Dao Dai Than)*, making him the emperor's personal instructor and advisor, especially in the subjects of the French language and Western philosophy. In 1903, the emperor no longer required Kha's instruction, but allowed him to keep this position and title. Whenever possible, Emperor Thanh Thai would ride to Phu Cam on horseback to enjoy a few hours of relaxation with his old and loyal friend under the pretext of seeking information from the learned man.

Kha represented a very small number of Catholics who achieved some of the highest positions at the Imperial Court. His presence at court, in fact his very life, which had been spared in the great massacre, was a miracle.

Until his death Kha's mind was constantly haunted by the memory of the holocaust that had consumed the Dai Phong church and his family. His veneration of all the martyred Christians never waned. He permanently displayed on his desk the first edition of Father Alexander de Rhodes' *La Glorieuse Mort d'André, Catechiste de la Cochinchine, qui a versé son sang pour la querelle de Jesus-Christ, en cette nouvelle Eglise* (The Glorious Death of Andre, Catechist of Cochinchina, who shed his blood for the cause of Jesus Christ in this new Church), printed in Paris in 1653. In it, Father de Rhodes offered a terrifying eyewitness account of the execution of the first Vietnamese martyr in 1644. Like many Vietnamese Christians of his day, Kha especially venerated the martyr André who had survived savage beatings and stabbing only to finally be beheaded.

Kha's daughter, Elizabeth Ngo Dinh thi Hiep, grew up listening to Aunt Lien's story of the night massacre. She marveled at the Dai Phong parishioners' courage under persecution and was appalled by the ugliness of religious intolerance. Hiep could not have known that a few decades later her own son, Thuan, would become a victim of such intolerance and would spend thirteen years suffering a living martyrdom for his faith.

As a child Thuan himself also had many opportunities to hear Aunt Lien speak of the events in Dai Phong some fifty-two years before his birth. He took pride in being related to martyrs, but could never have imagined that he would one day suffer in his soul and flesh for the cause of Christ, or that the glorious canonization of 117 Vietnamese martyrs in Rome by Pope John Paul II on June 19, 1988, would adversely impact his own imprisonment.

Born into this tradition of Christian pride and resilience and in a land filled with centuries-old memories of persecution and martyrdom, Thuan could later write in his brief and exquisite *Five Loaves and Two Fish* how "contemplating from my childhood these shining examples, I conceived a dream." Indeed, from his early childhood, Thuan dreamt about following the footsteps of Vietnamese martyrs and joyfully serving God in the most distressful circumstances. Incredible odds would at times challenge this dream, but the models he contemplated as a child would never fail to urge him on amidst disaster and tragedy; and these examples shone forth on both sides of his family.

----◆◆◆----

THUAN'S FATHER, NGUYEN VAN AM, was a descendant of Christians who had suffered greatly for their faith. Am's grandfather had become a legend in his own time because of his courage during the persecutions under Emperor Tu Duc. In 1860, Emperor Tu Duc attempted to wipe out Catholicism, but in his reluctance to shed blood, the emperor devised his *phan sap* (divide and integrate) policy. It was a despicable scheme that violated the most basic principle of Vietnamese society: the sacredness of the family.

Under the *phan sap* Catholic families were split up; the heads of families and other male adults were taken away to serve as unpaid laborers on farms owned by non-Christians. Non-Christian landowners were expected not to feed their laborers well and that large numbers would either die of starvation or exhaustion, or that this harsh treatment would cause them to renounce their faith. Meanwhile, their wives and children became servants in non-Christian households with the hope that they would forget their faith.

The emperor believed that his policy would eradicate the "imported" religion in a few years, and it might have worked, except for the compassionate and humane treatment of Christians by non-Christians who did not starve their laborers. However, the main reason for its failure was that the Christians endured that period of forced separation and servitude with heroic courage and resilience.

As a child Thuan listened to his father Am describe the horror of the *phan sap* policy and the pain and suffering his great-grandparents endured when they were forced to separate—his great-grandmother and her younger children were sent into servitude; his great-grandfather, Nguyen van Danh, worked as an unpaid laborer. Am told his son that it was thanks to Am's grandfather Nguyen van Vong that his great-grandfather Danh managed to survive.

Vong had been separated from both his parents and worked on a rice field some six miles away from his father, Danh. Somehow, Vong heard of the terrible conditions his father suffered under his cruel landlord. When Vong learned that his father was being starved, the young boy of fourteen approached his own landlord and asked permission to bring food to his father every morning. Vong did not stop to consider that he hardly received enough food to eat himself. Every morning, while it was still dark, Vong woke up, cooked his small ration of food, and carried half of it to his father. He had to run the twelve miles back and forth to be in the rice field on time to begin work alongside the other laborers at sunrise. He did this for several years.

Eventually the emperor realized the uselessness of *phan sap* policy and abandoned it altogether. Nothing seemed to break the courage of the Christians, and a growing number of non-Christians sympathized with and showed mercy toward the Christians, sometimes even at the risk of antagonizing the local mandarins.

When Nguyen van Danh, sick and emaciated, was at last reunited with his family, he was proud that none of his children had renounced their faith and that his wife had steadfastly continued to teach their children to fear God and love their neighbor. He also proudly admitted that he owed his survival to his eldest son. Not only had Vong brought him food every day, but the boy had also encouraged his father. Danh said that his son's indomitable courage had made his hell endurable.

Eventually Vong married Tong thi Tai, a close relative of Paul Tong Viet Buong, a military commander martyred under Emperor

Minh Mang on October 23, 1833. Buong was beatified by Pope Leo XIII on May 27, 1900, and canonized by Pope John Paul II on June 19, 1988.

The young couple moved to Phu Cam where they met Father Joseph Eugéne Allys, the future bishop of Hue. Father Allys recruited Vong as a unique kind of missionary. He was not to preach, but to settle in a small village, live the life of a virtuous Christian, and convert others through his example. Once there were enough converts in a village, he was to move on to a new village. This novel evangelization technique took Vong from village to village in a region located more than forty miles south of Hue.

Vong, Thuan's future great-grandfather, spent fifteen years evangelizing in this way. He was so enthusiastic that he would have spent his entire life as a missionary had not Father Allys asked him to return to Phu Cam to spend more time with his extended family.

Father Allys lent Vong some money to establish a farm and he became a prosperous farmer, the chairman of the parish council, and one of the most honored men in the Christian community of Hue. Later, Vong became a builder and constructed the landmark Pellerin Institute for the Brothers of Christian Schools and the Joan of Arc Institute for the Sisters of Saint Paul of Chartres, both inaugurated in 1904. These two institutions attracted elite students from Hue and all over the country. Vong and his son Dieu left their architectural imprint on the major public, religious, and private buildings of the city. They also did the maintenance and renovation work on most of the city's ancient monuments.

THUAN WOULD NEVER FORGET ALL THAT his family had endured, that he descended from martyrs. Later, when he suffered in his own flesh and soul for the Christian faith during thirteen years of detention, he would recall hearing about the martyrdom of his forefathers ever since he was a child. Strengthened by this example, he would embrace his own "martyrdom" as a cherished heritage. Thuan would venerate his ancestors, along with all the Vietnamese martyrs, until the day he died.

CHAPTER TWO

A Vocation of Patriotism

The LORD has make known his victory;
he has revealed his vindication
in the sight of the nations.
He has remembered his steadfast love and faithfulness
to the house of Israel.

Psalm 98:2–3

My mother taught me stories from the bible every night,
she told me stories of our martyrs,
especially of our ancestors.
She taught me love of my country.

Testimony of Hope,
F. X. Nguyen Van Thuan

I N PHU CAM, NGO DINH KHA AND HIS WIFE, Pham thi
Than, had six sons: Khoi, Thuc, Diem, Nhu, Luyen, and
Can; and three daughters: Giao, Hiep, and Hoang. Elizabeth Ngo Dinh thi Hiep, born on May 5, 1903, was Kha's fifth child. Without a doubt, she was the apple of her father's eye. Among his children, she was the only one who had no fear of him and who dared to take hold of his hand and ask him questions when he was tense or irritable. Even as a little child she was the only one who knew how to appease his anger and soothe his anxiety.

Amazingly, Kha took her into his confidence when she was as young as five. He told her everything and shared his innermost thoughts with her. To his own amazement, Kha heard himself speaking with her about his fears and hopes for Vietnam and of the complicated intrigues of the Imperial Court.

Hiep was allowed to listen as her father engaged in important political discussions. During a particular crisis, Emperor Thanh Thai, whom Kha loyally served, incurred the wrath of representatives of the French colonial administration and was about to be forced to abdicate. Kha stood by the emperor to the bitter end and, by doing so, made many enemies among his colleagues who had abandoned their sovereign. During this time, Kha lived in a state of continual tension and was uncommunicative at home. Yet, to the surprise of her mother and siblings, Hiep could still make her father talk and laugh.

Throughout the crisis Hiep heard most of Kha's grave discussions with Minister Nguyen Huu Bai, the future Duke of Phuoc Mon, concerning the emperor. Although a quiet child and a good listener, Hiep certainly could not comprehend everything her father and his powerful friend discussed. She was only a guest in that strange world of adults. She did not understand its rules, but she did understand why her father and Minister Nguyen Huu Bai had to fight for the emperor and battle the arrogance of the French officials in the colonial administration. After the two men concluded their meetings, Hiep's questions seemed to inspire rather than irritate the Grand Chamberlain. He would patiently explain why he and Bai took this or that measure to counter the intrigues of other mandarins who sided with the French and spied on the emperor.

When it became clear that there was no way to save Emperor Thanh Thai from being dethroned, the two friends decided that Bai would remain "loyal" to the Imperial Court and that Kha, instead, would fight against the French for the emperor's political sovereignty to the end. Ultimately, Ngo Dinh Kha, the only high ranking mandarin to openly oppose the French, was stripped of all ranks and honors and the French threatened to send him back to his grandfather's village of Dai Phong. Bai, however, managed to persuade the French to allow Kha to remain in Phu Cam, although he would have no further influence at the Imperial Court.

Kha began working a rice field in Phu Cam with his sons. Hiep helped her mother to carry food and tea to the field for her father and brothers. These were difficult years, but no one in the family complained about the dramatic reversal of fortune. During those years of poverty, Hiep continued to live in rapt admiration of her father's fortitude and patriotism. Kha was moved to tears at times as he watched his little girl courageously going about her chores with a cheerful smile.

Over time Kha prospered as a farmer, but the years of hard work and deprivation would never be forgotten. His sons, who would become important mandarins, had learned the value of manual labor and thrift; they had learned to value loyalty over honors and rank.

Kha's third son, Ngo Dinh Diem, who later became the first president of the Republic of Vietnam, would proudly recount how he and his brothers had worked hard as farmers. Western journalists and diplomats were required to sit and listen to Diem's long narratives detailing how he and his brothers plowed and irrigated the fields, how they worked on holidays and on school days, and how poor they were. Not everyone would appreciate Diem's pride in those lean years, thinking he was merely indulging in nostalgia. But Diem was constantly drawing fresh lessons from the joy, the pain, and the value of hard work his family experienced during those years.

Ngo Dinh Kha and his family were far from common farmers, however. Politics was their true vocation and patriotism their drive. After the French sent Emperor Thanh Thai and his son, Emperor Duy Tan, into exile off the coast of Africa in 1916, Ngo Dinh Kha and Minister Nguyen Huu Bai would spend the rest of their lives fighting for Vietnam's autonomy. This aim was Kha's sole ambition. He taught his children to love their country with passion, and hoped that one of them would one day lead Vietnam. Probably around the year 1912, Kha began to place his greatest hopes in Diem.

Diem was only twelve when his father, Kha, and godfather, Bai, began preparing the boy for the possible role of national leader. Kha and Bai spent a tremendous amount of time instructing Diem in everything they knew and in motivating him to model himself on the virtuous leaders of the past and present. Diem was not a docile student. Headstrong by nature, he constantly questioned what he was told until convinced of its truth.

In turn Hiep studied her brother carefully and came to know all of his strengths and weaknesses. Though Diem was two years her senior, he always turned to her when he faced critical problems and, despite her reticence, continued to do so when he become a national leader, the prime minister, and president. Diem had unshakable trust in his sister.

———————◆◆◆◆———————

UNTIL HE NEARED HIS DEATH IN 1925, Ngo Dinh Kha counseled his sons to be prepared to fight for their country's autonomy, though he insisted that it should be a non-violent struggle and the fruit of political negotiations.

On his deathbed, however, Kha no longer spoke to his children of Vietnam's autonomy. He realized how mistaken he and Bai had been in trying to groom emperor after emperor to wrestle back through negotiations some semblance of national sovereignty once Thanh Thai had been exiled. They had also been mistaken in preparing Diem to fight for their country's autonomy. Rather, the only goal possible was Vietnam's total independence.

The emperors Kha served had been either too impatient or too passive, characteristics that had led to one political disaster after another. Ultimately, none of them had succeeded in wresting any colonial prerogatives from the French. Kha knew that even with all his strengths Diem would not succeed in negotiations with the French. If peaceful negotiations could not work, his children must be prepared for even an armed struggle to liberate their country. All of Kha's children kept his last wish for an independent Vietnam uppermost in their minds. They would both live and die for that dream.

As he neared his death, Kha bound Hiep irrevocably to the political fortune of the Ngo Dinh family. When the moment arrived for Kha to give the father's traditional parting blessing, he surprised the entire family; he did not ask his eldest son Khoi to step forward;

he did not ask Diem. In a gesture heavy with consequences, he called for Hiep to receive the blessing. Kha told the family members gathered at his bedside that from then on Hiep would speak in his name on the yearly anniversary of his death. It was her duty to tell each of them where they had done right and where wrong. He said, "It is only natural that Hiep, who listened to me so well in my life, should speak in my name when I am gone."

The profound significance of the event was clear to all of them. Among the siblings, Hiep, the faithful listener of their father's ramblings and musings, possessed the greatest insight into their father's thoughts and dreams and, therefore, could rightly speak in his name.

Hiep thus became the most valuable resource for her brothers and sisters when they were in doubt. Whatever positions of political importance her brothers held—president, prime minister, governor, presidential advisor—on the occasions when Hiep addressed the family, they listened with bowed heads and invariably thanked her for her strong and reproving words. The annual ritual on their father's anniversary of death continued until, through a series of tragic events, all of Kha's sons were killed or forced into exile.

After Kha's death, his friend Nguyen Huu Bai also took Hiep into his confidence and respected her views and advice. "When I am listening to her," he once told Diem, "I seem to hear your father's voice."

Later Thuan would sometimes speak of his family's "political spirituality," which he shared particularly with Hiep and Diem. For his family it was a given that Christians made God's will the foundation of their political thought and action. Thuan had simply to look back on the living experience of his family to support this view. All Ngo Dinh Kha's children strongly believed that their dedication to the liberation of Vietnam and the welfare of its people was God's will. Their sense of justice, their righteousness, their humanity and heroism would make them some of the most tragic and misunderstood yet exalted figures of Vietnam's modern history.

In particular, Ngo Dinh Diem, a man who lived and died for his political spirituality, was a man of great contradictions. Diem, a meditative man by nature, was pulled into action by a government that needed direction. A naturally mild and kind man, he was placed in a leadership role at moments when the political and military situations in Vietnam were most violent. He took vows as a Catholic monk, but also embraced Confucianism, and at the same time, accepted the demanding position of president of a nation during uncertain times. Diem lived all these contradictions, and his spirituality gave him the courage to do every day what he believed to be right. Few Christian politicians could have shown Thuan a better approach to political spirituality than his uncle.

◆◆◆◆◆

INTENSE AS THEIR DREAM FOR THE INDEPENDENCE of their country was, Kha's children did not forget their first duty: the practice of their Christian faith. Kha himself had lived a devout Christian life and spent an exceptional amount of time in daily prayer and meditation. From his home's terrace that overlooked the Phu Cam Cathedral, he loved to listen to the clear, musical rhythm of the parishioners chanting morning and evening prayer.

The Ngo Dinh family would walk briskly across the street to the cathedral for Mass, and while he might speak with his children on the way, once inside Kha became completely unaware of them. The children watched in awe as their father prayed and became so absorbed in the presence of God that he seemed to enter a kind of trance.

Kha's children would learn to pray with similar attention and devotion, especially Diem and Hiep. Both were mystics in the sense that through their prayer and penance, they constantly felt God's presence within and around them. Like their father, they often became oblivious to the world around them when praying.

Pham thi Than was less educated than her husband, but she took very seriously her role as her children's first educator. She admonished them when they failed to answer correctly their catechism questions. With her, the children studied their faith and memorized the contents of their catechism text, written by the French missionaries.

By the age of six, Hiep knew her catechism by heart, and she often surprised her father with her quick answers to the trickiest questions he might pose. She had an incredible sense of balance, an absolute faith, and a genuine respect for the beliefs of non-Christians that was uncanny for her age.

Hiep's natural attraction to prayer led her to find joy in the family's devotional life. She delighted in retreating to her room to pray the rosary. When not helping her mother in the kitchen or listening to her father and his friends in the parlor, Hiep's brothers and sisters knew where to find her: on her knees in her room.

Thuan grew up in the midst of his extended family's collective political dream and religious fervor. Like his mother, uncles, and aunts, Thuan's patriotism and need for the presence of God in his life was boundless. His political spirituality took shape gradually and, as time went on, began to make more demands on him. It fashioned his world-view and his view of humanity. Ultimately, it significantly determined his relationship with God and where that relationship would take him.

CHAPTER THREE

Growing Up in Hue

When I look at your heavens, the work of your fingers,
the moon and the stars that you established;
what are human beings that you are mindful of them,
mortals that you care for them?

Psalm 8:3–4

You have a homeland, Vietnam…
love her mountains and her rivers,
her brocade and satin landscapes…
her raging rivers run
as does her people's blood;
her mountains are high,
but higher still the bones that pile up there….
the land is narrow, but the ambition vast.

Five Loaves and Two Fish,
F. X. Nguyen Van Thuan

DURING THE SUMMER OF 1924, Thaddeus Nguyen van Am, a successful businessman and builder like his father Dieu, his grandfather Vong, and his great-grandfather Danh, set his heart on Elizabeth Ngo Dinh thi Hiep.

Am urged his father to ask Ngo Dinh Kha for his daughter Hiep's hand in marriage. Dieu hesitated. What could he say to persuade Kha to agree to such a proposal? Though a wealthy builder, Dieu doubted Kha would accept not only because of the distance between their social classes—mandarin and commoners—but also because he knew that Hiep was Kha's favorite daughter and confidante. Dieu procrastinated for as long as possible, but Am showed such determination and persistence that Dieu finally complied with his son's wishes.

Dieu was cordially welcomed into the home of the Ngo Dinh family. Upon learning the reason for his visit, Kha said in all simplicity: "My wife and I have always had a profound respect for your father Vong and grandfather Danh. We would be honored to join our two families together. After all, both our families are descendents of martyrs."

Elizabeth Ngo Dinh thi Hiep married Thaddeus Nguyen van Am a few months after her father's death. Although tradition demanded a three-year mourning period, Kha had insisted that his death not be cause for delaying the planned wedding.

On her wedding day, it was customary in Vietnam for the bride to kneel before her in-laws as a sign of her permanent departure from her own family and her new and complete attachment to her husband's family. But on Hiep's wedding day Nguyen van Dieu disregarded this tradition and asked her to kneel before her own mother, saying that she would continue being a full member of the Ngo Dinh family. Thus, Hiep would be able to visit her mother every day and to speak with her brothers and sisters as often as she pleased.

Dieu's action and words that day reveal how profoundly he understood that Hiep was inextricably bound to her father's political dream for Vietnam's independence. Both Nguyen van Dieu and Nguyen van Am recognized the important though discrete role Hiep would have to play in the fulfillment of that dream.

━━━◆◆◆━━━

WHEN THUAN WAS BORN, his parents had already suffered the first major tragedy of their married life. One year after their wedding, Hiep gave birth to their first son, Xuan, meaning "springtime." The happy couple pampered and spoiled their first-born. Xuan was intelligent, independent-minded, and quick to smile. Hiep and

Am began to build all kinds of dreams for the future of this most promising child.

In October of 1927, while Hiep was expecting their second child, and Am, a proud father, walked on clouds, a cholera epidemic swept over Hue. Hundreds of children died in a matter of days, and two-year-old Xuan was among the fatalities. It was a staggering loss for Hiep and Am. They felt that with their son had also gone their own springtime. The young couple matured overnight. In the darkness of their chapel at home, they wept over their son's death and prayed to be able to accept such a great loss.

As her second child stirred in her womb, Hiep could not shake the many dark thoughts that plagued her mind. The fear of losing her second child was always present. While she accepted what she simply believed to be the will of God, the loss of her first child would remain an open wound for years. Even much later when she watched her other children: Thuan, Niem, Tuyen, Ham Tien, Thanh, Anh Tuyet, Thuy Tien, and Thu Hong running along a beach or playing in her garden, she would sometimes imagine little Xuan with them. Then she would turn to God and whisper: "Will I never forget the pain of losing my first child?"

Hiep and Am carefully chose a name for their new son: Thuan, meaning, "conforming to (God's) will." Under different skies and in another language, his name would be "Islam."

———————◆◆◆◆———————

IF HIEP DID NOT SEEM TO HAVE MUCH of a childhood because of her involvement in her father's political life, Thuan did have one, and a good one. His parents spoiled Thuan, though his relentlessly rigid father always tried, however unconvincingly, to be firm with him. All his aunts and uncles indulged Thuan; Ngo Dinh Thuc and Ngo Dinh Diem became his favorite uncles.

Thuc, who had been ordained to the priesthood and sent to study in Rome and Paris, returned to Hue in 1929 as Thuan celebrated his first birthday. Thuc spent as much time as possible with Hiep and her young son, feeling guilty that he had been away when Xuan had died.

From the first time Father Thuc held Thuan in his arms, he saw in the child a future priest. He imagined his little nephew going to the village of An Ninh to attend the same minor seminary he and his younger brother, Nhu, had attended, and then on to Phu Xuan Major Seminary in Hue, and ultimately to Rome and Paris, exactly as he had. Father Thuc hid his dream from Hiep, but as soon as Thuan began learning to read, his uncle whispered in his ears that God was calling him to the priesthood.

The fact that Thuc spent much time with Thuan was not an indication of an idle life. On the contrary, after returning to Hue, Thuc worked first as a professor at the Sacred Heart Monastery, and then at the Phu Xuan Major Seminary. In 1933, he became the director of Providence Institute, the first Catholic high school in Vietnam. But these institutions were not far from Hiep's family, and until he became one of the first Vietnamese bishops in 1938, he was a frequent visitor at his sister's home.

Ngo Dinh Diem, Thuan's other favorite uncle, enjoyed a highly successful political career. From the beginning of his service as a mandarin, Diem received successive promotions: district chief, chief of prefecture, and then to province chief. In 1933, hand-picked by young Emperor Bao Dai to be prime minister at the age of thirty-two, Diem headed a cabinet of young men who were supposedly to lead the country through a series of innovations and reforms. The French colonial power opposed all of Diem's proposals and regarded his demands for Vietnamese self-rule and democracy as disloyalty to France. When it became clear that the French would block his every move, Diem protested by resigning after only seventy days in the prime minister's office. Many Vietnamese patriots saluted Diem's resignation as an act of great courage.

Afterward Diem retired to his mother's home in Phu Cam and seemed content to spend his time planting roses in the garden and indulging his hobby of photography. Discretely, however, he began building a network of revolutionaries, according to his father's wishes and the advice of his father's faithful friend, Nguyen Huu Bai.

From 1933 to 1944 Diem lived only a few steps from his sister Hiep's home. He often strolled over to "steal" Thuan away from his parents, carrying his little nephew on his shoulders and walking all the way to the Ngu Binh Mountain. He would climb the mountain while making Thuan laugh at his absurd stories drawn from Chinese history, legends, and mythology.

Even as a child Thuan was awed by his uncle's fantastic memory. Diem seemed to remember the name of every person he had ever met and all the places he had ever been. He had a dozen anecdotes about each of the mandarins, from the highest to the lowest ranks. From Diem, Thuan learned how to reason logically, and to master Chinese "ideograms" quickly. Thuan had to listen to his uncle intently to grasp the true meaning behind Diem's words, since he constantly understated and rarely repeated himself.

Diem was also Thuan's godfather, and he took that role seriously, often speaking to Thuan about God and the Church. As he listened to his uncles Thuc and Diem, Thuan noticed the difference between the expressions of their faith. Thuan believed that Diem was a mystic; his relationship with God was simple and direct. Where Thuc relied on theology, Diem relied on intuition. Thuc's prayers were long and formal; Diem's were short—like simple greetings addressed to his divine Father.

Thuan always remembered with special fondness the family reunions when the whole Ngo Dinh clan spent the summer together at the beach house owned by his Uncle Khoi, who was Governor of Quang Nam province. During those relaxed vacations, Diem would take Thuan on daylong horseback rides. They would return to the beach house in the evening tanned, hungry, and happy. Then the whole family enjoyed a feast of seafood. Despite all the tragedies the family experienced over the years, Thuan always spoke of those moments of happiness with his uncles as if they were fresh memories.

Until the age of twelve, Thuan attended Pellerin Institute, which all of his uncles had attended, and he learned under almost all of the same teachers. Here, Thuan tested what he had learned from his parents and uncles against what the Brothers of Christian Schools taught.

After school Thuan would run back home or stop by his grandmother's house to visit Diem. His father owned and drove one of the first cars in town, and from time to time Am would pick Thuan up after school. Thuan delighted in that touch of an acceptance of modern convenience in his father's usually austere character.

As Thuan was growing up, it seemed to Diem that he was always struggling with an unresolved problem, and his brooding became more obvious with time. It did not take long, however, for Diem to discover the cause: Father Thuc's talks with Thuan about his vocation. Diem was very concerned and, though he dreaded confronting his older brother, he approached him one day and insisted that he "leave the boy alone." Diem believed it was not in Thuan's best interest to speak to him so often about his vocation. If God wanted Thuan to become a priest, God would let him know in due time.

Thuc pointed out that even Diem himself had to admit that he already knew Thuan would become a priest. But they were not prophets, Diem insisted. Rather than applying pressure, they should allow Thuan to consider the question on his own. He had time; after all, he was only a child! Diem believed it was best to leave the boy alone and he would make the right decision when the moment arrived.

It was not long after their discussion that Thuc was appointed bishop of Vinh Long and moved some 400 miles south of Hue. But Thuan's vocational seeds had already been sown.

◆◈◆

AS A CHILD THUAN BEGAN TO SENSE the first intimations of what was to become an important part of the groundwork of his unique spirituality. Gradually, the boy Thuan became conscious of the rich heritage he had received from both sides of his family, a three-fold legacy that he would later identify as the "culture of stone, of paper, and of breath." Though it took years to play out in full, Thuan early on discovered the intimate relationship between these foundational aspects of his inner life and how they shaped his mind and molded his heart.

During his childhood Thuan took for granted that his grandfather had built the spacious home in which he lived, and he rarely considered that the Phu Cam Cathedral, a magnificent work of art, had been renovated throughout the years by his great-grandfather,

grandfather, and father. He came from a family of great builders in Hue, a city with a passion for stone.

In Hue the massive ramparts of the Citadel, the splendor of the Imperial Palace, and the Imperial Tombs were lasting tributes to the labor and sweat of generations of builders. Am explained to his son in simple terms the symmetry and harmony of the different parts of construction work. He pointed out the beauty and ingenuity of the arches and vaults, the economy of lines, the profusion of ornamental designs, and where one could find the best sources for glazed tiles, bricks, and marble. Thuan listened to his father's knowledge and artistic appreciation and learned from him how to look at monuments and buildings with a skilled and artistic eye.

As builders, the men on his father's side of the family taught Thuan the value of hard work, the pride one could take in being able to contribute to the great masterpieces of human endeavor, and how to observe the tangible, measurable result of human effort. From these generations of men, he learned to appreciate and value the beauty crafted by architects and builders.

Thuan would one day surprise people with his natural architectural skill and gift for interior decorating. If he were given a cabin to live in, he could soon transform it into a villa; he could quickly renovate a warehouse into a livable residence. Thuan's love of stone, which had begun in Hue, developed further during the time he lived in Rome, where he spent hours in the heart of the Eternal City contemplating its architectural masterpieces.

These periods of contemplation in Rome strengthened his understanding of the culture of stone, and connected it to the other two foundational aspects of his family's legacy: the cultures of paper and of breath. Thuan could see that the stones of a grand cathedral had not arranged themselves, but neither was the building the result of merely physical effort. Behind the work of human hands (the culture of stone), there exists knowledge and skill (the culture of paper), and inspiration (the culture of breath).

If the culture of stone had a powerful influence on Thuan's life, the culture of paper inherited from his mother's side of the family was even stronger. For Thuan, this culture of paper encompassed all branches of learning and intellectual endeavors. However, going beyond literary masterpieces or scientific knowledge with its applications, it also embraced the schools, institutes, and universities that train and shape the minds of men and women.

Thuan's family made major contributions to the culture of paper in Vietnam. When Emperor Thanh Thai decided to introduce Western culture into the curriculum of Vietnamese schools and began looking for someone to create and implement a plan, Ngo Dinh Kha caught his attention. Kha was one of the few Vietnamese scholars who had knowledge of both traditional and Western cultures.

One day in the summer of 1897, Thanh Thai personally visited Kha at his home to ask him to build a "National Institute" for education where, along with traditional subjects, the students would study Western culture. Kha was inspired by the emperor's enthusiasm and the National Institute soon took shape. Kha had to go from door to door asking for support from the other mandarins, who did not believe that their children would benefit from the new institution. In the minds of many mandarins, the blend of Eastern education with Western knowledge that the National Institute heralded signaled the eventual destruction of pure Asian traditions. At first, the mandarins shook their heads, but Kha's insistence, and the emperor's steady support, eventually overcame their resistance.

It took Kha several years, but ultimately he made a national success of the institute. Many of Vietnam's future leaders would come out of it, including such men as Ho Chi Minh, Pham Van Dong, Vo Nguyen Giap, and Ngo Dinh Diem.

As an educator, Kha left a lasting impression on generations of Vietnamese and his children were very proud of him. They, too, promoted education and urged their fellow citizens to reach beyond the traditional to the modern world. They encouraged young and old to think strategically and globally. Yet, they were equally steeped in Eastern culture and the millennium-old philosophies and morality they inherited from their ancestors.

At least four of Ngo Dinh Kha's children made significant contributions to the culture of paper: Thuc became founder and chancellor of the University of Dalat, the first Catholic university in Vietnam. Diem worked tirelessly to develop the national education system, and founded the University of Hue. Nhu became the soul

and mind behind the philosophical movement of Christian person-
alism in Vietnam. Luyen was instrumental in improving the map-
ping of Vietnam.

Thuan often said that without the National Institute and the
efforts of Ngo Dinh Kha, the culture of paper in Vietnam would
have taken another direction or at least would have progressed at a
much slower pace.

The culmination of the cultures of stone and paper is what
Thuan called the culture of breath or the culture inspired by the
Holy Spirit. This highest of the three cultures is the life-giving force
of all human actions. The culture of breath is what sanctifies the
cultures of stone and paper.

Thuan lived the culture of breath throughout his life.
Watched over lovingly by his parents, he laid a solid foundation for
his spiritual growth as he learned to see God's providence in all
things, and to offer a constant *"fiat"* to the work of the Holy Spirit in
his life. He began to see all the political, cultural, and professional
work of his parents and family as a prelude to the work of the Holy
Spirit. Thuan's family never considered any work of their hands or
minds complete until it received the final touch of fire and breath,
that is, until it was offered to God. Victory or defeat, success or failure was never as important to Thuan's parents as their Christian
faith. Even the difficulties they encountered in bringing their
father's dream to reality were insignificant compared with their desire to fulfill God's will.

------◆◦◆◦◆------

WHEN THIRTEEN-YEAR-OLD THUAN was about to finish his
studies at Pellerin, he chose a quiet evening to speak to his parents
about the future. He sat next to his mother and father as they
sipped tea in the living room and asked their permission to join
the An Ninh Minor Seminary. Although An Ninh was only fifty
miles away, Hiep trembled at the thought of being separated from
her eldest child. She looked at Thuan, and then looked away to
hide her tears.

Am tried to hide his own emotions as he asked his son if he
had sufficiently considered such a serious decision. Had he prayed

[29]

long and hard enough? Had he asked God to show him his will in the matter?

Thuan did not answer his father because he knew from experience that Am would find fault in whatever he might reply. As he silently watched his parents, Thuan knew that they were in pain and were making every effort to calm their uncertainties, to discern God's will. But he felt confident of their approval. He was sure that the idea of opposing his vocation would never enter their minds.

After a long silence, Thuan's father began to discuss matter-of-factly the best way for Thuan to reach An Ninh: first, the train to Ben Hai, then the boat down the Ben Hai River—which would one day become the general demarcation line between North and South Vietnam. Hiep shuddered at the thought of Thuan traveling the river in late August—the height of the flood season. Am agreed it might be dangerous, but he trusted their son's good sense.

Finally, Am gave voice to his "wishful prediction" that Thuan, spoiled as he was by his mother, would not stay long at the seminary. It was a hard life, and the institute was known for its poor food. Thuan's uncle Thuc had made it through the seminary, but that did not mean Thuan would survive the discipline. They only had to recall how Hiep's brother Nhu had stayed in the seminary for less than two years—and he still talked about the terrible food. In addition, Am would have to ask the pastor of Phu Cam parish, Father Andre (Chau) Chapuis to sponsor Thuan for admission to the seminary. He was sure Father Chapuis would laugh at the idea!

Hiep disagreed softly; Father Chapuis would not laugh. If Thuan wanted to go to the seminary, they ought to let him. He might not stay long, but then again, he might have a true vocation to the priesthood. Am added his consent to hers but grumbled because *he* would be the one to have to speak with Father Chapuis.

Just as Thuan felt certain that his parents would agree to his joining the minor seminary, he knew he would persevere in his vocation, whatever the conditions at An Ninh. He had heard enough of what was in store for him from Thuc, who had told him how awful seminary food was and had warned, "More often than not you will have a boiled egg in fish sauce and a heap of sour cabbage to share between four boys. Don't touch the fish; they are never fresh. As for meat, you may see it six times in a year if you're lucky."

As bad as the diet proved to be at the seminary, the food in the prisons and detention centers Thuan lived in later would be a hundred times worse. And his survival was at least in part due to his conscious and constant effort to eat whatever he was served at the seminary. Unknown to him, every step of the way prepared Thuan for his future ordeal.

CHAPTER FOUR

An Ninh Minor Seminary

I will pour out my spirit on all flesh;
Your sons and your daughters shall prophesy,
Your old men shall dream dreams,
And your young men shall see visions.

Joel 2:28

The time of study is a time of prayer.

The Road of Hope,
F. X. Nguyen Van Thuan

As THUAN WALKED PAST the monumental gate of the seminary on a late afternoon in August 1940, he found himself entering an enclosed universe filled with history and legends. The fifteen-foot-thick bamboo wall that had once helped protect the defenders of the seminary more than fifty years earlier against the *van than* militia now stood guard over a vast ensemble of orchards, vegetable and flower gardens, and a wildlife refuge. As he followed the main walkway toward the central buildings, the songs of birds and insects and the fragrance of ripe fruit and tropical flowers overpowered his senses.

He soon noticed the two chapels on either side of the walkway, one dedicated to the Blessed Virgin Mary and the other to Saint Anthony. During the siege of the seminary in 1885, the Blessed Virgin had reportedly appeared over her chapel several times. The vision, according to the legend, had contributed far more to the victory of the seminary's defenders than had their own bravery. *Van than* militiamen reportedly had been frightened out of their wits by her appearance and in total confusion had turned their weapons against each other.

The main walkway led straight to a two-story building that housed the parlor, library, warehouse, and the priests' quarters. In the parlor, Thuan found looking down at him from the wall two large, familiar portraits: one of Ngo Dinh Kha, his own grandfather, and the other of Kha's friend, Nguyen Huu Bai, the Duke of Phuoc Mon. The prominently displayed portraits testified to the degree of reverence in which these men were held by Catholics in Vietnam. At An Ninh they were honored not only because they were the most prominent Catholics of their time, but also because they were alumni of the seminary, although neither had become priests.

On the opposite wall were portraits of the first Vietnamese bishops, among them Pierre Ngo Dinh Thuc, Thuan's uncle and mentor.

Thuan was led through a square courtyard to the second two-story building that constituted the living quarters and study rooms of the seminarians. He paused to look around. He almost expected to see his grandfather and his uncles—he felt their presence so strongly. He thought to himself with pride: *I will be living here as they did. I will be studying in the same classrooms, praying in the same chapels, and playing on the same grounds that were theirs.* Thuan felt at home. Life at the minor seminary seemed exactly as he had dreamed it would be. He believed that he would do well, and he did.

Though the days were quite hectic, Thuan found time to walk around his new world, filling his senses with the beauty of green leaves and blue sky, the scent of fruit ripening in the orchards, and the concert of insects loud even during the day.

However, he soon discovered that not everything was perfect in that little "paradise." As he had been warned, most of the time the food was very poor and either undercooked or overcooked. The meager diet of pickled cabbage, boiled eggs, and salted fish was a far cry from his mother's cooking, which he had enjoyed at home. He laughed, however, as he recalled his father's predictions and his uncle's serious advice to avoid eating the fish. He really did not have much choice: it was either steamed rice with spoiled fish or steamed rice!

Bishop Thuc had also told Thuan that being at An Ninh Seminary was a constant reminder of the last Christian persecutions. In fact, An Ninh Seminary was one of only two sites where Catholics had organized themselves, fought in self-defense against the *van than* militia, and won.

In 1885, seven seminarians had commanded seven rag-tag companies of forces totaling one thousand Christians from the An Ninh and Di Loan parishes. The men forced back the hordes of ferocious *van than* that attacked An Ninh. Meanwhile, the churches in An Ninh and Di Loan, only a short distance from the bamboo walls of the seminary, had been burned to the ground.

Every year on September 18, at the beginning of the academic year, the seminarians celebrated the anniversary of that final victory over the overwhelming forces of the *van than* troops. The display of ancient guns, rifles, flags, and banners that had been captured from the *van than* marked the parade. The commemoration was never meant to be a joyful event; instead, it was a reminder of the Christians who had not survived the other *van than* attacks of that month, carried out in the Quang Tri Province from the parishes of Dinh Cat, Nhu Ly, Bo Lieu, Dau Kenh, Dai Loc, Duong Loc, Thanh Huong, Ke Van, Cam Lo, Mai Xa, Van Thien, Bai Son, An Hoa, and An Bang.

An annual parade gave the seminarians a chance to see the very weapons that had been used by the *van than*, and to remember that the martyrdom of more than 150,000 Christians was no legend. Thuan and his fellow seminarians felt close to the Christians who had died for their faith.

———————◆◆◆———————

IT WAS IN AN NINH MINOR SEMINARY that Thuan became more aware of his particular spirituality. Under the instruction and influence of his mother, he had begun praying at the age of three, and had developed a great devotion to the Blessed Virgin Mary by the time he was eight. He had also received his First Communion two years before his admission to the seminary. But at An Ninh, Thuan began to feel the presence of the Holy Spirit within him. For the first time, he experienced a great truth: he had already begun to live the eternal life promised by his crucified and risen Lord.

At the minor seminary, Thuan met several holy men whose faith and spirituality greatly strengthened his own. The shining example of holiness in his teachers would permanently shape Thuan's spiritual beliefs. Indeed, he was fortunate to be close to priests who were widely considered to be "living saints."

Father Jean Baptiste (Thi) Urrutia of the Paris Foreign Mission Society was the rector of the seminary and would one day be named bishop of Hue. Father Urrutia dedicated almost his entire active adult life to Vietnam. Those who knew him recognized in him a man of sound judgment, even temper, absolute sincerity, and childlike simplicity. His characteristic mildness was legendary. Before he was sent as a missionary to Vietnam, he lived at the headquarters of the Paris Foreign Mission Society. The priests there had nicknamed him *le doux agneau* (the mild lamb).

Urrutia kept his childlike innocence throughout his life, even when he became one of the most competent bishops in Vietnam and when held in captivity by Japanese troops. He offered the same smile when he was asked to take on enormous responsibilities as when he went into semi-retirement at the sanctuary of Our Lady of La Vang.

Thuan learned from Urrutia a gentleness of behavior, a simplicity of expression, the discernment of truth, and a calm and unpretentious dedication to the service of God. Later, Father Urrutia was in Hue as vicar general of the diocese when Thuan entered Phu Xuan Major Seminary. As the vicar, he went often to Phu Xuan where his homilies moved his audience of seminarians to tears. Urrutia's weekly talks revealed to Thuan the wealth of an inner life dedicated to God.

Bishop Urrutia continued to give abundant encouragement to Thuan when he was a young priest. He was instrumental in Thuan being sent to Rome for further studies, and for placing him in the role as seminary professor after his return to Vietnam. When the Vietnamese hierarchy was established in Vietnam and Archbishop Thuc moved to Hue, Archbishop Urrutia went to La Vang and then to Dong Ha where he humbly served the people as a parish priest. After he was ordered to leave Vietnam in 1975, he continually asked to be allowed to return to the country he had loved so much.

Throughout his final years in France, he spoke almost exclusively about three things: Vietnam, Hue, and the An Ninh Seminary.

Urrutia's example of dedication and his words would accompany Thuan into prisons, detention camps, and cells of solitary confinement. They would continue to play a major role in Thuan's spirituality for decades.

Another outstanding priest at An Ninh Seminary was Father Jean-Mary Cressonnier. Also a member of the Paris Foreign Mission Society, Father Cressonnier came from a very wealthy family, but he lived like a pauper. A man who suffered from almost constant ill health, he endured one serious surgical procedure after another, but was always cheerful and never complained about his ailments. He would later be shot to death by the Viet Minh Communists during the Tet Mau Than Offensive in 1968 while carrying the Eucharist to the sick and injured.

Father Cressonnier introduced Thuan to the works of Dom Colomba Marmion, a Benedictine monk born in Ireland who wrote about the mysteries of the rosary, and who described the extraordinary role of the Blessed Virgin Mary in the Incarnation. Dom Marmion's writings profoundly transformed Thuan's spirituality. Years later, Thuan had the joy of attending Marmion's canonization, after which he hurried home to re-read selections from those works of Marmion which Cressonnier had especially recommended.

Father Cressonnier reinforced Thuan's devotion to the Blessed Virgin Mary. Thuan later commented that he had never seen Father Cressonnier without his rosary. Emulating his mentor, Thuan always kept a rosary in his pocket and volunteered to serve Masses at the Chapel of Our Lady. Thuan also requested permission to take piano lessons, which were normally given in that chapel. Nothing made him happier than to be in the Chapel of Our Lady, surrounded by the rich fragrance of the blossoms of the southern crabapple trees planted alongside it.

Father Cressonnier's life of poverty helped Thuan to value the virtue of poverty more fully as a priest. Thuan would also choose to live like a pauper. He would sleep on whatever was available—for instance, a hard bed covered with a straw mat—when he was a bishop in Nha Trang. That he led such a simple life proved providential during his captivity when mattresses were nonexistent. By adopting the lifestyle of a monk, Thuan unwittingly prepared himself for the forced poverty of prison.

Father Joseph Marie Nguyen van Thich was another of Thuan's teachers at the minor seminary. A saintly, cultured man, Father Thich possessed many talents and was a close friend of Thuan's uncle, Ngo Dinh Diem. He was the son of Minister Nguyen van Mai, a devout Buddhist and Confucian, who was co-director with Ngo Dinh Kha of the National Institute for education. Thich had braved his father's wrath to convert to Christianity and enter An Ninh Minor Seminary when already an adult. After two years of living and studying with young boys, he was allowed to join the Phu Xuan Major Seminary, although Thich had not minded studying with boys twenty years younger than he, perhaps because he was as innocent as a child and remained so throughout his life.

Father Thich was a poet and painter, an exquisite calligrapher, and an excellent composer. His spirituality was apparent in the songs he composed, the poems he wrote, and in all of his daily duties. He breathed an elegance and holiness into whatever he did, and he too would have a tremendous influence on Thuan's spiritual growth.

From 1936 onward, Father Thich published the first weekly, then monthly magazine, *For God (Vi Chua)*, an influential periodical in both the Christian and non-Christian circles of that time. Father Thich became known as Father Vi Chua: *the priest who lived for God*. A great teacher of Chinese, Father Thich was a strong believer in the pre-Christian values of Confucianism. As a professor at An Ninh, he sparked Thuan's interest in the subject by showing him how the cardinal Confucian virtues of benevolence or humanity, righteousness, propriety, and wisdom were very close to the Christian cardinal virtues of fortitude, justice, temperance, and prudence.

It was partly due to Father Joseph Marie Nguyen van Thich, and partly due to his Uncle Diem, who was at least once called "the last Confucian," that Thuan undertook a serious study of the Chinese language and classics and drew a great deal of wisdom from those sources.

Another great influence on Thuan was the man who succeeded Father Urrutia as rector of the minor seminary, Father
Andre Nguyen Van Tich. Father Tich played a major role in the lives
of all the seminarians at An Ninh from the 1940s through the 1950s.
Even the youngest seminarians felt that they were in the presence of
a holy man as soon as they met him. Rumors that Father Tich performed miracles were rampant among the boys. Such rumors certainly inspired awe, but it was Tich's genuine concern for the
spiritual welfare of each seminarian that won their hearts. When
Father Tich discovered that someone had broken the smallest rule
or regulation, rather than reprove the offender, he would simply
look at him with sadness. As a few tears rolled down his cheeks, he
would sigh and say, "Let's go to the chapel and pray together for
forgiveness."

Tich had the gift of being able to see into the heart and mind
of those with whom he spoke. Seminarians who came to him for
counsel often did not even have to state their difficulties. He seemed
to look into their eyes and see what was troubling them. He did not
need to say a lot, either; his eyes and silence were often enough to
assuage the pain of those who sought his counsel.

Even while rector, Father Tich remained a simple man with
simple tastes and a great sense of humor. He liked to laugh, play
dominoes, take long walks, and entertain the priests from the neighboring parishes. He also liked to sing, to teach, and to organize celebrations. The memory of the way Father Tich ran An Ninh
Seminary followed Thuan until the day he became its rector in 1960.

From living with these holy men, Thuan could not help but
believe in the abundance of God's grace. Years later, Thuan still recalled the overwhelming joy and light that danced in the eyes of
these holy priests. It gave him cause to thank God for them and the
small paradise he found in his years at the minor seminary.

Because of priests like Archbishop Urrutia and Father
Cressonnier, Thuan always acknowledged the debt he and his fam-
ily owed the Paris Foreign Mission Society. Even after 1945, when
Vietnam's sudden access to independence aroused the majority of
Vietnamese to anger and to accuse many of the priests of the Paris

Foreign Mission Society of being "colonialists" or worse, Thuan remained steadfastly loyal. He would remind those who tried to make him change his view that there had been so many good Paris Foreign Mission Society priests to compensate for the bad behavior or weaknesses of a few.

To his friends he explained his feelings in greater detail. His grandfather had studied for the priesthood at the Collège Général de Penang in Malaya—the college administered by Paris Foreign Mission Society priests whom Kha had loved and admired. Kha never forgot their solicitude after he lost almost his entire family in 1885.

It was certainly due to the priests of the Paris Foreign Mission Society that Thuan never harbored anti-French sentiments. Indeed, few Vietnamese fought against French colonialism with as much fierceness and tenacity as Thuan's extended family, but neither Ngo Dinh Kha nor any of his sons or daughters could be called anti-French. They continued to admire French culture and France's contributions to humanity and the Church. They honored and emulated the great men and women of France. Thuan did the same. As much as he hated colonialism, he never generalized when speaking about the French. France remained an attraction for Thuan, and its culture nourished him. He would eventually have great friendships with thousands of French men and women in Vietnam and Europe, and never believed being a Vietnamese patriot meant being anti-French.

——————◆◆◆——————

THUAN DID NOT LOOK UPON the minor seminary as only a high school. Rather, it was the place where his personality emerged, the secret garden where his spirituality grew. Guided by holy men who made it possible for him to see the abundance of divine grace in his life, Thuan might have taken them as models for his long journey to holiness, but these humble priests directed him otherwise. He chose as models of the spiritual life three saints from whom he drew great sustenance. First, there was Saint Thérèse of Lisieux from whom he learned to place his faith in the power of prayer. Second, there was Saint John Mary Vianney, the Curé of Ars, who taught him humility and the value of strenuous effort. Finally, there was Saint Francis Xavier, his patron saint and the great apostle of Asia.

Thuan's mother had first introduced Thuan to Saint Thérèse of Lisieux when he was a child of four. Hiep spoke often of "the Little Flower," the beautiful Carmelite who had died young and left behind *The Story of a Soul*. Thuan read more about her at the minor seminary and studied her writings seriously. He was struck by the spiritual journey she described as, "the way of spiritual childhood, the way of trust and absolute surrender." Years later, during his own spiritual journey in captivity, he realized how deeply Thérèse's poetry and thought had permeated his sensibility and thinking. Without reserve, he would quote Saint Thérèse in every one of his books and unsparingly praise her and her works.

Saint John Mary Vianney, the Curé of Ars, was a favorite patron saint at the minor seminary. His life was mandatory reading and, like all of his classmates, Thuan knew in detail the strengths and weaknesses of this man of God. John Vianney was not an intellectual, but he was a man endowed with an indomitable will. Thuan learned from him the virtues of patience, perseverance, and endurance. He learned from John Vianney how to "read people" simply by opening his own heart to them. As Thuan contemplated his models, his faith in the power of prayer grew, since it was prayer that made both Thérèse of Lisieux and the Curé of Ars strong in the face of pain and difficulty. Thuan spent long hours in prayer and these hours, along with the daily Eucharist, nourished him.

Thuan longed to be an obscure pastor of a small parish, inspired both by the example of Saint John Vianney and by the novel of George Bernanos, *Diary of a Country Priest*. Thuan even envisaged for quite a long time the possibility of spending the rest of his life as a Benedictine monk meditating in the quiet of a monastery cell. Ironically, he would spend many years in a cell, but not in a monastery.

From Saint Francis Xavier Thuan learned the importance of planning work to be done in the service of God. In spite of the passion that urged Francis Xavier to rush to new lands to spread the Good News, he took the time to carefully plan his journeys and activities. Thuan, passionate by nature, learned to do the same.

But the most valuable lesson he learned from the great Apostle of the East was Francis Xavier's indifference to success or failure. The saint trusted that ultimately God would make all his efforts bear fruit. Thuan was moved to tears when he meditated on how Francis Xavier had died on a desolate beach, almost within reach from his goal, China. Was this his final defeat? Thuan never believed so. Francis Xavier had died without bitterness, embracing God's will. Much later Thuan encountered the *Monumenta Xavarena*—the body of his patron's writings—but during his minor seminary years, Thuan was already greatly inspired by the saint's zeal.

Thuan also kept burning in his heart his devotion to the Blessed Virgin Mary. Naturally enough, his three models were all great devotees of Mary. In *Five Loaves and Two Fish,* Thuan recalled that John Vianney called Mary his "first love"; that Thérèse of Lisieux had once said, "I want so much to be a priest so that I can talk of Mary to everyone"; and that Francis Xavier always ended his catechism classes with a Hail Mary. Thuan declared without his usual reserve: "My mother instilled in my heart this love for Mary from when I was just a child." He was content that the major events of his life always coincided with Marian feast days. Thuan always drew strength from his love for Mary.

In the sheltered environment of the minor seminary, Thuan read, prayed, and meditated. He was happy most of the time, though he missed his family tremendously. He felt his spiritual life, still in its infancy, becoming stronger every day.

◆◆◆

THE SEMINARIANS AT AN NINH lived a very strict schedule that was enforced mostly by the seminarians of the senior class rather than the priests. The seminarians took care of ringing the bell that marked the activities of the day, kept watch over the dormitory and study rooms, began morning and evening prayers, and made sure that the younger seminarians did not whisper a word during the hours of strict silence. They also took care of the libraries, of dispensing first-aid, and they planned and supervised sports events and celebrations. Most importantly, they prepared the daily, weekly, and annual liturgies.

In his first year, Thuan watched and admired the seniors' effectiveness. He asked the older seminarians hundreds of questions about their individual backgrounds, their hobbies, their talents, and their dreams. Never satisfied with casual acquaintance, Thuan showed a characteristic concern for everyone he met. In the environment of the minor seminary, he was interested in learning what had inspired each of his classmates to respond to God's call. Before long, Thuan knew every little peculiarity of those who studied with him.

Thuan was a careful observer of the idiosyncrasies of the people around him, and to the great joy of his audiences he could mimic voices and mannerisms to perfection, although he never did so out of malice. His talent also enabled him to speak Vietnamese with all the local accents, in the purest dialects, and aided him in learning foreign languages with extraordinary ease. He became fluent in French, Italian, Spanish, Chinese, and English, as well as Latin.

Thuan was highly respected by his classmates—awed as they were by the fact that he was the grandson of Ngo Dinh Kha, the Grand Chamberlain, and nephew of Bishop Thuc of Vinh Long, and of Diem, the former prime minister. Yet, he was not singled out or spared any duties or responsibilities because of his family connections.

One such duty was drawing water from the well early in the morning. Sleepily, Thuan would crank the unwieldy handle of the windlass to lower the heavy bucket down into the well. Then came the difficult and dangerous part of the routine; the bucket was very heavy when full, and Thuan struggled to haul it up. Should the slippery windlass slide from his hands, it could strike him in the face or send him flying head-over-heels into his classmates. All the seminarians feared this particular task and had visions of broken jaws or worse when it was their turn to haul the water.

The care and cleaning of the seminary grounds on Saturdays was another task that Thuan approached with youthful energy. He did not mind digging, tending, and fertilizing the gardens. The experience of this kind of labor served him well when he was held in various prisons where he volunteered for even the most humble tasks.

The seminarians' well-regimented daily routine began with a wake-up call at 6:00 A.M. They would scramble to the nearby washroom to bathe hurriedly in the cold water drawn from the deep well.

Fully awake now, they would rush off to church for morning prayer and Mass, followed by a quick breakfast. An hour of study in the common study hall and three classes completed the morning's activities. After lunch and a half-hour walk, the seminarians enjoyed the small luxury of a half-hour rest. The afternoon schedule was organized in a similar manner: an hour of study and three classes.

Following the afternoon classes, the seminarians were allowed an hour to play soccer. The soccer field, located just outside the seminary gate, provided the greatest physical exercise of the day. Thuan was a good soccer player and he would rush exuberantly from one end of the soccer field to the other until he was literally exhausted.

After a quick shower, the seminarians studied for a solid hour before dinner, which was followed by another half-hour walk, the recitation of the rosary, and evening prayer. Then it was time to retire to the large dormitory. Because they all followed the same schedule, the seminarians were rarely alone, day or night.

During the week, meals were eaten in silence while someone read from the life of a saint or the history of the Church. After lunch, the Martyrology, a catalogue of martyrs honored by the Church, was read in Latin. The seminarians welcomed weekends and major feast days because they could converse at mealtimes.

Saturdays were devoted to long hours of study and hikes to parishes in the region or to the beach. Cua Tung Beach was beautiful with its white sands, high promontories, dark rocks, and ancient pine trees. The heights that dominated the beach were dotted with red and white French villas. Thuan loved to swim, and the view of distant islands off the coast and the nine Elephant Head promontories jutting out into the sea stirred Thuan with a longing for distant lands and new horizons.

Sundays were special days. The most pleasurable time for Thuan was the chanting of vespers. Meals were always a little better prepared, and the seminarians were free to study or recreate or pray and meditate as they wished. Thuan excelled in Chinese chess and eagerly spent hours playing one game after another.

Major feast days interrupted the weekly routine at regular intervals. Thuan had the habit of remembering events by the feast days on which they occurred, perhaps instilled in him at home, where his family annually celebrated the feast day of their patron saints rather than birthdays. Thuan especially honored the feasts of the Blessed Virgin.

Remembering the cycle of the liturgical calendar and the major feast days of the calendar year contributed to Thuan's exceptional memory. Like other family members, including his uncles Diem and Can and his own mother, Thuan could remember faces and dates, locations and events with uncanny accuracy. By the end of his first year at the seminary, he had gained the reputation for being a walking almanac.

He did not find his studies difficult since the classes were based largely on the student's ability to memorize lessons. Because Thuan had already passed the certificate of primary school before joining the seminary, the faculty admitted him immediately to the third year, which meant he would only have to study in An Ninh for six years instead of eight.

This placed him at a level with a curriculum that included Latin and Chinese. Although many students dreaded languages, Thuan loved them. Many seminarians found Latin studies particularly discouraging. Thuan and his classmates had to memorize hundreds of grammatical rules, complete with examples and exceptions, and were then required to formulate sentences based on such rules and exceptions.

The seminarians also had to memorize the book of Genesis, one verse each day. Naturally this was easy at first, but as the amount of text increased with each passing day, some seminarians could not keep up with the class. Thuan had no such problem; and because he did not have to spend much time memorizing grammar or Genesis, he found time to study and memorize Latin poems, which he could recall throughout his life.

Chinese calligraphy was another aggravation for some of his classmates, but Thuan loved the smell of rice paper and China ink, and he enjoyed putting his personality into the brush strokes that formed the simplest or the most intricate ideograms. With Father Thich, the consummate teacher of calligraphy, hovering over him, Thuan would mentally visualize the characters before transmitting them to paper. Nevertheless, Thuan realized the importance of practice in order for an ideogram to be perfect, and likewise, he did not usually mind even the tedious aspects of his other studies. Time seemed to stand still in An Ninh, and Thuan had all the patience in the world.

The seminarians only went home during the summer, and it was one of Thuan's greatest pleasures to be able to reconnect with his siblings during those months. In the summer of 1942 Thuan went home to find that Niem, his oldest sister, had grown into a young lady of twelve, capable of helping her mother around the house and of holding her own in discussions with him on any religious subject. And Tuyen, at the age of nine, was not shy. He asked Thuan all kinds of questions about seminary life. Thuan thought that Tuyen might have a vocation, but it was Niem who eventually felt the called to religious life and entered the convent. Thuan enjoyed playing with Thanh, age seven; Ham Tieu, age four; and little Anh Tuyet, who was just two years old.

He felt some concern that being away most of the time meant that he could not fulfill his role as their eldest brother, but he loved each of his brothers and sisters so deeply that there was no awkwardness when he came home for vacation. As postal services became more reliable and telephone lines began to appear in Vietnam, Thuan would communicate with his siblings more often and offer them, on a more regular basis, his much-appreciated guidance and encouragement.

Despite his love for them, Thuan was shy regarding dramatic displays of affection for his brothers and sisters, but he was never reluctant in showing his respect. Even when they were very young, Thuan always treated their ideas seriously, listened to them attentively, tried to understand their perspectives, and considered their opinions with deference.

Vacations were also a time when Thuan enjoyed his mother's cooking, and she tried to compensate for the months he had been undernourished at the seminary. Thuan relished the special dishes she prepared, but above all, he valued the treasure of her keen memory. Mother and son spent hours talking and Thuan listened carefully to the woman who had inherited, in a special way, the wisdom of her father, Kha.

From his father Thuan learned patience. Am found fault in everything his children did or said, but this apparent penchant for criticism and reproach did not disturb but rather amused Thuan. He did not doubt that his father adored his children and truly worried when one of them became sick. Thuan came to accept his father's negative comments as his way of loving his children. Later the children nicknamed their father "Thaddeus the Difficult." Thuan would smile at this somewhat disrespectful name, but felt grateful that their father had always kept them on their toes.

During his vacations, Thuan went on short trips with his father and siblings to temples, pagodas, imperial tombs, and other architectural wonders in and around Hue. He listened to his father's running commentary on builders, building materials, and the strengths and weaknesses of the monuments they visited. Thuan continued to marvel at his father's knowledge and his appreciation of architectural beauty.

The summer was also the time when Thuan could meet with Diem. He was always available for Thuan, and Thuan treasured every minute spent with his uncle, whether they shared enthusiastic conversations, sat quietly in the orchard listening to the chorus of cicadas, or climbed Ngu Binh Mountain, which towered above the landscape a short distance from their homes.

Diem was a walking dictionary of names and places, clans and families, plants and birds. He had an eager curiosity toward every subject and a superb memory that kept everything he learned fresh. He always questioned traditions, customs, regimes, policies, and philosophies. He invited Thuan to do the same and smiled encouragingly whenever Thuan faltered in his attempts.

Politics, political philosophies, intrigues, and interpretations were not the only things Diem discussed with Thuan. Though usually reluctant to speak about spiritual things with others, because he was Thuan's godfather Diem made an exception with regard to Thuan. He spoke about the development of the inner life, the role of Mary in the Church, and the importance of meditating on the mystery of the Incarnation. Thuan was often moved by Diem's simplicity, readiness to listen, and his shyness when speaking about his own ideals and dreams.

Thuan never doubted Diem's sincerity and goodness. After his family's downfall, when the foreign media that had once heaped praises on Diem began to malign and accuse him of being a corrupt dictator and worse, Thuan would close his eyes and picture him in his mind. He would see someone who was gentle and think to himself, *They must be talking about someone else.*

Although the summers were golden seasons for Thuan, by the end of August each year he felt impatient to return to the seminary. Going back and forth between An Ninh and Hue, Thuan was fortunate to find a perfect haven at either end. When tragedies began to strike his family, Thuan remembered with gratitude the seasons he lived in An Ninh with his classmates, and the summers he spent with his beloved family in Hue. The joy and wonder of those years intimately shaped his life, a life that he incredibly described as "overbrimmed with joy." Thuan shared memories of both places with only a small number of very close friends. These memories would light up his darkest days and help him start out on the road of hope.

CHAPTER FIVE

The World in Turmoil

If I go out into the field,
look—those killed by the sword!
And if I enter the city,
look—those sick with famine!

Jeremiah 14:18

Conflict and war is one of the most frightening wastes of
human potential in today's world.

F. X. Nguyen Van Thuan,
Address on Global Ethics and Governance at UNESCO
(Paris, September 18, 2000)

TWO YEARS BEFORE THUAN had joined the seminary,
World War II had erupted. Most children in Vietnam
were barely aware that there was a war going on, but
eleven-year-old Thuan was. His family's involvement and interest in
politics made them keenly attentive to the coming tidal wave of
change. They read newspapers, listened to the radio, and discussed
the political situation and world affairs daily.

From the time the family first owned a radio, Thuan's mother
always turned it on to listen to the news saying, "Let us hear the
good and the bad news of the day." Even when, more than two decades later, the coup d'état of 1963 ended in the assassination of
Hiep's brothers Diem and Nhu, Thuan would watch his mother sitting by the radio for hours listening to the outrageous reports of
the trial that ultimately sent her third brother Can to his death be-

fore a firing squad. His father, fearing that the hostile comments would depress Hiep, would turn off the radio. She would turn it back on, insisting, "I want to know the lies and the facts. I want to hear how the trial is reported and who is saying what on the witness stand."

During the years 1939 and 1940, the international news was mostly upsetting. Nazi troops crossed into Poland and crushed Polish defenses in a lightning campaign. The Ngo Dinh clan had always detested the Nazi party, and their victory over Poland grieved them beyond words. The family then heard reports that French troops were digging foxholes and trenches in preparation for a German assault; that the French armed forces seemed to have been lulled into a state of boredom as they waited; that the air of unreality hovering over the western front caused the French to believe that they could wait forever. They even began to refer to the conflict as *la drôle de guerre* (the funny war).

It was no longer amusing when Nazi troops turned their full fury on the Netherlands, Belgium, and France. The French, who had once laughed behind the fortified and seemingly impregnable Maginot Line, now watched helplessly as German troops bypassed it. Suddenly they realized that their country was defenseless.

On June 14, 1940, the Germans captured Paris, and the eighty-three-year-old World War I hero, Marshal Philippe Pétain, signed an armistice with Germany. According to the terms of the armistice, France was divided into a free French zone under the control of Pétain's government, with its capital in Vichy, and a German-occupied zone that covered three-fifths of France, including Paris.

Diem and the entire Ngo Dinh clan did not rejoice at the humiliations endured by the French. After this defeat of France, however, the French colonial administration in Vietnam was more vulnerable than ever. Vietnamese patriots of all political leanings in Vietnam and overseas—especially the large number of Vietnamese revolutionaries in Southern China—looked upon French isolation in Indochina as a clear opportunity to overthrow French rule and achieve their nation's independence.

Indeed, the situation in Indochina soon forced the French colonial administration to accept increasingly humiliating concessions—to the Japanese. Japan's defeat of Russia in 1906 convinced

Asians that the superiority of the "white man" was purely a myth. Vietnamese Prince Cuong De and other patriots had gone to Japan and China to develop political and revolutionary structures, and they encouraged Vietnamese youth to study in those countries in order to prepare for the future overthrow of French rule. Thousands of Vietnamese responded to the call and, assisted by the revolutionaries, traveled to Japan and China to attend schools, universities, and military academies in those countries.

At that time, Japan had been engaged in a lengthy military campaign in China. The Chinese, under the leadership of Chiang Kai-shek, had been forced to withdraw from all coastal provinces and were then encircled in the Si Chuan, Guang Dong, Guang Xi, and Yun Nan provinces and adjacent areas. The Haiphong Harbor and the railroad that linked Haiphong to Yun Nan province was one of their main Chinese supply lines.

The Japanese reasoned that cutting off that supply line would crush Chinese resistance. They demanded that the French stop supplying goods, ammunition, and weapons to China. They also requested the use of certain airports and permission to station their troops in various cities in North Vietnam to be close to the Chinese border.

Then, while elsewhere political and military accords were negotiated, signed, and renegotiated, Japanese troops fighting in Southern China turned, crossed over the border, and invaded North Vietnam on September 24, 1940.

In the fighting that ensued, 800 French soldiers died in and around the border town of Lang Son. Units of Prince Cuong De's *Kien Quoc Quan* (Army of National Rebuilding) followed the Japanese into Lang Son in an attempt to overthrow the French colonialists.

However, not long after the capture of Lang Son, the Japanese withdrew their troops and declared the invasion a mistake, and asked Prince Cuong De's revolutionaries to return to China. When some elements of the *Kien Quoc Quan* refused, the French massacred them pitilessly while the Japanese stood by and watched with indifference.

Though Diem never spoke of it, Thuan knew of his close ties with Prince Cuong De and his network of revolutionaries in Vietnam and overseas. Diem also had enduring friendships with many Japanese who were key players in the making and implementing of Japan's policies in Indochina. But Thuan and most Vietnamese did not know—before the Lang Son conflict—that Vietnamese revolutionary units had been armed and trained in China until these units materialized in North Vietnam and fought alongside Japanese troops against the French.

For a few days, those who could listen to the radio followed the battle in Lang Son. After school, the young Thuan sat beside his mother and listened to the reports on the fighting. Then he would run to his grandmother's home in the evening and wait for Diem to comment on the day's events. Diem was not optimistic. From the very first report that the Vietnamese revolutionary forces had invaded Lang Son, Diem had shaken his head and said: "This is not a good move." Then the news came of the massacre of *Kien Quoc Quan* soldiers. Thuan grieved over the massacre, as he had grieved a week earlier for the French soldiers killed by the Japanese.

Diem was distraught for days and he hardly spoke. When he did communicate, it was to say, "Never trust allies who do not see you as an equal, especially those that are a hundred times stronger than you." The duplicity of the Japanese in Lang Son radically changed Diem's views regarding Japan's government. He preserved his friendship with many Japanese, but he lost his confidence in Japanese policies in East Asia. He decided that the Japanese military could not be counted on as allies of Vietnamese revolutionaries.

One day he confided to Thuan, "I had thought the Japanese, being readers of Confucius and the Chinese classics like us, would make good allies. I was wrong. They are always trying to impress us with their talk about respecting the 'warrior's code,' but in this they have acted without honor. Never trust people who act without honor."

The Lang Son incident revealed how weak France had become in Indochina. The French colonial administration was both frightened and profoundly humiliated. Vietnamese patriots watched the French quandary and knew that France's days in Vietnam were numbered. The French colonial government made one concession after another in an effort to placate the Japanese, but to little avail. Soon the Japanese landed in Haiphong, occupied all the airports in

North Vietnam, and took control of Cam Ranh Bay for their naval units. They then signed an agreement with the Vichy regime back in France by which Japan recognized French sovereignty over French Indochina and France allowed Japan the use of all airports in Indochina. Japanese troops landed in Nha Trang and took effective control of all Vietnam's airports in Da Nang, Nha Trang, Saigon, Soc Trang, Bien Hoa, and Phnom Penh.

Physically cut off from support from France, the French armed forces in Indochina and the French colonial administration could not resist Japanese demands. Eventually, Japan would be rid of them for good.

For the first time in sixty years of French domination, Vietnamese revolutionaries and patriots saw the definite possibility of the end of colonial rule in their lifetime. From north to south, diverse Vietnamese revolutionary cells began mushrooming. Rebellion and revolt were in the air, despite the presence of the French secret police.

AFTER ENTERING THE SEMINARY, Thuan found An Ninh Seminary to be a small island of peace and quiet on the stormy ocean of events that were shaping and reshaping the world scene. During his first year at An Ninh (1941–1942), Thuan kept informed of the major political and military events taking place, even though the world's turmoil came to him filtered through his teachers, delayed by slow mail, and distorted by his own focus on study and prayer. He accepted this seclusion, knowing that over the summer his mother and Diem would detail whatever he had missed during the academic year. Nevertheless, Thuan seemed to live in two worlds: in An Ninh he was protected but ignorant; in Hue he was informed but vulnerable.

In 1941 the French in Indochina faced a dilemma. Unable to resist the Japanese, they reluctantly adopted a policy of collaboration with them, thereby risking the wrath of China and its allies. By April and May of 1942 Allied planes began bombing Japanese military installations in Vietnam as well as centers of transportation, especially railroads. The planes came from Si Chuan, in China. Though the bombing was sporadic and limited to the north, it was

Thuan's first taste of warfare. He watched as his country was drawn inexorably into the maelstrom.

By August 1942 bombing had intensified, with Hanoi and Haiphong in North Vietnam becoming the key targets. In the month of August 1942 fifty French and Vietnamese were killed and seventy-one injured. On December 22, 1942 the bombing killed forty-five and injured forty-one, most of them civilians.

During his summer vacation of 1942 Thuan scanned the newspapers and discussed the situation with Diem whenever he could. The French had cast their lot with Japan and official media constantly sang the praises of Japanese military genius. Had not Japanese troops vanquished the British in Hong Kong, Malaya, and Singapore? Had not they destroyed most of the American naval units in Pearl Harbor? Had not they defeated the Americans and Filipinos in the Philippines and taken over the Indonesian islands from the Dutch? But Diem no longer believed in Japan's good will or their widely touted goal of establishing a "Greater East Asia Sphere of Co-Prosperity."

Diem tried to teach Thuan how to look at the broader context of the war. The December 1941 attack on Pearl Harbor had finally drawn the United States into the war. With U.S. troops fighting alongside the Allies, Diem predicted that the expanding Greater Japanese Empire was moving steadily toward collapse. Thuan listened with ever greater respect to the man who seemed cut off from the outside world in his Phu Cam retreat, yet could so convincingly analyze the political and military situation of the world.

Thuan's uncle wanted him to learn how to look at any situation with the eye of a strategist. Diem often said, "Our struggle against the French has, so far, never been effective because our leaders—be they emperors, mandarins, or party leaders—have never practiced strategic thinking. They failed because they improvised. They failed because they focused on the details and not on the total picture. We are now approaching a great opportunity. The evident weaknesses of the French colonists tell us that the day is near when our country will become independent. Yet, our leaders must learn to think strategically or they will miss the opportunity and will lead the country toward great disasters."

In late August 1942, as he prepared to return to the seminary, Thuan went to Pham thi Than's house to say good-bye to his uncle. He found Diem tending the rose bushes in the garden. They embraced and Diem asked Thuan to pray for Vietnam and to remember him to the French priests at the seminary. Diem sounded more sorrowful that day because of the reports of widespread famine in the north, where the impact of the monopolistic and aggressive purchase of rice for export to Japan was causing great hardship. Diem was bitter about the French Governor General's acquiescence (on July 18, 1942) to a Japanese monopoly on such basic commodities. The more aggressively the Japanese bought rice, the higher the price rose, and the stricter the rationing of rice became in Vietnam. People starving in rural areas migrated to the cities, but found no relief in the urban centers. Death by starvation was beginning to spread.

———◆◆◆———

FROM ALL THAT HE WAS READING and hearing, Thuan formed his views on the nature of war. As he returned to An Ninh, he was convinced of the grim truth that war was evil. It killed and maimed innocent people, it increased poverty, and it caused starvation. This first taste of war had made of him a peace lover, or rather, an apostle of peace.

Thuan began to pray day and night for world peace, and for the end of war in his own country. He analyzed the evils that accompany war and as he gradually questioned his admiration for the great warriors of world history, Caesar, Alexander, and Napoleon fell from their pedestals. The rapid campaigns of Nazi Germany in Europe, and the lightning expansion of the Japanese Empire south and eastward, no longer impressed Thuan. Each military victory necessarily demanded the loss of human life and bred human misery.

Thuan had always focused only on the number of Vietnamese casualties in any conflict. Now he looked more closely at worldwide statistics and was horrified by the number reported in the newspapers. He suddenly became aware of the Second World War's global devastation. The more he looked at the numbers, the more disgusted he became with war. He felt helpless before the reality of immense human suffering experienced all around the world.

In the fall of 1942, refreshed from their vacations, Thuan and a small group of seminarians from Hue decided to go to the shrine of Our Lady of La Vang to pray for peace. Thuan and his classmates spent the whole day at the shrine. They felt happy and at peace as they prayed and meditated, and explored the site. In the surrounding jungle, they found traces of the ruins of the shrine's original chapel, which had been built in 1820 and subsequently burned to the ground in 1885 by the *van than* militia. On the exact site of the present-day shrine, a new church had been built in 1886 and consecrated in 1901. That church soon proved too small for the large number of pilgrims that flocked there for special events, and the larger shrine was built.

The history of La Vang and the story of the apparitions of the Blessed Virgin were familiar to the seminarians. Catholics in the last decade of the eighteenth century had fled to the jungle to escape the persecution initiated by the Tay Son dynasty. They arrived at the site with nothing but fear of their cruel persecutors and hope to preserve their faith. Then one night a Lady came and spoke to them and her words quieted all their pain and fear. She lifted the refugees out of their misery and strengthened their hope in eternal life.

The Lady did not appear just once, but she came back night after night until all their worries had been vanquished, until they understood how precious they were to her. They were not just a crowd of hungry, frightened people; they were *her* children, chosen and purified by the blood of her Son, carrying within them the seed of divine life on their way to eternal life.

Later, from 1820 to 1886, during more periods of persecution, Catholics fled into the same jungle. And again the Lady came back to strengthen their faith and restore their hope, to assure them that she would never leave them orphans.

That day, with his fellow seminarians, Thuan experienced for the first time in his life an almost physical, powerful presence of the Blessed Virgin Mary over the sanctuary grounds and in the nearby jungle. Thuan prayed for the return of peace in the troubled world around him. He would visit that holy ground as often as he could to pray for world peace and the end of war in Vietnam.

Many decades later, in the Jubilee Year 2000, Thuan began a new worldwide movement for young people: the global Community of Our Lady of La Vang.

------◆◆◆◆------

As Thuan settled down for another year of study and prayer at the seminary, two major disasters struck Vietnam. On October 10, 1942, the passenger ship *Laos* sunk in a typhoon in the Gulf of Tonkin, killing fifty-eight people. On November 16, two passenger trains collided just outside Hanoi, killing twenty-six people and injuring another fifty-eight.

Though these events were unrelated to the war, Thuan viewed them as part of the larger tragedy afflicting his country. He made no distinction between the victims of natural or man-made disasters; neither did he separate the dead and injured into the categories of French or Vietnamese. Once, when a classmate mentioned the difference, Thuan exclaimed with irritation, "They are no longer French or Vietnamese *now*, are they?"

The French missionaries at the seminary faced the turmoil stoically and kept a calm countenance even when the worst occurred. The young seminarians received news of the outside world through the mild and cautious comments of their teachers who, by common accord, attempted to shelter their students from the violent conflicts around the world.

Yet, Thuan and his fellow seminarians could not be sheltered from the fact that the world they had known as children was fast disappearing, and that war waited for them just outside of the seminary's gate. They were aware that a significant number of Vietnamese, who had gone to fight alongside the French against Nazi Germany, had been captured and were being held in detention camps by the French Vichy regime. They felt their inability to alleviate the misery of their fellow countrymen who were now prisoners of war. It was obvious to all of them that if the war were to continue for a few more years, they might all be called up to fight on some battlefield.

The seminarians had seen how Japanese propaganda for a Greater East Asia had won many adherents in Vietnam, and the boys knew that Vietnamese secret parties had been actively organizing in Vietnam and Southern China in preparation for Japan's invasion of North Vietnam. For some, the scene was too complicated and disturbing and they tried to focus on their studies to shut out the outside world. But there was no escape for Thuan. His grandfather, uncles, and mother had inspired in him a vocation of patriotism, and while Thuan loved peace and hated war, he believed he must somehow "live the war." He had to keep in mind the mounting number of casualties, and pray for all those who were killed or maimed. He also had to keep watching for weaknesses in the French rule and for opportunities that would aid patriots to rid themselves of colonial domination.

———— ◆◦◆◦◆ ————

GERMANY'S STRATEGIC ERROR OF TAKING ON the Soviet Union in June of 1941, and entrance of the United States into the war in December of 1941, sealed the eventual defeat of the Axis powers. At the same time, Japan's rapid conquests in Southeast Asia—to the detriment of the British, French, and Dutch colonial empires—and its anti-white propaganda enflamed Asians with fervent enthusiasm for national independence and, in many cases, hatred of white colonialists.

The French missionaries at the seminary were as discreet as ever about world events. By never indulging in discussions about the war, they succeeded in ensuring that An Ninh Seminary remained a peaceful haven. Yet, even there the ferment of revolution had already begun working. Many of the seminarians had never imagined the idea of national independence and had never been encouraged to work toward such a goal. Japan's humiliation of the French, British, and Dutch colonialists opened their eyes to the fact that the white man *could* be defeated, and that they were not "superior" to Asians.

French Governor General Jean Decoux tried to organize Vietnamese youth to create a larger force to counter Japanese ambition in Indochina. He asked the youth to follow the shining example of Joan of Arc in defending and loving France, their Metropolitan

Motherland. However, his efforts only managed to incite Vietnamese youth—including the young seminarians in An Ninh—to follow instead the example of the Trung Sisters (who had rebelled against the Chinese in A.D. 40–43 in defense of Vietnam) and to feel a greater love for their own country.

Many of the seminarians believed that after the war there would rise a new era of national independence. Along with other educated people in Vietnam, they began to consider the evils of colonialism. They regarded the "civilizing mission" of Europe pure arrogance, and resented the fact that the majority of the French in Vietnam, even the educated, looked on the Vietnamese as an inferior race. The seminarians now recognized that even in the most compassionate of official French writings during the more than sixty years of domination, the Vietnamese had never been treated as equals. They reread French textbooks, which made it clear that in the eyes of most French people, the Vietnamese were childish, quarrelsome, mischievous, lazy, and unreliable indigenous people in need of civilizing.

But as much as the growing resentment against the French permeated the thick bamboo walls of the seminary, the French missionaries continued to receive the loving respect of their students. Thuan never forgot the fortitude and the understanding of the French priests at An Ninh during this time. Sharing the sadness of war and the hope for national independence with his classmates, Thuan continued to study, pray, and meditate, and he longed to see his uncle Diem during the summer.

Before leaving for the summer vacation of 1943, Thuan received the good news that he had another baby sister, Thuy Tien. He also learned that his uncle, Khoi, had been forced by French Resident Superior Emile Grandjean to resign his positions as governor of Quang Nam province and viceroy of the Southern provinces. This did not surprise Thuan. He did not know exactly what had happened, but he could guess. Ngo Dinh Khoi had been working closely with Diem, and had thus drawn upon himself the wrath of the French authorities. Diem was not simply a retired prime minister with a passion for rose gardens and a camera and darkroom. Diem was secretly organizing a vast network of patriots affiliated with Prince Cuong De. Thuan realized that Diem must also be in great danger, and the thought tormented him.

When he arrived in Hue, however, Thuan found Diem at peace, living as if nothing could possibly happen to him. When Thuan asked Diem about Khoi's dismissal, Diem answered: "By now you should know that our lives are in God's hands and that honors and positions are of little value. Your grandfather also had a high position in the imperial court's hierarchy, but when the emperor was forced to abdicate, the French dismissed him without a pension. I was once prime minister, but when I resigned from my office the court and the French stripped me of all honors and rank. We must do what we must do and leave everything else in God's hands. Your Uncle Khoi did what he had to do, and was prepared to take the consequences."

Once again, Thuan was struck by Diem's interior peace. Secretly heading a revolutionary network while surrounded by French spies, Diem did not seem to have a care in the world.

That summer Diem again took time to chat with Thuan and test his knowledge. He encouraged Thuan to study Chinese and Asian philosophy, saying, "I know that you have four hours of Chinese study a week in the seminary, but that's not enough. Chinese is so essential to Vietnamese cultural life. You have to have a good handle on the Chinese classics. Don't let anyone fool you. Chinese is not a dead language, and Chinese philosophy will answer many questions."

Diem's words would stay with Thuan for years and he gradually came to understand that Christianity should be imbedded in the cultural tradition of a country. In a way, he was already predisposed as a young man toward the Church's teachings on inculturation, which would be fully developed after the Second Vatican Council.

Diem and Thuan climbed the pine-covered Ngu Binh Mountain at least three times that summer. Once, watching Thuan's face, Diem said, "Only a few years ago when we climbed Ngu Binh Mountain, I had to carry you on my shoulders." Thuan did not say anything, but he thought, *Yes, I am older, but you seem not to have changed a bit.*

It was true that Diem never seemed to change. When he returned to Vietnam in 1954 after a long self-imposed exile, he looked almost the same as he had in 1943.

Once Thuan's tutor in political strategies, Diem had also become his spiritual guide. He spoke more often about the things of God and the necessity of leading a life of prayer and meditation. His behavior and attitudes, more than his words, impressed Thuan. Thuan's devotion to his uncle became boundless.

————◆◆◆————

IN THE SUMMER OF 1943, Thuan was fifteen years old and began facing teenage "growing pains." Like most adolescents, Thuan began to assert himself and to challenge the views of adults. For the first time in his life he was easily provoked to anger. He had never before dreamed of talking back to his parents, but now Thuan suddenly found himself ready to challenge his father's critical remarks and sometimes had to control himself in order to avoid explosive confrontations. He knew his father did not mean to hurt his feelings or to be unjust, but it was difficult to be patient with Am's criticism. Outlandish as his father seemed at times, Am was always rational, and Thuan tried to gain from him valuable lessons and perspectives, uncommon views and intriguing opinions.

Perhaps in response to this, Thuan also spent more time that summer reading biographies of saints and praying. Meditating on the mysteries of the rosary helped calm his anxieties. The daily Eucharist gave him renewed strength; he never missed early morning Mass.

Thuan needed physical activity, too, and was faithful to a regime of morning exercises. He also took long walks and went mountain climbing whenever he could. A good swimmer, he made the fifteen-mile trip to the Thuan An Beach on holidays to spend the day swimming. He took long rides to the Imperial tombs and Buddhist pagodas and found peace in those secluded places.

When Thuan returned to An Ninh in the fall, he found that his classmates had also grown up quickly over the summer. They had lived outside the walls of the seminary and learned about the war in Europe and the Pacific. They had also listened to discussions on the future of a post-war world.

Thuan and his fellow seminarians tried to stay focused on their studies, which required so much of their time and energies. For many, Latin and Chinese continued to prove insurmountable. Thuan was far ahead of his classmates in both subjects and could discourse convincingly on Confucian classics. He loved reciting Virgil's poetry. His continued ease in memorizing gave him more leisure time, and so he turned his energy to the seminary library, a genuine treasure.

Many French missionaries, upon returning to France, had left behind the books they had read or used in the seminary. Most prominent among these was Father Léopold Cadière. One of the greatest scholars of his time, Cadière was a universal scientist whose curiosity ranged from botany to geology, from archeology to linguistics, from astronomy to anthropology. The volumes he had given to the library were made more valuable by the notes and comments he had written in the margins or at the end of the chapters. Thuan enjoyed deciphering Father Cadière's scribbling as much as he enjoyed reading the books.

The library also contained quite a respectable collection of saints' biographies. Thuan studied these and tried to learn something new from each saint. During that year Thuan discovered Theophane Venard and began to read anything he could find on this martyr. Venard, a French missionary, was forced to spend months locked in a cage and then was killed in 1861 during the Christian persecutions under Emperor Tu Duc. While he lived in the cage, he wrote inspiring letters to friends and family. Thuan was moved by Saint Thérèse of Lisieux's poem in Venard's honor. The spirituality of Theophane Venard would permeate Thuan's future life and works. When he wrote *The Road of Hope* in 1975, Thuan kept in his mind's eye the vision of Venard writing letters from his cage.

As his studies in Chinese advanced, Thuan recognized for himself the pre-Christian values of Confucianism and in the Confucian social order. He readily admitted that the Confucian hierarchy of values had sometimes baffled him. In its three relationships, for instance, Confucianism places the king above the teacher and the teacher above the father. That seemed illogical or at least completely outdated. Still, the more Thuan thought about it the more he comprehended its meaning, and the more it corresponded to his own spiritual heritage.

The king, called Son of Heaven, was not only a political ruler, he was the link between heaven and his subjects. He was the one who each year, in the name of the nation, performed the offerings to Heaven. He was the link between God and men and represented spirituality. Thus, for Thuan, he represented the "culture of breath." The teacher was honored before the father because he shaped the mind of his students. He worked with their intellect and brought them knowledge and wisdom and so represented the "culture of paper." The father was honored last because the physical realm was lower than the intellectual and the spiritual level. The father represented matter or, in Thuan's comparison, the "culture of stone."

Thuan recalled his uncle's explanation of the hierarchy of the Confucian social order: "In the traditional social order, the scholar was put above the farmer, the farmer above the craftsman, and the craftsman above the merchant. You may wonder why the Confucians adopted that kind of hierarchy." Diem had stopped then, and added thoughtfully, "You can see that the world around you offers quite a different picture. Evidently, the merchant is richer than the craftsman, the craftsman richer than the farmer, and the farmer richer than the scholar. So why do Confucians refuse to see that?"

When Thuan did not attempt an answer, Diem offered a response: "The scholar works with his intellect. That is why he was thought to be superior to those who work with their hands. The farmer works with his hands like the craftsman, but he respects nature and needs its cooperation to obtain good crops. The craftsman modifies nature while he works. He changes nature and so is judged inferior to the farmer who preserves and collaborates with nature. Finally there is the merchant who, rightly or wrongly, is believed to be unproductive. He trades with what the scholar, the farmer, and the craftsman what they produce with their minds or their hands. In the eyes of Confucians, he does not add any value to the work of others.

"Today that social order has apparently become obsolete. Your parents and grandparents on your father's side have been builders and craftsmen. On your mother's side, we are all scholars and were once farmers. Yet, you do not see any difference between the two sides of your bloodline. We are all men and women of faith; we are all descendants of martyrs from whom we inherited courage and spirituality."

––––––––––◆◆◆––––––––––

THE FOLLOWING JUNE 1944, Thuan arrived in Hue for vacation. A few weeks later he went to visit Diem, despite a warning to stay away from his grandmother's house because the French were expected to take some action against Diem for his suspected revolutionary activities. When Thuan arrived, Diem seemed reluctant to send him away, and he asked Thuan to stay for lunch. As they ate, Diem analyzed the consequences of the Allied landing in Normandy on June 6, 1944, and predicted the inevitable collapse of the Axis powers. He also spoke of his dream that an independent Vietnam emerge out of the war.

As always, God kept coming back into the conversation. Thuan could not help but think that if not for Kha's dream of Vietnamese national independence and his expressed wish that Diem fight for that goal, his uncle would have been happy as a contemplative monk.

On July 7, 1944, the French secret police surrounded Pham thi Than's house and entered to arrest Diem. They discovered that that he had already escaped. Somehow forewarned, Diem had disguised himself as a priest and slipped away. Authorities interrogated Pham thi Than for hours, but she could only tell them that she did not know where Diem had gone. They spent days interrogating Thuan's uncle Nhu, who worked at the French Residence General. But he truly did not know Diem's whereabouts.

Thuan worried about Diem until reassuring messages came into his mother's hands. The family learned that Diem had fled to the Japanese Consul in Hue, and had taken a Japanese plane to Da Nang and then to Saigon. Despite his inclinations to distrust the Japanese at that time, Diem had relied on a network of Japanese friends because he knew that the French would never dare do anything against Japanese officials.

Thuan missed Diem and their discussions, but he hoped that Khoi might replace Diem as his mentor. Thuan was therefore distraught to discover that he could not meet with his uncle Khoi, because it was too dangerous. Khoi was being closely watched by the French secret police and was virtually under house arrest.

In late August 1944, Thuan made the trip back to An Ninh entirely by boat because Allied planes were continually bombing the railroad between Hue and Ben Hai.

CHAPTER SIX

Japan's Victory and Defeat

All those things have vanished like a shadow,
and like a rumor that passes by;
like a ship that sails through the billowy water,
and when it has passed no trace can be found,
no track of its keel in the waves.

Wisdom 5:9–10

We need to succeed in disarming ourselves,
I have fought this war for years and years.
It was terrible. But now I am disarmed.
I am no longer afraid of anything,
because love drives out fear.

Patriarch Athenagoras quoted in *Testimony of Hope*,
F. X. Nguyen Van Thuan

THUAN CELEBRATED THE COLDEST Lunar New Year of his life on February 13, 1945 at the seminary. Actually, there was not much of a celebration. Just one week before, American planes had bombed Saigon and its nearby district Cho Lon, killing 154 people and injuring fifty-four. More people died of starvation every day in the North and, according to different sources, the number of victims was around ten thousand.

Despite the widespread famine in Vietnam, the Japanese continued to force Governor General Jean Decoux to increase the quota of rice sold to Japan. The Vietnamese, even those who once had some sympathy for the Japanese, now rejoiced at American victories against the Axis in the Philippines and elsewhere.

The daily, heavy attacks on Tokyo by American planes based in the Philippines and the imminent landing of U.S. troops on Japanese islands, strengthened Japan's resolve to take over Indochina permanently. On March 15, Japan sent an ultimatum to Governor General Decoux demanding a written guarantee of French military support of Japan if the Allies landed anywhere in Indochina. Given two hours to consider the terms of the ultimatum, Decoux rejected them. But the French in Indochina were no match for the Japanese. That very night the Japanese launched attacks on all French garrisons and met almost no resistance. In less than twenty-four hours they defeated the French.

Emperor Bao Dai was on one of his regular hunting trips when he heard of the coup de force. He hurried back to the capital to find that Japan had become Vietnam's new master. With Japan's encouragement and consent, Bao Dai declared the independence of "Greater Vietnam" from France on March 11.

In An Ninh the French missionaries did not comment on the events. They had good reason to be unhappy, but tried to act as if the events had nothing to do with them. In reality, they actually expected to be arrested and interred by the Japanese at any moment.

The seminarians in An Ninh were divided as they passionately discussed the events. Some argued that after sixty years of French domination the Vietnamese should rejoice over their new national independence. Others, like Thuan, were concerned and argued that the Japanese might prove worse than the French, and they insisted that Bao Dai's announcement of independence was a farce. A weak ruler, Bao Dai had grown up in France and, for all practical purposes, depended on the French colonial administration to run the government. He had deferred to the decisions of the French officials in even the most insignificant of matters. Now he would relate to the Japanese in the same way. He would not be permitted to make any major decisions just as in the past.

The Japanese coup de force and the proclamation of independence had two major consequences, both of which hit very close to home for Thuan and his fellow seminarians. Immediately after the surrender of the French armed forces in Indochina, the Japanese arrested all French men living in the former colony and forced them into concentration camps. In the week following the coup, a detachment of Japanese soldiers arrived at An Ninh Seminary to escort the French priests to Hue, where they were imprisoned at Providence Institute.

The injustice of such indiscriminate punishment on the vanquished population became tangible to the seminarians. It was heartrending for them to see their teachers led away under military escort. Now they realized more fully the important role Father Urrutia and Father Cressonnier had played in their lives. They also learned a difficult lesson: no one is safe in wartime.

The departure of the French priests was devastating to those left behind at An Ninh. Although Father Urrutia had long prepared Father Andre Nguyen Van Tich to succeed him, the sudden departure left a void that was hard to fill.

Thuan and his classmates waited anxiously for news of the missionaries. Before long, they began to receive letters and messages from the imprisoned priests, which reassured and consoled them. The priests did not complain about difficult conditions, but maintained their wonderful sense of humor and laughed at the unfortunate incidents in the camp. They seemed oblivious to their surroundings and wrote beautiful messages to their former students, telling them of their hopes for the future and promising their prayers.

The missionaries did not lose their courage during those trying times, and when he became a prisoner Thuan gratefully recalled his teachers' letters from prison. They had shown him the joy and the hope that even captivity could not destroy.

The second consequence of Japan's coup de force was Emperor Bao Dai's desire that Ngo Dinh Diem be the new prime minister. Within a week of the change of power, the emperor had requested the resignation of his entire cabinet. The move was not unexpected. The cabinet under the direction of Prime Minister Pham Quynh had been a tool of the French colonial administration and obviously could not stay on. The emperor was relieved that

Pham Quynh left with good grace, but agonized over who would head the new administration in a time of crisis. Emperor Bao Dai's finally decided to nominate Diem and his offer was conveyed through the office of Ambassador Yokoyama. Bao Dai waited for Diem's response, but no reply came.

When news of Diem's nomination spread at the seminary, Thuan became the center of attention. His classmates surrounded him and wanted to know if he believed Diem would accept the offer.

Thuan laughed them off. He had no privileged information. As he told them, their guess was as good as his. This was only partly true, however. From earlier conversations with Diem, Thuan was almost certain that Diem would never agree to become prime minister under such circumstances.

Thuan believed Diem would decline the offer because he had already seen the writing on the wall: the Japanese were losing the war. It was only a matter of weeks, perhaps even days, before the total collapse of the Axis powers. The Japanese had not returned any real power to Emperor Bao Dai, and the so-called Independent Greater Vietnam was neither greater nor yet independent. Also, Diem would not accept such an offer because he had seen Japan's duplicity and it was obvious that the Japanese had simply replaced the French as "masters" of the country.

On April 17, with no response from Diem, Emperor Bao Dai announced the formation of a new cabinet with the historian, Tran Trong Kim, as the new prime minister. As Diem had predicted, it was a "cabinet of technocrats" without real power. In fact, all the key positions previously held by French officials were "temporarily" handed over to the Japanese. Governor General Jean Decoux was taken prisoner, and Japanese Ambassador Yokoyama "agreed" to assume the role of the emperor's supreme advisor in his stead.

One of the first tasks the new cabinet faced was to provide relief assistance to the northern provinces where famine had reached catastrophic dimension. Resources were scarce, and neither Emperor Bao Dai nor his previous ministers had been able to offer anything beyond symbolic aid to the starving population.

The cabinet also quickly abolished the French education system and attempted to replace it. Their only accomplishment of lasting consequence was making Vietnamese the official language in the school system.

◆◦◆◦◆

As THUAN FINISHED HIS FOURTH YEAR in An Ninh, the Nazi regime in Germany came to a violent end. On May 1, 1945, Russian and Allied troops penetrated further into the heart of Berlin. Hitler's alleged suicide and the fall of Berlin left Japan alone on the final battlefield against the Allied forces.

In June, Thuan returned to Hue for vacation to find that the Japanese had stationed a large garrison in the Imperial City. He saw anti-aircraft artillery pieces everywhere, especially along the banks of the Perfume River where its two bridges were bombed regularly. Almost every day piercing sirens announced the approach of American planes. The alarm that could be heard all over the city came from the power plant located less than half a mile from Thuan's home.

When Thuan heard the wailing of sirens he prayed that stray bombs would not kill innocent civilians and that no damage would be done to the city's historical sites. He also prayed for the safety of his younger brother Tuyen, who was studying at the Pellerin Institute located near the White Tiger Bridge—a frequent target—and within walking distance of the family's home.

When Thuan arrived in Hue, twelve-year-old Tuyen was waiting for him. Tuyen told Thuan that after the Japanese coup de force, the family had temporarily moved to a distant village near the sea. The boy took Thuan by the hand to show him where the Japanese had built a road through their garden. The road led to large, camouflaged sheds at the extreme end of the property. They had been built to hide locomotive engines, and Thuan was shocked to see the heavy equipment still on the family's property. Fortunately the Japanese were no longer around. They had left the engines in the care of Vietnamese conductors and engineers. Perhaps they had even forgotten about them; after all, the Japanese had more important matters to consume their attention.

Thuan's family moved back to Hue in late July, and two weeks later, on August 5, 1945, Tran Trong Kim and his entire cabinet resigned, but then stayed on as a "caretaker government." Just one day later, an atomic bomb destroyed Hiroshima. Bao Dai had asked Kim to form a new cabinet, but after the atomic attack it became impossible. Japan was already on its knees and collaboration with the defeated nation would have been a foolish move. Emperor Bao Dai now knew it was time to once again ask Diem to head the government; but again, there was no response.

———————◆◆◆◆———————

THUAN WOULD ALWAYS REMEMBER August 6, 1945. Radios blared the news of the total destruction of Hiroshima, and at first Thuan could not comprehend the massive destruction and immense holocaust; he was in denial. Over the next few days, however, reports of the details of the devastation made the nightmarish vision of Hiroshima unbearably real.

Then another bomb was dropped on Nagasaki. All Thuan wanted to do was go back to An Ninh and bury himself in his books. He tried to pray, but the thought of the two destroyed cities overwhelmed and preoccupied him.

Only after the atomic attacks did the Japanese lift their strict censorship and allow local newspapers to report on Japanese losses: the fire bombing of Tokyo and other Japanese cities. Those who hated the Japanese said: "They have sown the wind; now they reap the whirlwind." Thuan could sympathize with the logic of their statement, but he also felt the pain of the former victors.

In Hue, every day before sunset, the Japanese soldiers climbed to the top of the ramparts of the Mang Ca Fortress. Arm in arm in the twilight, their thousands of voices echoed throughout the city as they sang heartbreaking songs of their vanquished army and broken dreams. Although the citizens of Hue had disliked the Japanese, the sadness of their songs moved them so deeply that many wept.

Late one evening, Hiep and Tuyen went to watch the Japanese on the ramparts. Finally, Thuan himself went to see the surreal spectacle. He returned home that night terribly shaken. Human ambition and so many futile victories seemed to melt on the dark walls of the city of Hue. For the longest time Thuan was haunted by the memory of the Japanese soldiers standing in the dusk, their faces wet with tears, their silhouettes gradually fading in the night.

The end of World War II brought no joy to Thuan. Peace had returned, but he could not celebrate. He sat for hours in the chapel of his home feeling overwhelmed by the events. What struck Thuan most profoundly was how rapidly the "glorious" Japanese Empire had collapsed. The more Thuan thought about it, the more he was convinced of the fragility of all human dreams and undertakings. Later on, the inscription on his episcopal ring would read *Todo Pasa,* "Everything passes."

Everyone waited to see what would happen next. Then one morning in early August, the people of Hue woke up to see red flags flying here and there around the city, and especially on the citadel of Hue. By noontime people had begun discuss who might be behind the red flags. Then, in fear, they whispered the words *Viet Minh.*

The military commander of the citadel asked Bao Dai if the flags should be pulled down; the emperor just shrugged. Bao Dai did not really know what he should, or could, do. He was waiting for Diem's return; only Diem would know what to do. But there was no sign of him.

CHAPTER SEVEN

An Era Ends

A king is not saved by his great army;
a warrior is not delivered by his great strength.
The war horse is a vain hope for victory,
and by its great might it cannot save.

Psalm 33:16–17

A leader must be brave, he must be calm in the face of the
unexpected event, whenever or wherever it crops up. If he
observes these rules he will be able to overcome the
severest of challenges.

The Road of Hope,
F. X. Nguyen Van Thuan

THUAN HAD BEEN BORN under the last emperor of the
Nguyen dynasty; his grandfather had loyally served
Emperor Thanh Thai; two of his uncles, Khoi and
Diem, had served Emperors Khai Dinh and Bao Dai. The Nguyen
dynasty had ruled their country for years, even though the last emperors acted mostly as figureheads. Thuan had grown up in chang-
ing times, but it never crossed his mind that the Nguyen dynasty
would end. Yet, before Thuan left for the fall 1945 semester at An
Ninh, the Viet Minh had already begun to take power.

Better organized than other revolutionary groups and patri-
otic parties, the Viet Minh was created in 1941 by Ho Chi Minh,
himself a Communist leader. The group developed a strong core of

seasoned Communists and had succeeded in taking Hanoi on August 19 after engineering massive street demonstrations. The Japanese, still garrisoned all over Vietnam as they awaited disarmament by the Chinese and British troops, offered to help Bao Dai wipe out the Viet Minh. The emperor hesitated. When the first red flags had appeared in Hue, the number of local Viet Minh cadres could be counted on the fingers of two hands, but Bao Dai refused their offer.

Diem had reportedly been on his way back to Hue from Saigon. For days the emperor and the people of Hue waited for Diem's return. He could now be made prime minister without fear of being tainted by the perception that he was either pro-Japanese or merely a tool in their hands. But where was he?

The emperor turned to Khoi and asked him to step in to save the country. Khoi declined saying that Diem alone could save the situation. He advised the emperor to wait for Diem and to stand firm against the Viet Minh Communists in the meantime. No one knew at the time that Viet Minh cadres had already captured Diem in South Central Vietnam and were escorting him to North Vietnam. No one knew that, sick and starving, he had to walk most of the almost eight hundred miles, to a remote tribal village near the Chinese border.

Thuan only had to observe his mother to know the gravity of the situation. She seemed to posses her characteristic peace, but Hiep spent a great deal more time in her home's chapel during that month of August. Thuan had heard her sighing heavily when she thought no one else was home.

Thuan felt a great catastrophe closing in on the people nearest to him. He knew that Khoi had put his life in jeopardy by strongly advising the emperor to resist the Communists. If the Communists took over the whole country, what would happen to Khoi?

Even though he still was under the French police's surveillance, Khoi had managed become a substitute mentor to Thuan in Diem's absence. During the summer of 1945, Thuan frequently visited Khoi's home on the other bank of the An Cuu River, less than half a mile away from his own home. Khoi was rarely alone. His friends, followers, and disciples seemed to set up permanent

A family photo (from left to right):

Back row: *second from left, Ngo Dinh Huan (Khoi's son).*

Second row: *Nguyen Van Am (Thuan's father), Nguyen Van Le (Hoang's husband), Ngo Dinh thi Hoang, Ngo Dinh thi Hiep holding Ham Tieu, Ngo Dinh Can, Ngo Dinh Luyen.*

Third row: *Ngo Dinh Diem, Nguyen thi Hoa (Khoi's wife), Ngo Dinh Khoi, Thuan's grandmother, Bishop Ngo Dinh Thuc, Nguyen thi Giao, Ngo Dinh Nhu.*

Front row: *Francis Xavier Nguyen Van Thuan; fourth from left, Nguyen thi Niem; seventh from left, Nguyen Van Thanh; eighth from left, Nguyen Linh Tuyen.*

Inset: *Thuan.*

Portrait of Thuan's grandfather, Ngo Dinh Kha.

While Thuan's younger brother Thanh plays in front of the family home, Thuan (third from right) stands near his brother Tuyen (second from right) and their paternal grandmother (farthest right).

Family photo (from left to right standing): Thuan, Ngo Dinh Nhu, Ngo Dinh Diem, Bishop Ngo Dinh Thuc, Nguyen Hoang Anh (Thuan's cousin), Thuan's mother Hiep (directly behind her mother, seated), Madame Nhu, Ngo Dinh Thuy, Hoang Anh's husband Tran Trung Dung, Ngo Dinh Can, and furthest right Ngo Dinh Luyen. A portrait of Ngo Dinh Kha hangs on the wall behind the family.

President Ngo Dinh Diem.

Thuan's family home in Hue.

Ngo Dinh Can's beach house in Thuan An, Hue.

Photograph taken on the steps of Thuan's family home in Hue. Standing in the back row from left to right: *Thuan's paternal grandmother, Thuan's father Am, and Thuan kneeling next to his father. The child standing farthest right is Thu Hong.* Seated in second row: *Thuan's mother Hiep, Ham Tien, Tuyen, Thuy Tien, and Niem.* Seated in front: *Anh Tuyet and Thanh.*

Thuan, a seminarian at Phu Xuan Major Seminary, holds his youngest sister, Thu Hong.

For Thuan, Archbishop Urrutia (at the center of the photo) was a living example of holiness and a spiritual guide. Thuan stands farthest right in the group of young seminarians.

A family photo after Thuan's ordination. Back row from left to right: *Tuyen and Thanh;* second row: *Anh Tuyet, Hiep, Niem, Am, Father Thuan, Ham Tieu;* front row: *Thu Hong, Thuan's paternal grandmother, Thuy Tien.*

Thuan on his motorbike at the Phu Xuan Major Seminary in Hue.

While studying in Rome, Thuan and his uncle, Archbishop Thuc, at a private audience with Pope Pius XII. Thuan (in front of his uncle) kneels beside Father Tran Ngoc Thu, future private secretary of Pope John Paul II.

While studying in Rome, Thuan (foreground, standing closest to the grotto) visited Lourdes in the summer. It was at Lourdes that Thuan felt the Blessed Virgin Mary asking him to accept great suffwering in the future.

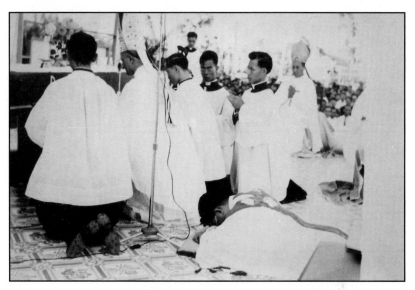

Thuan's episcopal ordination on June 24, 1967.

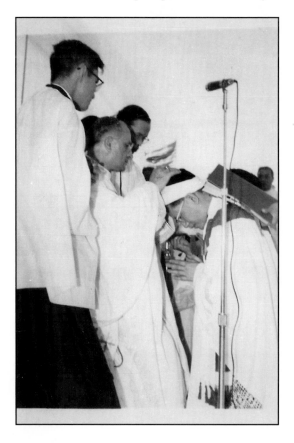

Apostolic Nuncio Angelo Palmas lays his hands on Thuan's head during the Mass of episcopal ordination.

The new bishop concelebrating at his episcopal ordination.

Bishop Thuan seated at his episcopal ordination.

After the Mass, the newly ordained Bishop Thuan (center) blesses the crowd. On his right is Archbishop Urrutia, and on his left Arch-bishop Nguyen Kim Diem.

Bishop Thuan's coat of arms. His episcopal motto is the title of the Consti-
tution, Gaudium et Spes *(Joy and Hope) from the Second Vatican Coun-*
cil. Thuan desired to be an apostle of joy and hope.

Apostolic Nuncio Angelo Palmas (center) posed with Thuan and his family. Thuan's mother is on the left of the nuncio, his father on the right, and Thuan behind and to the right of his father.

Bishop Thuan with his parents after the episcopal ordination.

Formal portrait of the bishop of Nha Trang.

The new bishop in his parents' home in Hue.

The newly ordained bishop.

The new bishop offering a word of thanks to his parents, family, and friends.

The young bishop of Nha Trang.

camp around him. But whenever Thuan came Khoi would speak with him privately.

Thuan recognized that Khoi was as intelligent as Diem, but more decisive. Khoi also chose his collaborators more wisely and inspired loyalty in his followers. Yet, when Diem was only twelve years old and Khoi already a young mandarin, Kha had groomed Diem to be the leader of the clan rather than his eldest son, Khoi. Traditionally an eldest son was not passed over unless he had committed serious mistakes. However, this was not the case. Khoi had always made his father proud. He had even married the daughter of Nguyen Huu Bai, Kha's closest friend and the most powerful man at the Imperial Court.

Surprisingly, Khoi never disputed his father's decision that Diem be prepared as a future leader. He always supported Diem, followed his advice, and did whatever he asked. When Diem resigned as prime minister in 1933 and began building his network of revolutionaries, Khoi helped Diem as much as possible. After Khoi's 1943 forced resignation from governorship of Quang Nam—a direct consequence of his involvement with Diem's activities—he spent all of his time and effort in strengthening Diem's network, despite being under the constant scrutiny of the French secret police.

Khoi did not share with Thuan as openly as Diem, but Thuan understood. Khoi was a man of action more than of words. He funneled his energy into wanting Diem to accept any offer Emperor Bao Dai made to prevent the Viet Minh Communists from taking over the country. Khoi kept saying: "If we let them take over now, our country will suffer for the next one hundred years."

Khoi had placed himself in jeopardy when he advised not only the emperor, but also some of his ministers to fight the Communists. People in the capital and around the country were terrified at the approach of the Viet Minh and no one wanted to oppose them. Though no one had yet been killed, fear was palpable everywhere.

The terror was understandable. People still remembered the Communists' excessive violence during an uprising in 1930. Khoi was vehemently against such terrorism, declaring, "I hate terror.

Nothing is as effective against freedom as terror. Look at a terror-ized horse, its body is covered with sweat and all its muscles tremble uncontrollably. It is a horrible sight. When people are terrorized, they act like that frightened animal. They lose control of their minds, their actions, and even their muscles. I don't like to see people terrorized and that is why I hate those who use terror as a military or political tool. I will fight them until my last breath."

But the wave of terror continued to grow, so that people were soon claiming that when the Viet Minh Communists approached even the dogs stopped barking.

Surrounded by officials who betrayed him and who now worked in favor of the Viet Minh, Emperor Bao Dai finally saw no other alternative but to surrender. Acting against Khoi's advice, Bao Dai signed the Edict of Abdication on August 25, 1945, saying he preferred to be "a citizen of an independent country, rather than the emperor of an enslaved nation." On August 25, following mas-sive street demonstrations, the Viet Minh took power in Saigon. Be-tween August 18 and 28 the Viet Minh's control spread like wildfire throughout the country.

Thuan went to say good-bye to Khoi before returning to the seminary. "We should never submit ourselves to a reign of terror," Khoi said firmly. "In the future, you will see more clearly what I am telling you today. The Viet Minh will claim a monopoly on patrio-tism. They will say that they were the only ones who fought for our country and, worse still, that they are the only ones who love our country. Anyone who dares to stand against them will be called a traitor. I will fight them to the end!"

That day as Thuan shook his uncle's hand, he had a premoni-tion that this was the last time they would see each other. As if shar-ing Thuan's foreboding, Khoi confided, "I have no fear of death, and as long as I live, I will do all I can to stop them."

A few years later at the major seminary, Thuan came across *The Three Ways of Spiritual Life* by Garrigou-Lagrange and meditated upon the distinction between "material goods" and "spiritual trea-sure." He suddenly understood why the monopoly of patriotism by an individual or party had seemed so frustrating and ridiculous to both Khoi and himself. "Spiritual values," like the love of God or the love of one's country, grow when shared, unlike "material goods," which diminished in quantity. His favorite argument in Garrigou-Lagrange's treatise was that if one refused to share God, even with just one person, one's own love for God diminished and eventually evaporated.

Thuan applied the same argument to patriotism. It must be a spiritual rather than material value and ought to be shared among all citizens. Remembering his last meeting with Khoi, Thuan thought: *If you monopolize patriotism, if you do not allow a single person who is your fellow countryman to love Vietnam, then your love of the country is no longer authentic. It would be like a brother refusing to let his siblings love their own mother.*

The full impact of Khoi's prediction that Vietnam would suffer for a hundred years then hit Thuan. As long as some Vietnamese prevented others from loving their country, there would be no end to their misery. Thuan coined a kind of motto: "Do not turn spiritual values into material possessions." It became clear to him who the authentic patriots were.

———◆◆◆———

THUAN LEFT HUE BEFORE EMPEROR Bao Dai's abdication. Traveling by boat at that time of the year was quite dangerous, but he had no alternative because some of the bridges between Hue and Ben Hai had been destroyed. So, in the company of the other seminarians from Hue, Thuan rented a boat and its crew of sailors, loaded it with food and supplies, and set out for An Ninh.

As the boat sailed east, following the An Cuu River and heading toward the Tam Giang Laguna, Thuan looked back. His city and home were still there, but he felt in his heart that he was looking at a fast disappearing world.

He was right. On August 29 a huge demonstration was staged at the stadium in Hue to welcome the delegation of Viet Minh Communists sent to finalize the agreement on the emperor's abdication. On August 30 Bao Dai gave up his sword and the imperial seal, the two symbols of the mandate of the Nguyen dynasty, to the Viet Minh. His gesture represented the official end of the Nguyen dynasty and marked the end of an era.

On September 2 Ho Chi Minh declared Vietnam's independence. In Thuan's eyes the craftily worded declaration was a mock-
ery and a lie. Vietnam had passed from foreign domination and an
enslaved imperial court to the rule of a small group of Communists
who proved more cruel and oppressive than their predecessors.

By the time Thuan obtained a copy of Ho Chi Minh's Declaration of Independence, he had already learned of the arrest and
disappearance of his uncle Khoi.

CHAPTER EIGHT

The First of Many Tragedies

I have passed out of mind like one who is dead;
I have become like a broken vessel.
For I hear the whispering of many—
terror all around!—
as they scheme together against me,
as they plot to take my life.

Psalm 31:12–13

When love dries up in the human heart, when there rises
the tidal wave of selfishness and revenge, the time of
extermination is near.

The Road of Hope,
F. X. Nguyen Van Thuan

NGO DINH KHOI AND HIS SON HUAN were arrested on August 31, 1945, just one day after Emperor Bao Dai surrendered his sword and seal to Viet Minh representatives. Thuan learned of the arrests a few weeks later. The priests of the seminary and his classmates tried to reassure Thuan: Khoi was a patriot, and no one would kill patriots during the first days of national independence.

But Thuan fostered no false hopes. As soon as he learned of Khoi and Huan's arrest, he knew that they would be killed. As the eldest son of the family, Khoi was the nominal head of the Ngo Dinh clan because he accepted Diem as the leader. Huan, his only son, would follow as the head of the clan for the next generation. Thuan thought, *If something happens to them, then the future of my whole clan is decimated.*

His heart went out to Khoi's wife, Hoa. With their marriage, Hoa and Khoi had united the two most powerful Catholic families in Hue. She was a model wife and an ideal mother. What would become of her now? He pictured her, sitting alone in her garden by the An Cuu River. Would there be a miracle? Would the "robots" who received orders from an unidentified "upper echelon" suddenly have the courage or heart to release his uncle and cousin? Thuan shook his head. He knew better.

A few weeks later, Khoi and Huan's execution at the hands of the Viet Minh was confirmed. A newsletter reported their trial by a revolutionary court, their conviction, and their execution before a firing squad. The newsletter also announced that the tribunal had condemned former Prime Minister Pham Quynh and he had been executed by the same firing squad. In his lifetime Pham Quynh had been an adversary of Diem and Khoi. In the end he shared Khoi's fate.

Thuan was filled with anguish and anger. That his uncle and his cousin had been condemned and executed as traitors to their country was too great an injustice to accept. He still remembered the way his uncle had talked about independence for Vietnam, and how he had refused to kowtow to the French. He thought about Huan and the hope that his family had placed in him. He had been brilliant, so youthful and yet so mature! Now he was gone. Those who had "invited" Khoi to a meeting with "representatives of the People's Committee" reportedly had not "invited" Huan. The young man had simply volunteered to accompany his father. Was filial devotion a crime? How could any revolutionary court convict him? Thuan's mind reeled with unanswered questions as he struggled to accept what had happened.

Thuan's sense of justice and righteousness led to a kind of anger he recognized could harm him spiritually. He found it very difficult to forgive. Though he could say to God, "I genuinely accept your will," he knew he could not be at peace with God unless he rid himself of intense anger. He tried, but at times the struggle seemed useless.

The anger Thuan felt in 1945 would return in 1963 and 1964 when murder and execution finally destroyed his family. It would come back in 1975 with his first taste of captivity. On his "road of hope," that is, his own "pilgrim's progress," Thuan found that unchecked anger was the strongest impediment to reaching a state of total surrender to God's will. The process of dealing with his anger would not be an easy one for him.

Ngo Dinh Khoi's murder was the first tragic death his family experienced, and Thuan's efforts to forgive those who had killed his uncle and cousin were painful. When he prayed for his uncle and cousin, his heart was full of bitterness. He had always known that following Christ's teachings would not be easy, but he now realized that loving those who grievously offended him was not optional. He could not follow Christ if he could not forgive. But his heart felt closed to such an act of forgiveness.

Thuan tried to imagine how his mother was reacting. He knew that while he was struggling with his anger and grief, she had probably already accepted what had happened as "God's will" and had forgiven those who had murdered her brother and nephew. Thuan's heart went out to her. He believed he would never have her courage and strength, but he so much wanted to emulate her.

———◆◦◆◦◆———

SOON AFTER THESE TRAGIC EVENTS, Thuan read the story of Father José Ramon Manual Pro Juarez, a Jesuit from Mexico. Arrested by the secret police of the Mexican Communist government, Father Pro died a martyr's death. Without a trial, he was sentenced to die before a firing squad together with his brother, Humberto, in Mexico City in November 1927.

Thuan felt a great affinity for the young Jesuit martyr, who had died under a volley of bullets a few months before Thuan was born. Father Pro's ability to forgive those who were about to kill him was an inestimable lesson for Thuan at that moment of his life.

Thuan became familiar with the smallest details of Father Pro's life: his family, his dreams, his studies in Mexico and abroad, his illnesses, and his sense of humor. What Thuan loved most about Father Pro was his indomitable courage. "He was afraid of nothing, because he had put his life in God's hands once and for all." Thuan knew he would have to do the same.

The details of Father Pro's long ordeal filled Thuan's mind with ideas of how to face disaster, and helped to make his own pain more tolerable. Thuan regained the courage to focus on his studies and meditation. Pro, who could laugh at pain and mortal danger, became a friend with whom Thuan held lengthy conversations in his moments of distress. He was grateful to Father Pro for his example, and he would revisit the Mexican martyr's story during the most crucial times of his life.

But total surrender to God cannot be accomplished in one day. Thuan would have to journey through many tragedies before he could finally put his life in God's hands without reservation.

During those dark days, Thuan also drew courage from the reading of Saint Paul's epistles, beginning a lifetime study of the man and his writings. During his years at the major seminary Thuan continued to memorize the letters until he could recite them all. Memorization was not simply a matter of remembering a text but the profound meaning of the text as well. Saint Paul's Letter to the Romans challenged Thuan most particularly. He found there all the elements for the foundation of his spirituality.

In addition, Thuan began memorizing psalm after psalm, and some of them became his favorite prayers. He found in them the best expressions ever written to address God in moments of sorrow or joy, in times of victory or defeat. For Thuan, praying certain psalms acted as a quick salve to his open wounds. He loved to think that by memorizing the psalms he enshrined them in his mind and carved them on his heart so that he would never forget them.

Yet, after his captivity, Thuan confessed to Cardinal Jean-Marie Lustiger, archbishop of Paris and author of *First Steps Toward Prayer*, a book which emphasizes the beauty and historic significance of the psalms, that sometimes during his imprisonment he could not remember a single psalm.

Cardinal Lustiger had raised his eyebrows: "Not even a short one?" Thuan shook his head: "I know you wrote that Jesus learned the short psalms when he was a child because they were easier to memorize. But no, I could not remember a single short psalm. In solitary confinement, living in a cell without light, sound, or any sign of a human presence, I was once unable to remember so much as the *Hail Mary*. It was the only time during my captivity that I was really afraid."

With the daily Eucharist, the rosary, the help of Father Pro, the psalms, and Saint Paul, Thuan began the process of allowing his anger to heal. Whenever he thought about Khoi and Huan, the anger would flare again, but for gradually shorter periods of time.

———————◆◗◆◗◆———————

FOR THE TWO YEARS FOLLOWING THE END of the Nguyen dynasty and the first major tragedy that struck Thuan's family, Vietnam drifted into a swirl of "wind and dust." The tumultuous events that took place seemed incomprehensible at best and insane at worst. People, especially the young, lived in a state of total confusion.

Secluded at An Ninh, Thuan could hardly keep up with the news. He was anxious to know the details of what was happening around him and all over his country. There was of course the radio, but only the priests had access to it, and the stations the priests could tune in to broadcasted propaganda designed to misinform.

The Viet Minh government had hardly been in place when it had to contend with the Chinese and British troops sent to disarm the defeated Japanese. The British had jurisdiction over the southern half of Vietnam and the Chinese over the northern half. It became immediately clear that the Chinese were hostile to the Viet Minh and were assisting Vietnamese nationalist parties opposed to them. In the south, the British were helping the French former prisoners to rearm themselves, and eventually they left the scene after arranging for the French to replace them.

By October 1945 French troops under the command of General Leclerc arrived in Saigon and began the re-conquest of Southern Vietnam from the Viet Minh. The First Indochina War was underway and would go on until the fall of the French stronghold of Dien Bien Phu in 1954.

In 1945 the Viet Minh negotiated unsuccessfully for peace, while it called upon citizens to resist the French and gain control of the southern provinces. The Vietnamese resistance against the Viet Minh assumed the form of guerrilla warfare, while the French continued to advance. Meanwhile, in the north the Viet Minh government tried to appease the nationalist parties supported by the Chinese. It invited nationalist opposition leaders to join a coalition government, and cajoled the Chinese in an attempt to avoid a civil war.

In 1946, however, the Viet Minh Communits experienced another series of major setbacks. First, the French came to an agreement with the Chinese to replace them in the north. Then, the coalition government formula did not satisfy the Vietnamese nationalists, and civil war seemed inevitable. During this time, both pro-government and anti-government agents were hired for political assassinations which took place on a daily basis.

Before Thuan went home for summer vacation in 1946, the French had managed to install a separatist government in Saigon. French troops replacing the Chinese then arrived in Hue to protect and arm the French civilians and ex-prisoners.

Although several months' time had elapsed since the execution of Khoi and Huan by the Viet Minh, the sorrow was still fresh in Thuan's family. When he arrived home, Thuan saw how his mother's hair had grayed. Aunt Hoa, Khoi's widow, tried to put on a brave face. Thuan went to visit her frequently. Somehow, Hoa was the one who found the words to comfort him. He was grateful when she asked him to pray the rosary with her.

With such political unrest on all sides, the Ngo Dinh family's safety was questionable. Both Thuan's father and his uncle Can spent each night at a different home. Can, who had never been interested in politics before Khoi's death, now seemed to have stepped into his shoes and taken over Diem's network of friends and allies in Diem's absence. Because Diem was known to be a devout Catholic, Can knew that he and other Catholic leaders were being watched closely by the Viet Minh authorities; zealous pro-government elements might murder them at any time and with total impunity. The only truly good news for the family was that the Viet Minh, who for a while wanted to play the national unity card, had released Diem. They were relieved to know that he was safe and well, though his whereabouts around Hanoi remained sketchy.

Thuan walked around the city of Hue without recognizing it. The French, preparing for an all-out attack by Viet Minh forces, stretched barbed wire around their quarters and piled sandbags everywhere. Thuan and the people of Hue wondered when the battle would begin.

In the Phu Cam parish, people dug tunnels to link one house to another; foxholes dotted sidewalks at regular intervals. The parish self-defense militiamen, armed with swords and antiquated rifles, trained day and night in preparation for an attack. Many knew that besides the expected attack on the French, they might also have to deal with government assassination squads being sent into the villages to kill their parish leaders. Some of the Catholic parishioners who had been prominent supporters of the Viet Minh structures in its first days in August 1945, began to realize that they had been deceived and went into hiding.

Thuan lived in a world of uncertainty and unreality. In Hanoi and other cities, opposing nationalist and government forces were already engaged in a civil war. Ho Chi Minh and his Communist government had tried and failed to negotiate a peace treaty with France. Thuan realized that his country was sliding faster and faster toward a major catastrophe.

<hr />

THUAN FELT DEEPLY TROUBLED when he returned to An Ninh that fall. He sensed the inevitability of war with France, and that the battle of Hue would be bloody. He and his classmates had all become more serious and mature over the summer. They had seen enough to know they were about to face several years of war and strife.

[87]

With his classmates, Thuan tried to focus on studies and reading. He discovered the life of Pier Giorgio Frassati in that final year at the minor seminary. Frassati was a fun-loving young man who died at the age of twenty-four after much time dedicated to working with the poor and sick. Thuan read everything he could find on the young "Servant of God" and his activities as a member of the Society of Saint Vincent de Paul. Frassati became a great inspiration for Thuan's love and concern for young people.

Thuan also returned to his study of the life of Father Pro. He constantly thought about the Mexican martyr who had also lived in a time of confusion. Thuan wanted for himself Father Pro's courage, his ability to laugh even when everything went wrong, and his strength in enduring pain without complaint.

Earlier that summer, Thuan had grown tired of the confusion in Hue. To escape it for a time, he and his friends had gone to climb the high mountains southwest of Hue, where Thuan had contracted malaria. After he returned to the seminary, he suffered month-long bouts of horrible fever and chills, but Thuan saw God's hand in this illness. He was beginning to realize how much more he needed to learn from such models as Father Pro about enduring physical pain with calm and courage. Thuan's physical weakness from the malaria and his prolonged poor diet resulted in major health problems that would plague him for years.

Even more than from illness, Thuan continued to suffer from the turmoil in his country. The Viet Minh government had arrested hundreds of opponents, and everywhere Catholic parish leaders had gone into hiding. Several bloody incidents took place: French troops that were now garrisoned in the north repeatedly confronted the pro-government militia in deadly clashes. In December 1946, Vo Nguyen Giap, Viet Minh minister of defense, ordered a general offensive against the French in Hue, while the rest of the Viet Minh government fled to the mountains.

Thuan received the news that the battle of Hue had begun and that his family had fled to the countryside, where Pham thi Than and Can had become separated from Thuan's parents. Then he lost all contact with his family. Sources also reported the Viet Minh's assassination of great numbers of Catholic leaders, including those who had willingly followed them into the mountain strongholds.

In February 1947, after the French had driven the Viet Minh troops out of Hue, Thuan's family returned and he finally received news from them. Unfortunately, the suffering his grandmother had endured during the flight from Hue had made her an invalid.

Before Thuan said his final farewell to the minor seminary, French troops had reached Quang Tri and Quang Binh, and French units were garrisoned at Cua Tung Beach, only a few miles from the seminary. In Hue, Governor Tran van Ly, an old friend of Thuan's family, had set up a provisory administration to govern Central Vietnam.

Thuan left the minor seminary with a heavy heart. For six years it had been a kind of paradise for him, a refuge from the turmoil of the outside world. There, sheltered by the thick walls of bamboo, he had been able to focus on his studies and prayer, even though his country was practically on fire around him. He had been surrounded by the living example of holy men, and he had absorbed himself in the lives of holy men and women. They had strengthened his faith and his dedication to the service of God.

He thanked God for those years, for the innocence of his classmates, and for the gentle guidance of his teachers. In that earthly paradise Thuan had experienced despair and anger; there he had regained his hope and peace. At An Ninh Thuan had left behind his childhood and entered his adolescence. Now he was leaving for the major seminary as an adult. His memories of the minor seminary remained with him throughout his life, and were part of his spiritual strength.

Sad as he felt to leave An Ninh in the summer, Thuan was also eager to enter the Phu Xuan Major Seminary. A new chapter of his life was about to unfold.

CHAPTER NINE

Phu Xuan Major Seminary

Now the LORD came and stood there, calling as before,
"Samuel! Samuel!" And Samuel said, "Speak, for your
servant is listening."

1 Samuel 3:10

To respond "yes" is easy, but see how the Lord followed
his call up to his death on the cross. You must deny
yourself, carry your cross every day, and nail yourself to
that cross.

The Road of Hope,
F. X. Nguyen Van Thuan

THE NEXT SIX YEARS THAT THUAN spent at the Phu
Xuan Major Seminary were hectic for many reasons,
not least of which were the events outside its walls.
Although Vietnam appeared to have entered a period of stability, it
was actually still adrift. When Thuan left An Ninh in the summer of
1947, the French occupied most of the cities in Vietnam. Having
fled into the mountains for a time, the Viet Minh government now
began to wage a modest guerrilla war against French troops.

In response, many Vietnamese that had celebrated Bao Dai's
abdication now organized mass demonstrations to demand the
former emperor's return. It would be another two years before Bao

Dai reassumed power. In the meantime, three regional administrations governed Vietnam, with the French holding all the real power.

———————◆◆◆◆◆———————

THUAN'S FIRST THREE YEARS at the Phu Xuan Seminary marked a phase of spiritual growth that forced him to discern all the options open to him and his future. He had always assumed that he would become a diocesan priest and his one dream was to become like the Curé of Ars. As soon as he arrived at the major seminary, however, he learned that it was also possible to join a religious order or congregation. Now he had a choice to make, and Thuan began a discernment of his future.

Thuan had read enough to know something about the Society of Jesus because his patron saint, Francis Xavier, and one of his models, Father Pro, had been Jesuits. He began a serious study of the life of Saint Ignatius of Loyola, its founder, and his *Spiritual Exercises.*

The Jesuits had first come to Vietnam in 1615, and they had an extensive impact on the country, especially through Father Alexandre de Rhodes. They left Vietnam following the dissolution of the Society by Pope Clement XIV in 1774, and did not return to Vietnam when Pope Pius VIII re-established the Order. (It was only in 1957 that the Jesuits returned to Vietnam.)

Thuan was impressed with the Jesuits' missionary work and their structured exercises for reflection and contemplation. He knew how hard Jesuit missionaries in China and Vietnam had worked for inculturation of the Gospel with Confucianism and with the Asian practice of honoring ancestors, maintaining that both had value. But if Thuan decided to join the Society of Jesus, he would have to go to the Philippines to enter the Jesuit school. This was a problem he could not resolve, and Thuan eventually abandoned the idea of joining the Society of Jesus with much regret.

Thuan's love for meditation and prayer and his attraction to contemplative life subsequently led him to consider joining the Benedictine Order. A new Benedictine monastery had been built in the mountains of Thien An in 1940. The monastery, nestled among the pines, was five miles southwest of Hue. Christians from near and far went there to speak with the Benedictine monks, to pray and meditate, or to enjoy a walk in the beautiful surroundings.

Thuan was very fond of Dom Romain, a saintly man who had spent most of his adult life in Vietnam and had dedicated all his energy to assisting the Vietnamese. Thuan also felt great admiration for Dom Benoit Nguyen Van Thai, the first Vietnamese Benedictine priest. Both men became Thuan's close friends. Under their guidance he continued to read the works of Dom Marmion, which he had discovered at An Ninh. He read and reread *Christ in His Mysteries, Christ the Life of the Soul,* and *Christ the Ideal of the Monk.* He was deeply touched by Dom Marmion's emphasis on love "which turns all that it touches into gold," the mysteries of the rosary, and liturgical life.

Dom Marmion's motto, "To serve rather than to rule," inspired Thuan to accept leadership roles with humility and to search for joy and peace in every circumstance. Thuan memorized many of Dom Marmion's simple words, such as "joy is the echo of God's life in us," and "the life of union with God can only develop in a soul filled with peace and joy."

The Rule of Saint Benedict appealed to Thuan and added to his desire to join the Benedictines. He went to many retreats organized by the Benedictines in Thien An Monastery and earnestly began to prepare himself to become a monk there. Still, Thuan had some misgivings about leaving the major seminary, and he prayed for God's guidance.

Many decades later he smiled when he recalled, "I prayed for God to show me his will. I did not hear his voice or see him in a vision. All I knew was that each time I went on a retreat at Thien An Monastery, I came back a really sick man. Was that God's way of telling me to stay at the major seminary? After several such bouts of illness, my enthusiasm for becoming a Benedictine monk began to wane."

Thuan finally decided that he would stay at the Phu Xuan Major Seminary and prepare himself for priesthood there. After two years of philosophy, Thuan began his theological studies.

Father Simon Hoa Nguyen Van Hien was the rector of Phu Xuan Major Seminary and taught dogmatic theology. He was one of the rare Catholics of his time to have a Vietnamese for his patron saint: the Venerable Simon Phan Dac Hoa, who suffered martyrdom on December 12, 1840. In 1955 Hien became the bishop of Saigon and of Dalat in 1960. As a bishop, he chose for his motto *Praedicamus Jesum crucifixum* (We announce Jesus crucified).

Father Hien was an ascetic who was severe with himself, but treated others with leniency. Thuan listened with pleasure to Father Hien's anecdotes about life in Rome and his studies at *Propaganda Fide,* the institute founded by Pope Urban VIII in 1627. The stories were similar to those his Uncle Thuc had often told. Thuan never really dreamed he would go to Rome, which seemed a stepping-stone to honors and important positions. In fact, one of the chief reasons Thuan had considered joining a contemplative order was to avoid worldly distinctions. He wanted to be close to the humble people and to live in poverty—a far more attractive life in Thuan's eyes.

Father Dau was the seminary's professor of fundamental theology and philosophy and Father Danh was professor of moral theology. When Hien left for Saigon to assume his duties as bishop there, Father Dau took on his role as rector of Phu Xuan. Dau and Danh were more than professors to Thuan. They were friends who offered him the treasures of their wisdom and knowledge.

Thuan also felt blessed to continue having contact with Father Urrutia. As the vicar general of the diocese, Urrutia frequently visited Phu Xuan Seminary where he regularly gave moving lectures and sermons on the interior life. Father Urrutia's talks taught Thuan how to build lofty themes, views, and visions by using simple words and ideas to which people could easily relate.

◆◦◆◦◆

At Phu Xuan, Thuan had more time to himself, and he used his time on subjects such as philosophy and theology that demanded far greater personal reflection than similar topics he had studied at the minor seminary.

As he studied, Thuan felt drawn to Saint Thomas Aquinas, a Doctor of the Church who had originally prepared himself to become a Benedictine monk, but instead joined the Dominicans, because of their total dedication to the study of sacred sciences. He spent months on Aquinas's *Summa Theologica*. The vast dimensions of the work amazed him, and as he read he thought how much Christianity could have Christianized the Confucian and Buddhist world just as, in the thirteenth century, Thomas Aquinas had Christianized Greek philosophy, especially that of Aristotle.

To aid him in studying Thomas Aquinas, Thuan used the commentaries of the renowned Thomist, Reginald Garrigou-Lagrange. A Dominican himself, Garrigou-Lagrange's work on the *Summa Theologica* rendered them more accessible to the reader. When he became familiar with Garrigou-Lagrange's style and reasoning, Thuan read and reread with increasing pleasure his *Three Ages of the Interior Life*, finding it to be an effective guidebook for his own journey through various phases of spirituality.

During these years preceding his priestly ordination, through reading and meditating on Aquinas and Garrigou-Lagrange, Thuan began to nurture the hope that he would one day be capable of total surrender to God's will.

Besides the Benedictine and Dominican spirituality, Thuan also developed a real veneration for Saint John Bosco, the founder of the Salesian Society. Don Bosco's great love of the poor and work with youth inspired Thuan, and he loved his educational philosophy that focused on reason, religion, and kindness. He believed it was so successful because it aimed at coming to a deeper understanding of young people and their particular problems. This approach appealed to Thuan, whose enthusiasm for being at the service of young people would be a life-long characteristic.

Thuan also discovered *The Little World of Don Camillo* by Giovanni Guareschi. Thuan claimed that Guareschi's novel had a tremendous influence on him and his spirituality, and he always kept a copy within reach. In the character of Don Camillo, who was a country pastor, Thuan found a model of simplicity, candor, righteousness, childlike trust in God, and courage. Thuan especially admired the author's genius in using brief dialogues between Christ and Don Camillo. The humor and ideological struggle between Don Camillo and his Marxist adversary, Peppone, was a more or less nonviolent one; both men respected at least some common rules of fair play and Thuan often lamented the fact that this was often not the case in the struggle between Communists and Capitalists in the real world.

Thuan also began the daily reading of the *Imitation of Christ* and praying the *Little Office of the Blessed Virgin Mary*. He was faithful to these practices, except during times of serious illness. Besides the Eucharist and the rosary, it was the *Imitation* and the *Little Office* that gave Thuan strength during his many ordeals.

Being at the seminary in Hue had its advantages. Thuan received permission to visit his parents over long weekends and during the Lunar New Year festivities. Many of Thuan's siblings had grown up, but the youngest, Thu Hong, was born in October 1947, a few months after Thuan's entrance into the major seminary. Thuan's oldest sister, Niem, had entered a Carmelite convent nearby and Thuan visited her frequently. He also spoke with the abbess, a holy woman whose words always had a strong and positive effect on those who met with her.

The six years at the major seminary went by all too fast. Thuan prepared himself to receive Holy Orders and he searched for an understanding of God's will in his own life. He rarely cast a glance over the political scene during that time.

◆◦◆◦◆

FROM 1947 UNTIL 1953, when Thuan was about to be ordained a priest, the political situation in Vietnam remained unchanged. Former Emperor Bao Dai, now Chief of State, was an absentee ruler. He lived mostly in France and left the country in the hands of a series of equally ineffective prime ministers. The French controlled everything: banks, treasury, budget, economy, and the Vietnamese army. Viet Minh guerrillas continued to fight both French troops and the Vietnamese army with some victories. The Vietnam of 1953 appeared very much like the Vietnam of 1947 on the surface with the French, through the Bao Dai regime, controlling most of the cities, and the Viet Minh a large part of the jungles and the countryside. But Thuan did not trust appearances. He perceived that the country was sliding toward the Viet Minh and that the French were losing the ongoing war.

From time to time Thuan's mother received short letters from Diem, who had left the country in early 1950 in order to study the developments of industrialized countries and some day bring this knowledge and experience back to Vietnam. Thuan knew that his mother and the rest of his family truly believed Diem would one day be the leader of Vietnam. Kha's dream still inspired them, but even they had to wonder what Diem could do in such an impossible situation. As the day of Thuan's ordination approached, he prayed fervently for his war-torn country, his family, and especially for Diem and his grandfather's dream: the real independence of Vietnam.

CHAPTER TEN

The Young Priest

All people are grass,
their constancy is like the flower of the field.
The grass withers, the flower fades...

Isaiah 40:6–7

The Lord commands you, "Go out into the whole world
and proclaim the good news to all creation" (Mk 16:15),
but he doesn't issue a timetable or draw up a plan. He
leaves the initiative—and the difficulties to overcome—
to you. He asks only that you carry the Gospel wherever
you go.

The Road of Hope,
F. X. Nguyen Van Thuan

THUAN COULD HARDLY CONTAIN his joy as he celebrated his first Mass in the Phu Cam Cathedral in
the presence of his parents and siblings, his grandmother, Uncle Can and Aunt Hoang, Aunt Hoa, and distant relatives from both sides of the family.

As he prayed the opening line of the Holy Mass, "I will go to
the altar of God, to God, the joy of my youth," his whole body
trembled with emotion. Thuan had learned to control his emotions,
but that day at the altar he broke down many times and wept.

He was a priest *forever.* The finality of the priesthood had impressed Thuan on Thursday, June 11, 1953, when Bishop Urrutia

ordained him. He was a priest forever, anointed by one of the men who had been instrumental in shaping his life.

Now a priest at the altar, Thuan felt the enormity of the grace and responsibility of the priesthood. God had called him to re-enact every day the death and resurrection of Christ, to consecrate the bread and wine and to give with his own hand Christ's body, blood, soul, and divinity to God's people. Among those people on that day were his loved ones.

Thuan began and ended his first homily by thanking his parents and all those who had contributed to his intellectual and spiritual growth. He looked at his parents and saw in their eyes such pride that he knew he would never totally meet their expectations. His mind felt numb when, for the first time, he gave the Eucharist to his invalid grandmother, his father and mother, his uncle and aunts, and then his brothers and sisters.

Over the next few days in Phu Cam, Thuan went through a dizzying series of celebrations organized in his honor. Soon, however, he received his assignment: he would serve at a parish in Quang Binh, a hundred miles north of Hue. He bid farewell to family and friends and, with only a small suitcase, took a slow bus to Tam Toa parish.

Travel at the time was very dangerous because, in their efforts to regain control over the country, Viet Minh troops were ambushing civilian and military vehicles, blowing up bridges, and laying land mines on all national highways and provincial roads. It was necessary for civilian transports to be accompanied by a military presence for protection. Thuan's bus was part of a convoy of old and overloaded buses under heavy military escort.

The dirty buses, laden with passengers, luggage, and merchandise, rumbled along the dusty road under the scorching sun until, at control posts erected near forts or blockhouses along the way, soldiers signaled for them to stop. The forts, most often built into the side of a hill overlooking the highway, had a few squat buildings and a series of watchtowers. However, here and there could be seen half-buried machine gun nests. The rows of barbed wire around them were an inadequate defense for the tall brick and concrete blockhouses.

Viet Minh Communist guerrillas regularly blew up such block-houses with rocket launchers and, as they passed the control posts, Thuan thought about the poor soldiers who were virtually sitting ducks in their high towers. They were completely helpless against such attacks at night, and one hit could pulverize a blockhouse.

As he sat in the stifling hot bus at one control post, Thuan prayed that the soldiers would permit the convoy to leave soon. It was becoming unbearably hot; at least when the bus was moving, there was a chance that the passengers might feel a little breeze. From the outset of the trip, Thuan had noticed how the bus driver trotted down the steps to present the soldiers with one or two bottles of liquor at each stop. The bribe worked every time. Shortly after the soldiers received their bottles, the bus would be motioned to move on. Thuan could only shake his head.

From time to time, a heavy machine gun from the armored car at the head of the column would suddenly open fire on the sur-rounding hills or into the jungle. The soldiers seemed to be shoot-ing randomly, like frightened men.

Thuan had never witnessed first hand the reality of war dur-ing the years he had spent at the major seminary. Now he had a taste of it, and he sensed that the French and the Bao Dai regime were losing. The war escalated as Viet Minh conducted raids at bat-talion level. Eventually, it was clear that guerrilla warfare would no longer be confined to jungles and countryside, but would enter the cities as well. Then all of Vietnam would fall under Commu-nist rule.

The possibility of ambush made the trip extremely tense, but that did not cause Thuan as much discomfort as his profuse sweat-ing and persistent cough. He thought that perhaps the red dust, raised high into the air like a large cloud by the long convoy, was causing the cough.

TAM TOA PARISH, LOCATED IN the heart of the city of Dong Hoi, was one of the most important parishes in the diocese. The bishop had sent Thuan to assist Father Tam in serving the rather large Catholic population.

Tam Toa was also the native city of the most important Catholic poet, Han Mac Tu. Thuan, who loved Han Mac Tu's poetry, visited the sites that had anything to do with him. The poet had died in a leprosarium near Nha Trang in 1940. His poems, written in honor of the Blessed Virgin Mary, had always been a source of inspiration for Thuan.

Father Tam was a good mentor. He took time to talk to Thuan about pastoral duties, parishioners, parish politics, and the histories of the families within the parish. Yet, the longer he knew Thuan the more Father Tam became concerned about the young priest's health. Thuan ran a high fever each afternoon and suffered a persistent cough that caused him to shake convulsively. Father Tam was worried, but did not want to alarm Thuan. After a month or so, he suggested that Thuan consult a doctor. Thuan, who never complained about pain or illness, was reluctant to submit himself to a medical exam and he kept procrastinating. However, when he coughed up traces of blood, he finally followed Father Tam's advice.

The diagnosis was devastating: advanced tuberculosis. Perhaps Thuan had presumed too much on his physical strength when he had studied and worked so hard in his last year at the major seminary. Perhaps the malnutrition he had suffered in the minor seminary had predisposed him to the disease.

Thuan had only been in Tam Toa parish for a total of ninety days when he was rushed by plane to the Central Hospital in Hue, because Dong Hoi did not have a medical facility equipped to treat a case as serious as Thuan's.

As Thuan flew back to Hue, a feeling of doom hung over him. Three months earlier he had begun to fulfill his dream of living with and serving poverty-stricken parishioners. Now he was going back to Hue with a serious illness. More than the illness, Thuan feared the pain and anxiety it would cause his parents. When they took him to the Central Hospital in Hue, his parents were fully aware of the seriousness of the situation. The doctors said that Thuan would probably require major surgery and, if that were the case, he would have to go to Saigon if there was to be even a slim chance of success.

Thuan expected his mother to fall apart upon hearing what amounted to a death sentence for her oldest son, but she stayed calm. Hiep and Am spent hours at the hospital praying the rosary with Thuan. They encouraged him not to be afraid; they told him he would be all right. Thuan was shocked when one day his mother said that even if he did die now, at least he had already achieved what he had wanted most in life: to be a priest. Thuan had always believed his father was the more unshakeable of his parents, but now he often saw his father with a trace of tears in his eyes.

Doctor after doctor was consulted, and all of them said the same thing: Thuan must have major surgery to remove a large part of his right lung, if not the whole lung. Thuan was unaware of the possible implications of such a surgery until his mother told him simply: "According to several doctors, *if* you survive such surgical intervention, you may be an invalid for the rest of your life." It took Thuan some hours to recover from the news, but his mother's serenity reassured him. Whatever the doctors' verdict, he would be all right. Thuan would wait for them to decide how to best proceed.

—◆◈◆—

WHEN THUAN WAS NOT PRAYING or talking with his parents, he listened to the radio. The war had spread as far as Laos, and the Communists were organizing their larger units into divisions and brigades. The face of the war was changing drastically. On the defensive, the French were abandoning one position after another. French Commander in Chief General Henri Navarre revealed the presence of seventy-eight Communist battalions in the delta of North Vietnam alone.

From France former Emperor Bao Dai stirred from his usual lethargy and demanded more extended power for the Vietnamese government and more independence for Vietnam within the French Union. But he did not persist. The French were not ready to yield a single shred of their power in Vietnam to Bao Dai or to the Viet Minh.

Thuan's heart grew sadder as Vietnam drifted further from the shore of peace. His mother sometimes said that only Diem could save Vietnam from falling under Communist control. Thuan did not dare contradict her; she always had such an unshakable confidence in Diem's destiny. But the last the family heard, Diem was thousands of miles away in Belgium.

Thuan eventually heard the news that the French were deploying large numbers of troops to Dien Bien Phu. Clearly their intention was to cut off communication between Communist troops in Vietnam and Laos. They were obviously hoping that the Communists would employ all their divisions to surround Dien Bien Phu, where the French planned to use their air power to crush the Communist divisions.

Thuan thought he might live long enough to witness this decisive battle. In his mind's eye he pictured the Dien Bien Phu valley and its imposing defense system of strongholds and fortresses so beautifully named: Claudine, Huguette, Anne-Marie, Dominique, and Elaine at the center; Gabrielle and Beatrice to the north and the northwest; and Isabelle to the south.

He also imagined the men and women of Dien Bien Phu. More battalions were soon to join the ten already in place, and Vo Nguyen Giap's divisions had already begun moving into position. Thuan saw this battle as the beginning of the Armageddon of the Indochina War. How many French and Vietnamese men and women would die in that God-forsaken place?

———◆◆◆◆———

IN THE HOSPITAL ONE COLD October afternoon, Thuan contemplated the life of Saint Ignatius, who had undergone a number of surgeries to restore the full use of the leg he had injured in battle. Ignatius had been ready to accept the pain of surgery without anesthesia because he wished to walk normally and with fashionable elegance. If Ignatius was willing to endure pain out of his sense of vanity, then Thuan ought to out of a sense of dedication to God's service. Thuan also remembered how his Aunt Hoa had prayed the rosary with him after Khoi and Huan had been killed. She had been so strong then, praying amidst the total ruin of her life. She had encouraged and consoled him. The memory of her courage brought tears to his eyes. Thuan decided that if God so willed, he would go to Saigon for surgery, no matter how painful and dangerous, and then he would return to Hue to continue his duties as a priest. More determined than ever, Thuan asked his parents to find some way to send him to Saigon.

In early December 1953, Thuan flew on a plane for the second time in his life, this time to Saigon. He had never before left Central Vietnam, had never been in the former Cochinchina, and had never been to a big city. When the plane landed, he was taken to Saint Paul's Hospital in the center of the city.

Saigon was a sprawling metropolis and people seemed to spill onto the streets from every direction. The gap between the rich and the poor was starkly evident to Thuan even on the ride from Tan Son Nhat Airport to Saint Paul's Hospital. The car passed through the slums where squatters lived and drove by gorgeous villas with their red roofs and green shutters standing behind high fences.

Thuan was admitted to Saint Paul's Hospital and, after several days, doctors determined that the complicated surgery he needed could not be performed there. While they could do nothing for him, the staff invited him to remain for as long as he wished, and his stay become more a time of retreat for his soul than cure for his body. Thuan grew progressively weaker and noticed that his morning and evening walks on the hospital grounds left him completely exhausted.

Despite various medications, Thuan's condition continued to grow more critical. He knew how common it was for people in Vietnam to die of less serious illnesses. Thuan prepared himself for the worst. He had never feared death, and now he simply accepted its possibility as God's will. He thought about his great models: Father Pro, Father Venard, Saint Thérèse of Lisieux, and Pier Giorgio Frassati. They had all died young. His only regret was not having worked harder to attain the holiness of his models. For this he asked God's forgiveness.

While in the hospital, Thuan listened to the radio every day to keep informed of the news, which became even more depressing. Dien Bien Phu was under siege, with at least four Communist divisions surrounding the stronghold. Thuan prayed for the men on both sides of the battle. He was horrified at the thought of the unavoidable carnage. He thought he might die before the battle be-

gan, but on March 13, 1954, Communists overran the fortress called
Beatrice.

———————◆◦◆◦◆———————

WHILE THUAN WAITED TO DIE at Saint Paul's Hospital, Father
Richard, a French priest who was the pastor of Saint Francis Church
in Hue, contacted Thuan's family. He told them that he had connections with surgeons at a French military hospital in Saigon. After
he obtained the agreement of Thuan's parents, Father Richard contacted his friends at Grall Hospital where Thuan was admitted in
April of 1954.

At Grall Hospital, Thuan was amazed at the technological ad-
vances of medical science. A battery of tests confirmed, however,
that the tuberculosis had badly damaged Thuan's right lung and
that radical surgery was indeed necessary.

The doctors impressed Thuan as being quite capable and he
entrusted his life to them and asked them do whatever they deemed
necessary. They told him that they were relatively confident he
would survive the surgery, but that his life would never return to
normal. Thuan thanked them for the "good news" and prayed.

By the time Thuan transferred to Grall Hospital, Communist
troops had destroyed the fortress Anne-Marie and had closed in
around the central defense system in Dien Bien Phu. The French and
Viet Minh had initiated peace talks in Geneva, while former Emperor
Bao Dai uselessly protested the French "negotiating with the rebels."

As the French were losing one stronghold after another in Dien
Bien Phu, rumors of a possible partition of Vietnam into two zones
began circulating. The French vehemently denied such an eventu-
ality and assured the Vietnamese that they would respect Vietnam's
territorial integrity in their negotiations with the Viet Minh.

———————◆◦◆◦◆———————

THUAN LAY IN HIS HOSPITAL BED the day of his surgery wondering if the bleak day in May would be his last. The weather in
Saigon often changed without warning. The sun had shone in the
morning, but by noon a huge storm seemed to be gathering. Birds
were beating their wings wildly as they flew past his window.

Thuan imagined his mother, who had returned home. What might she be doing at that moment? What would she do if he died? Would the hospital notify her by telegram? She would learn about his death on her forty-first birthday. He tried to imagine her reaction. Would she open the telegram with trembling hands and faint after reading the first line? Would she rush to the chapel to pray? Would she stay in the chapel all day until her pain and bitterness were gone?

Thuan patiently waited for someone to wheel him into the operating room. Instead, one of the doctors decided to have yet another x-ray taken of Thuan's lungs before administering general anesthesia.

After the x-ray, Thuan went back to his room and waited for a long time. He watched his two physicians walking past his room from time to time. Each time they seemed engaged in an intense discussion. Sometimes when they passed his room they glanced at him apprehensively. Finally, one of the doctors came into the room. His face looked flushed when he announced, "It is incredible!" Thuan assumed that the doctor must have meant there was another setback, and he asked, "What is it? Has the tuberculosis spread to the other lung?" The doctor shook his head, "No. *That* would not be so incredible! What's incredible is that now we cannot find a trace of tuberculosis in *either* lung. I don't know how this happened." He looked somewhat reproachfully at Thuan as if he were somehow responsible for the unexplained recovery.

They looked at each other for a moment and then Thuan said simply, "It is a miracle." The doctor nodded gravely. "I suppose you could say that. Your lungs are perfectly clear. You do not need surgery. You are healed. You can leave this afternoon if you wish." The doctor started to leave the room, but turned around once more to add, "You are in good health now, and I cannot explain why. Maybe you will live to see many of *us* die!"

Thuan would indeed live to see many people die—among them, those he cherished most. For the moment, however, Thuan was jubilant. He thanked God and the Blessed Virgin Mary for the miracle that had occurred in his own body. He knew God had prolonged his life for a purpose, and he prayed he would not fail to do what God expected of him. He tried to find words for the telegram to his mother: "Dear Mother, a miracle has taken place. My lungs are clear. I am coming home."

———◆◆◆———

FOUR DAYS LATER THUAN WAS BACK in Hue with the radio in the background announcing the news that Dien Bien Phu had fallen. According to General Navarre the Viet Minh had lost two divisions while the French had lost 12,000 of its men: 4,000 dead or wounded in action and 8,000 prisoners of war.

In Geneva the partition of Vietnam into two zones became the prevailing solution. The Viet Minh would rule over the northern half of the country, and the French and the Bao Dai regime the southern half. Many people expressed their opinion that Bao Dai should turn again to Ngo Dinh Diem. Thuan heard people saying that only Diem could "save the country."

Shortly after his return to Hue, Thuan spoke with Bishop Urrutia to ask about his next assignment. Bishop Urrutia told him to rest at home for a while, that he had something in mind for Thuan after his convalescence. Thuan was impatient to return to work. The whole country seemed to be in a state of suspense, as if something was about to happen, but no one knew exactly what. They did not have to wait for very long.

On June 14, 1954, Pierre Mendès-France became prime minister of France. He promised to reach an accord with the Viet Minh without delay.

On June 16, 1954, the cabinet of the latest Prime Minister Prince Buu Loc, who had demanded full independence from France, resigned. It was soon announced that Ngo Dinh Diem had accepted the office of Prime Minister and would return to Vietnam, with the mission of forming a new cabinet with full power over civil and military affairs. Thuan saw Diem's decision to lead the country at that precise moment as a selfless act of sacrifice. Diem had agreed to step in while everything was collapsing and the French were ready to sell out.

Thuan ran into the chapel of his home, fell on his knees, and prayed that God would help Diem. God knew everything: how frightened and humiliated the French troops were, how betrayed and helpless the Vietnamese felt, and how the Viet Minh had for all purposes won the war—and the peace as well. Without God's help, what could Diem hope to do? Without a miracle his uncle would fail. *Yet, who am I to question the possibility of a miracle?* Thuan thought. *Wasn't I completely cured only forty days ago?*

CHAPTER ELEVEN

Ngo Dinh Diem Comes to Power

The stone that the builders rejected
has become the chief cornerstone.

Psalm 118:22

True leadership is founded in a spirit of humility and
charity as shown in the Gospel.

The Road of Hope,
F. X. Nguyen Van Thuan

O ONE KNOWS THE PERSONAL struggle Diem endured before accepting of his new "mission" as prime minister of Vietnam. When Bao Dai had approached Diem to offer him the position, Diem had hesitated for some time. Diem told the emperor that he had already prepared himself to embark on the journey of a contemplative life in a Benedictine monastery. Five months earlier, at the Abbey of Saint Andrew in Bruges, Belgium, Diem had professed vows as an oblate of the Benedictine order. He was still a patriot, and he had not forgotten his father's wish, but Diem had begun to think that living the life of a monk could also be a great contribution to his country.

Bao Dai and Nguyen De, Bao Dai's Chief of Staff, pressed Diem to accept the appointment. At first Diem countered their arguments by simply saying he had actually already become a monk. Bao Dai was desperate and he responded angrily, "You chastised so many politicians for their unwillingness to make sacrifices for their country; now you of all people refuse to make a sacrifice? Are you a hypocrite after all?"

Historians and journalists later talked about the role the United States and France played in Diem's appointment. In reality, the French did not care who Bao Dai chose as his next prime minister. Their sole interest was to end the war before the Viet Minh slaughtered their demoralized troops. The United States likewise had no say in the person Bao Dai appointed. Bao Dai himself had mixed feelings about Diem, whom he hated because of Diem's resounding resignation in 1933 as prime minister, but whom he also respected for his patriotism and his integrity. When Bao Dai turned to Diem, he clearly did so not under pressure from either the United States or France, but out of desperation.

Thuan had only to look around to see how desperate the situation was becoming. The Viet Minh had won the war. The French, who had been holding things together for Bao Dai, no longer cared: the Mendès-France cabinet was ready for a sellout.

People who had not supported the Viet Minh were frightened; once the French left Vietnam, the Viet Minh would retaliate against them. The partition of Vietnam, which kept the Viet Minh to the north, would be temporary. There would be a general election within a year's time and then all of Vietnam would fall under Communist rule.

On June 26, 1954, Ngo Dinh Diem arrived in Saigon and, after a brief trip to Hanoi, returned to Saigon. He announced the formation of his cabinet on July 7, and for the next nine years, the "double seven" would be a national holiday.

A few weeks later Diem was in Hue visiting his family for the first time since coming to power. The family gathered in the home of Thuan's parents. Thuan listened politely while Diem spoke and marveled at his joviality and optimism. By the looks of it the new leader did not have a care in the world.

Diem made sure to tell Thuan, "You have a standing invitation to come and see me at the palace anytime. You are always welcome. Please come to celebrate Mass for us. It will be a great joy for me to receive the Eucharist from your hands."

While Diem was in Hue, Hiep attended an all-day meeting with Nhu, Luyen, Can, Hoang, and Diem at Aunt Hoa's home. Hiep came home and gave no indication how the discussions had gone or how Diem planned to address Khoi and Huan's murders. Since Hiep seemed unwilling to talk, no one asked her about the meeting. Afterward, however, she was absentminded and she often stared into space. Hiep spent a great deal of time praying in the family's chapel.

Thuan knew his mother was quite disturbed and that the situation must be very serious. Diem had not accepted his position for his own glory, but out of his belief that he had a mission to accomplish. From the way Hiep looked, the situation was much worse than Diem had expected.

Two weeks after Diem announced his cabinet, the Peace Accords were signed in Geneva between the Viet Minh and France despite the protest of Diem's representatives and the U.S. delegation. The treaty demanded a cease-fire and the partitioning of Vietnam into two zones, with the Ben Hai River as the general demarcation line. It contained provisions for the regrouping of Viet Minh troops to the north and the French and nationalist troops to the south.

More troubling was the date set for general elections. The authorities in the north and the south were required to begin negotiations on the procedures to be followed in the general elections scheduled as early as July 20, 1955. Indeed, the Communists believed that within the next two years they would reunify the country under their rule and win through rigged and pro forma general elections.

THUAN DISREGARDED WHAT HE read in the newspapers. There were two people in Hue who could give him the best information about the country's situation. The first was his mother, but she would not talk. The second was Can, who lived with Thuan's grandmother.

In Hue, Can was Diem's most important supporter at that moment. Can had taken over the leadership of various groups of Diem's followers while Diem lived in exile; he had also succeeded in assembling and arming two loyal battalions. These soon left for Saigon to protect Diem, who there found himself surrounded by people who hated him, knowing that under him their ill-gotten wealth and power would soon be gone. The battalions would be Diem's backup specifically against the army units in Saigon, which answered to the Army Chief of Staff General Nguyen Van Hinh alone. Besides General Hinh, who wanted to oust Diem, half a dozen warlords wanted to move in for the kill. In response, Can was also organizing a secret military base in southcentral Vietnam from which the forces loyal to Diem could operate.

Can spoke freely with Thuan, and Thuan became quite attached to his uncle. In Can Thuan saw a great intelligence and extraordinary memory, and in Thuan Can found a good listener. Gradually, Thuan grasped the strategy of the Ngo Dinh brothers. They used their weaknesses to vanquish much larger opposition—a lesson Thuan would never forget: one must use to one's advantage one's own weaknesses to defeat powerful enemies.

Can took pains to fully explain the situation to Thuan. "How can the weak overcome the powerful? Why do your uncles Diem and Nhu, who is now Diem's most trusted advisor strategist, expect to win this game of cat and mouse? It is because the powerful make wrong assumptions about their own strength.

"The Communists are indeed stronger than Diem. They have just won the war against the French. Their armed forces, however, were destroyed during the battle of Dien Bien Phu. They were afraid that the French would recuperate more quickly from their losses, so they agreed to sign the Geneva Accords. They were also afraid that the Americans would jump in to fight alongside the French or in place of the French. That would have been a terrible blow. Thus, the Viet Minh signed the Accords and, once signed, they assumed that they had won by negotiation what they failed to win on the battlefield. They now assume that, within a year or two, they will rule all of Vietnam. The Geneva Accords give them such a guarantee; they assume that their strength rests mainly on those Accords.

"But they are wrong. The Accords are not binding for us because we did not sign them. In Geneva, the Communists were so arrogant that they refused to give us equal footing in the negotiations. They dealt directly with the French and made the French command in Vietnam the co-implementer of the Accords. They were not overly concerned when we refused to sign. The Americans, too, did not sign. Now, suppose we don't implement the Accords. What value will they have? Furthermore, if we succeed in convincing the French to leave Vietnam, as your Uncle Diem wants, then the French command in Vietnam would no longer exist. The Communists in Hanoi would no longer have a co-implementer of the Accords, and of what value would they be then?"

Thuan nodded. "So the Communists, the stronger party in the equation, are actually weaker because of their false assumption about their strength, which rests primarily on the Geneva Accords?"

Can nodded and continued, "Now look at General Nguyen Van Hinh. He is the real Commander in Chief of the army and he has the backing of the French. He is stronger than Diem, who seems not to have any loyal troops and whom the French do not love. Yet, your uncle is stronger. Hinh has made two false assumptions about *his* strength: he thinks that the army under his command will fight for him, but he is wrong. The army does not want to fight for him or anyone else. When Hinh orders the army to fight for him, his army will vanish.

"Hinh also assumes that the French will fight for him. The French may be on his side, and they will harass and threaten your uncle, but they will not fight. The French troops are completely demoralized and it will take them a decade or more to rebuild their morale. If in the near future General Hinh challenges your uncle, your uncle will have to fire him. Then Hinh will suddenly see his weaknesses—especially when he realizes that I have formed four battalions of soldiers loyal to your uncle and transported them to Saigon."

Thuan then asked Can about the warlords. "The warlords," Can explained, "lead small bands of rebel fighters jousting for power during times of unrest. They are much stronger than your uncle; even with battalions on his side, Diem would be no match for them. The strongest of them is General Le Van Vien, who controls Saigon and Cho Lon, all the vice empire and the national police; and the Hoa Hao Generals Tran van Soai and Le Quang Vinh.

"But they also make wrong assumptions about their strength. Le Van Vien is commander of the national police and he pays handsome sums of money to Emperor Bao Dai out of his ill-gotten revenues from opium, gambling dens, and prostitution networks. He has a strong military base right on the other side of the Saigon River, which could finish off your uncle whenever Vien wants. Yet, he is wrong to presume that his police force will fight to the death for him. He is wrong to presume that Emperor Bao Dai, faced with a choice between him and Diem, will choose him instead of your uncle. He is also wrong to think that an absentee chief of state's word would have absolute power over your uncle's decisions."

Thuan agreed, though he was terrified at the thought that Diem would willingly gamble his life on this reasoning. Thuan then objected, "You did not mention the Cao Daist generals." Can nodded, "I didn't mention them because they will not fight Diem. Your uncle Nhu has made connections among them, and Diem had an extensive network in the predominantly Cao Daist provinces east of Saigon when he worked with and for Prince Cuong De.

"As for the Hoa Hao generals, they have wrongly assumed that the Cao Daist generals will join them in a war against your uncle, that your uncle will fight them both at the same time, and that the whole Hoa Hao population backs them. They are wrong on all three counts.

"As for the French, they have more troops than you can count. They still control the treasury. They can wipe out your uncle in an instant. Yet, they have no more strength here without political support. French parents have been demanding the repatriation, at any cost, of their children in the Indochinese Expeditionary Forces. Though they would never admit it, if your uncle were to ask the French to leave, they would be grateful for an honorable way to abandon Vietnam."

The events that unfolded over the next two years proved that Diem, Nhu, and Can had been right from the beginning. General Nguyen Van Hinh was fired and, after his noisy protests, exiled to France. The warlords were also eliminated, one by one. Diem had exposed General Le Van Vien's hefty payments to the emperor. Enraged, Bao Dai had begun asking for Diem's resignation, but it was

General Le Van Vien who disappeared, fleeing to France. General Tran van Soai surrendered, and General Le Quang Vinh was captured, condemned to death, and executed.

The political role of Emperor Bao Dai himself ended with a referendum on October 23, 1955. On October 26 the Republic of Vietnam was born, with Ngo Dinh Diem as its first president.

April 25, 1956 was the deadline for all French troops to leave Vietnam. On April 26, 1956, after a final parade through the streets of Saigon, the last French units departed. Vietnam had finally become an independent country.

The deadline for the general elections in North and South Vietnam, July 1956, came and went without any preliminary steps toward the referendum needed to prepare for the elections. Diem believed that there would never be a truly honest election in a Communist zone, and many of his fellow-countrymen agreed. Neither France nor the United States pushed for elections, and they never took place in the North or in the South.

In the meantime, nearly one million people left North Vietnam and migrated to the South. The resettlement of the refugees was one of the largest operations Diem's new government had to undertake. The refugees arrived outside Saigon in the midst of both political chaos—the partition of Vietnam into two separate zones—and military chaos, as the warlords, the national army commanded by General Nguyen van Hinh, and the national police commanded by General Le van Vien (Bay Vien) were readying to fight Diem.

However, Diem moved quickly in resettling the refugees at the gates of Saigon. He succeeded in his appeals for humanitarian help from many world nations. The refugees themselves were good farmers and foresters and soon became not only self-sufficient, but a civic and political force to reckon with. A large number of those refugees were Catholic, and their successful resettlement near Saigon would have very important political consequences. They provided popular support for Diem during the first years of his administration when he was otherwise surrounded by the hostile forces of the warlords, the Binh Xuyen in Saigon, the Cao Daist generals northeast of Saigon, and the Hoa Hao generals west of Saigon.

Thuan believed that Diem and his brothers would never have been able to achieve such miracles without their strong faith in God and their dedication to the goal set by their father on his deathbed: the total independence of Vietnam.

———◆◆◆———

THUAN MADE HIS WAY ALONG the Ben Ngu River, crossed the Phu Cam Bridge, and once more stood at the gate of the bishop's residence. After only one month, Thuan was amazed at how well he felt. He had expected to die, but was now fully recovered. He realized, however, that he would have to take better care of his health.

At the first knock, Bishop Urrutia opened the door and, seeing perspiration on Thuan's forehead, embraced him. "You are not going to die on me, are you?" Thuan shook his head, "No, Excellency, at least not for the moment. I was just walking too fast."

The bishop ushered Thuan into a parlor cluttered with books. There were books on shelves, on tables, desks, sofas, and even a pile of them on the floor. Urrutia laughed apologetically, "A little disorder does no harm. Anyway, I feel more comfortable when the house is not too tidy." He pointed to an armchair and motioned Thuan to sit down as he told the young priest of his new assignment at Saint Francis parish.

Thuan felt exhilarated. Saint Francis was one of the largest parishes in Hue, located in the French district. The majority of its parishioners were French. With the issue of repatriation of French citizens looming ahead, it would be a challenge to live and work there, especially since the pastor, Father Richard, had been instrumental in Thuan's admittance into Grall Hospital.

The bishop seemed to read Thuan's mind and asked, "I understand that Father Richard played a part in the improvement of your health?" Thuan nodded: "Yes, he made it possible for me to be treated at the French military hospital."

The bishop closed his eyes for a second and then repeated, "… French military." Was there pain in his words? Thuan would never know. The bishop opened his eyes. "After the disaster of Dien Bien Phu, many of the French families who have been here for decades came to ask if I thought they should leave Vietnam before it was too late. I advised them not to panic, that things would stabilize after the signing of the Geneva Accords.

"Now your uncle Diem is in power. He promised to protect the interests of the French population here. But I know, and you know, and many French families in Hue know that he wants total independence for Vietnam. So whether your uncle succeeds in establishing an independent South Vietnam, or the Communists win and rule over the whole country, French civilians will need to be repatriated in the near future."

Thuan had always known Urrutia to be a man of good judgment, and he recognized that the bishop had come to the right conclusion.

Urrutia continued, "I would not normally speak to you about politics, but politics will be part of your duty at Saint Francis parish. You will help Father Richard with the transition from a French majority in that parish to a Vietnamese one. You will be serving both populations. However, you will have the responsibility of making the parish viable, even after most of the French parishioners are gone."

Thuan felt pained as he listened to the bishop. The French presence in Hue would soon become a thing of the past. Without the French population, Hue would lose much of its special charm; without them, perhaps the church of Saint Francis would be almost empty. *Everything has an end,* Thuan thought. *Only the word of God remains.*

◆◆◆

FATHER RICHARD WAS HAPPY to have Thuan as his assistant pastor. The young priest's efforts to build up the new Vietnamese parish amused him. Father Richard would joke, "You are robbing Peter to pay Paul," and it was true in part. Where could Thuan recruit parishioners if not from the Gia Hoi and Phu Cam parishes? The two adjacent parishes had large Catholic populations and did not mind if some of their parishioners wandered off to Saint Francis Church.

Thuan also made many new friends among the French parishioners. They knew he loved to read and many of them dropped by the rectory to bring him books. But it was disheartening when some came to unload their whole libraries because they were about to leave for France—never to return. They were not eager to leave Vietnam, which was their second home, and as they prepared to leave, they already missed it. Thuan tried to find the right words to comfort them, and he encouraged them to remember their most enchanting moments living in Hue. These memories would be treasures that they could take with them.

The French parishioners often asked, "Were we so bad for Vietnam? Have we given Vietnam nothing?" Sometimes they posed their questions plaintively, sometimes irritably, sometimes resentfully. Thuan always responded with a smile and, although his answers varied, he offered the assurance that over time the best of French character and culture would be remembered and the worst forgotten. Thuan never engaged in confrontation, even when one French woman aggressively insisted that French colonialism was good for Vietnam. Thuan had smiled and said, in effect, that it had indeed been good for some Vietnamese and bad for some French, and left it at that.

Long before the last units of French troops left Saigon, the French names marking the pews in the church of Saint Francis were removed. Father Richard laughed as he remarked, "I hope that our Vietnamese parishioners will not want to reserve their pews by marking their names on them." To which Thuan jokingly rejoined, "Never fear; unlike the French, Vietnamese never want to sit in the same place. They would never commit themselves to returning to the same pew every Sunday!"

Within a few months, Fathers Richard and Thuan had completed the creation of the Vietnamese parish at Saint Francis. Father Richard warned Thuan that there would soon be changes for them both. Thuan shrugged this off, with his familiar saying: they were both good foot soldiers, going where they were asked to go. He was not about to worry about his future.

Not long after, Bishop Urrutia asked Thuan to come to his residence. Thuan walked the two miles to his destination and was amazed by the changes he saw in the French district. The Vietnamese were gradually moving in, but the empty homes and office buildings were already beginning to look run down. An air of desolation hovered over the district. *And this too will pass,* Thuan said to himself. He imagined the district a few years in the future, even more beautiful and prosperous than before.

At their meeting, Bishop Urrutia was direct. "I recall that you studied at the Pellerin before entering An Ninh Seminary. Am I correct?" Thuan nodded. The bishop played with his long beard for a moment and then said, "You are not going to like this, but I am appointing you the chaplain of the Pellerin Institute..." Thuan's mind went blank; he did not react. The bishop added, "...and of the Central Hospital...." Thuan felt a little better. The bishop smiled as he watched Thuan's facial expression change. He said finally, "...and the provincial prisons, too."

Thuan laughed, "I will certainly have to learn how to ride my bicycle better."

He was consoled to know that his assignment would allow him to work with educators and students, medical staff and patients, wardens and prisoners. He had never dreamed of such a possibility, but he could visualize the three distinct worlds he was about to enter.

Walking back from the bishop's house that night, Thuan prayed for the mission ahead of him. He was familiar with the Pellerin Institute and the teaching friars and students. He had experienced being in and out of hospitals, including the Central Hospital in Hue. But he was concerned because he had no idea what it was like inside a prison. During his thirteen years in captivity, he would often remember the apprehension toward prison he had felt on that balmy night in Hue.

◆◆◆◆◆

ON JULY 16, 1956, ANOTHER SYMBOL of Thuan's past vanished with the death of Father Léopold Cadière. The Communists had taken the great scholar and missionary to Vinh where they had imprisoned him for seven years. They finally released Cadière in 1954, but his long captivity had permanently damaged his health. He never recovered and died only two years after his release.

The day Cadière died, Thuan was walking along the Perfume River on his way to the Central Hospital. Thinking of Cadière's death, he became almost physically sick with sorrow. Thuan remembered how much he enjoyed reading the books Father Cadière had left at An Ninh Seminary—and the notes and comments Cadière had penciled in the margins. Reading them, Thuan had felt very close to the great man.

Not only had Thuan benefited from the books, he had also enjoyed the botanical garden planted by Cadière on the property of the Di Loan church. As a boy, Thuan had often walked to Di Loan, only a few miles from the minor seminary. He had strolled among the thousands of species of plants and flowers Cadière had collected over the years, and each time he returned he found something he had missed the time before. The memories triggered a painful yearning to return to An Ninh and Di Loan.

An Ninh Seminary and the Di Loan church with its garden were only a hundred miles north of Hue, but anything north of the demarcation line was as inaccessible as the moon. They "belonged" to North Vietnam, and Thuan was in South Vietnam. He suddenly grasped why Diem had insisted in the strongest terms that the country never be partitioned. He had said, "To partition a country is to cut open its soul." As he walked along the Perfume River that sunny morning, Thuan realized that his yearning was an impossible dream. It lay beyond reach, and would remain so for the rest of his life.

Instead, Thuan tried to focus on Father Cadière and his life, wholly dedicated to God, missionary work, and the sciences. Jailed, almost starved to death, illnesses ignored and untreated, the man had been freed only after he was totally broken. Thuan could not know that, two decades later, he would remember Father Cadière almost daily, when he himself experienced the same suffering of long years in Communist prisons.

———◆◆◆———

BISHOP URRUTIA HAD NOT MENTIONED to Thuan that his new assignment was temporary—very temporary! Only a few months after his appointment as the chaplain of Pellerin Institute, the Central Hospital, and the provincial prisons, Bishop Urrutia met with Thuan and told him, "You are fulfilling your duties as a chaplain very well. Therefore, I am going to send you away as soon as I have made all the necessary arrangements."

Thuan simply asked, "Where are you sending me?"

The bishop smiled and said, "To Rome."

Thuan had to swallow hard to maintain control. He finally asked, "Why Rome?"

The bishop smiled and answered, "You possess the necessary qualities for a leader of the Church. A long stay in Rome will give you some familiarity with the way things work in the Vatican, which could come in handy. Anyway, you need to do some graduate studies. You also need to see the world. You have never been abroad. Look at your family: your grandfather went to Malaya, and your uncles Thuc, Diem, Nhu, and Luyen have all been to Europe."

Thuan was so surprised by the news that he did not even thank the bishop. Urrutia seemed to read his mind and used one of his favorite expressions, "You are a good foot soldier. You will go where your bishop asks you to go."

After their meeting, Thuan spent much of his time reading about Rome and practicing Italian. He tried to envision what his life would be like in Rome, and realized that he felt some misgivings. Perhaps his time in Rome would put an end to his dream of being a simple pastor of a country parish.

Actually getting to Rome was much easier said than done at the time. It was no small matter for a Vietnamese priest to just pack up and leave the country. There were hundreds of bureaucratic procedures and financial and material arrangements to be made. Thuan thought that the paperwork would never end.

Diem and Thuc were keeping an eye on Thuan from a distance and one day in late summer both uncles showed up in Hue. Thuan had heard of their arrival, but had not found time to see them. He was counseling a young student at Pellerin Institute when he heard a knock on the door. Huynh Dinh Trong, Thuan's former classmate who had been Chief of Staff for Can and had become a presidential advisor, entered and said, "President Diem and Bishop Thuc want to see you right away."

Thuan asked, "Why the urgency? May I see them this evening?"

Trong laughed, "Well there's no *real* urgency. But the president and the bishop have come to Hue especially to see you. They have no other business planned. As a matter of fact, they are planning to fly back to Saigon as soon as they have seen you."

Thuan felt moved and yet concerned by the gesture. It was hard for Thuan to believe that Diem and Thuc would fly to Hue just to meet him. To hide his concern he asked lightly, "Am I in trouble?" Trong laughed again, "I don't really know. I did overhear the president saying something about not receiving a call about you wanting to go to Rome. 'He tries to do everything himself.' That's all I heard. Now, does that sound like trouble? You tell me."

Thuan left with Trong. As the black government car sped alongside the An Cuu River, Trong said, "The president seemed a little irritated when even your mother did not call him to ask for help.'"

Thuan nodded pensively. He had not wanted to trouble Diem with his paperwork, and his mother would never ask any favor of the president. Thuan then asked what Can had thought. Amused, Trong said, "Can only heard about your plans to go to Rome today when the president told him. He was quite angry. A word from him would have solved all your bureaucratic problems. Now, because you have not told anyone, the president and the bishop have to come to Hue. Don't you think that you will have some explaining to do?"

When Thuan met his uncles, he listened quietly to Diem's gentle reproach. Though he spoke calmly, Diem's words stung, "We are a family. To take care of your passport and visa is not a big problem; it would only mean a telephone call from your Uncle Can, Nhu, or me, and you could have them within an hour. Arrangements for your stay in Rome would only take another call from your Uncle Thuc. Why didn't you come to us?"

Thuan was embarrassed, but he had been careful to avoid asking Diem, or his other powerful uncles, for any favor. He loved them and he did not want to be the cause of any rumors about preferential treatment.

He finally replied, "I did not want to bother you with such a small problem. God knows you already have more problems than you need."

Diem shook his head, "You talk just like your father. He acts as if I am no longer his kin and friend just because I happen to be the president. And your mother! Do you know that I have to call her because she'll never initiate a call?" Thuan answered calmly, "They love you, and you know it."

Diem's countenance changed. He looked at Thuan a moment and then said, "The bishop and I came here to see you and help to work things out for you. Do you have any objections?" Thuan shook his head no.

Diem smiled. "Then consider everything done. Now, the bishop wants to give you all the contacts that he has in Rome. He wants to discuss some things with you...about life in Rome, the Vatican, and *Propaganda Fide.* I will leave tonight, but the bishop may want to stay to talk to you a little longer."

Thuan wondered why, if he could have taken care of everything quickly, Diem had come to Hue to see him at all. As if reading his mind, Diem said, "My coming here today is to tell you, and maybe to send a message to your parents, that I do not want our family to become estranged because I am president. This is unfair; I need my family now more than ever."

Thuan remembered this encounter for the rest of his life. Later, when people accused Diem of nepotism, Thuan could hear in his memory Diem's cry from the heart: "I need my family now more than ever."

It was still daylight when Thuan's parents arrived to sit down for a family dinner. Diem kept looking at Hiep as if he were about to say something, but seemed not to have the courage. Finally, Bishop Thuc said, "We are drifting apart, Hiep. This is not good at all. And you, too, Am. You both seem to think that your sense of decency and pride must keep you away from the president. This must not be. Hiep, on his deathbed our father asked you to speak to us from time to time..."

Hiep quickly corrected him. "Father said I should speak in his name once a year, not from time to time; once a year on the anniversary of his death!"

Diem sighed sadly. Hiep looked up and said, "I can, of course, speak in my own name as often as I wish." Diem laughed, "Then why don't you start right now?"

Hiep bowed her head, and Thuan prayed she would say what she felt in her heart. Hiep did not smile when she spoke: "In the last two years you have accomplished more than anyone expected; you have worked miracles. Now people who fawn over and flatter you surround you. You don't like this treatment, yet you haven't told a soul how much you dislike it. And you rely too much on Nhu and Can; you show too much respect for Bishop Thuc. So, people have begun talking about a government of 'family rule.' The reason we don't call you often is because my husband and I do not want to be included in this 'ruling family.'"

Diem listened to Hiep and remained silent after she finished speaking. Then he asked, "Can you tell me who in all of Vietnam is as intelligent as Nhu? Can you give me the name of one person in Hue who knows as much about Central Vietnam as Can? And as for the bishop, is he not our eldest brother? But you are right, of course. I will be more prudent. I must spend more time seeking other advisors."

Thuan was glad to hear his mother and Diem speaking this openly. He saw that Diem looked happier as the conversation went on. When he stood up after the meal to leave for Saigon, Diem smiled broadly and asked Hiep, "Please call me at least once a week." As he walked out to the waiting car, he looked like a man without a care in the world.

Thuan watched as Diem's car and accompanying motorcade drove down the slope in front of the cathedral and crossed the Phu Cam Bridge. Thuan felt an immense sadness. He could see how lonely Diem was, so lonely that he begged for his sister's attention. At the same time, Thuan felt proud to be the nephew of a man who would come all the way from Saigon just to say that he cared deeply about his family. Diem was a man inspired by a great political spirituality, trying to do what he sincerely believed was right. He was a man with a mission, yet surrounded by flatterers and perhaps people ready to betray him.

Bishop Thuc stayed in Hue and spent all his time with Thuan. He spoke to him in detail about Rome and also about Paris, and gave him a thousand pieces of advice. What worried Thuan were Thuc's probing questions about what he wanted to do once he returned from Rome. What frightened him was Thuc's prediction, "You will go farther, much farther than I."

When Thuc left Hue, the reality suddenly dawned on Thuan: he was the nephew of the president and a bishop. Both would do anything for him. Their love for him was obvious, but precisely because of his gratitude for their concern he resolved never to take advantage of them. He now understood more clearly why his parents acted the way they had with Diem. They excluded themselves as much as they could from the "ruling family" and made it plain that they did not want to fall under the presidential mantle.

Thuan said to himself, *Fortunately, I will be ten thousand miles away for at least a few years.* He felt remorse as this thought crossed his mind, recalling Diem's longing: *I need my family more than ever.* When the time came to return to the Pellerin Institute, Thuan turned down the offer of a ride. Instead, he walked back in the moonlit night along the An Cuu River. His heart was heavy. He already missed Hue, his family, and his uncles.

He sighed and prayed to the Blessed Virgin Mary to protect his family and especially President Diem. Once again, the calm beauty of Hue soothed his anxiety. He looked toward the bishop's residence and saw that the lights were still on. Urrutia was probably still at his desk working. Then he went past the residence of the late Duke of Phuoc Mon, where Khoi had lived until his arrest. Thuan kept walking and feeling himself a part of everything around him. He was taking in, perhaps for the last time, the serenity and beauty of his homeland. He was saying good-bye to Hue.

PART TWO

THE
SPIRITUAL
JOURNEY

Give ear, you that rule over multitudes,
*   and boast of many nations.*
For your dominion was given you from the LORD,
*   and your sovereignty from the Most High.*

WISDOM 6:2–3

Jesus cast fire on the earth and he desires the
earth to be set ablaze with its brilliant light
(cf. Lk 12:49). You must be the bright flame
kindled by apostolic zeal; from your bright light
other torches must be kindled until the whole
world is a vast sea of living flame.

The Road of Hope,
F. X. NGUYEN VAN THUAN

CHAPTER TWELVE

The Urbana Institute

I have seen many things in my travels,
and I understand more than I can express.

Sirach 34:12

The more knowledgeable we become,
the more we realize our limitations.

The Road of Hope,
F. X. Nguyen Van Thuan

BISHOP NGO DINH THUC and Bishop Simon Hoa Hien had told Thuan so much about their time in Rome, and Thuan had read so many books about the Eternal City, that even on his first day the city looked familiar. However, Thuan found the actual city far more engaging than the one painted by his reading or conversations with his mentors.

Thuan's fascination with Rome had begun with his first year of Latin at An Ninh Minor Seminary. Rome had been the city with a capital "C," the hidden dream of all his classmates. Thuan knew early on that if he was chosen to go to Rome for studies, his goal of being a pastor in a country parish would be over. All the same, he yearned to see at least once in his lifetime the Eternal City, the former center of the world and heart of the Universal Church.

Now he was in Rome, walking its streets, finding shade in its gardens, climbing up and down the marble steps of its buildings, and contemplating its architectural wonders. Thuan liked to go to Saint Peter's Square at night. Whether under moonlight or in the dark, he stood in the square and listened to the mysterious rumble that seemed to come from the center of the earth. It gave him the feeling of being so close to the entire Church.

In Rome Thuan, a born architect, found immense and varied architectural treasures, which provided him with hours of immeasurable joy. He visited all the ancient churches and temples and all the vestiges of the infant Church. There was a sense of physical closeness to the life and death of the early Christians in the catacombs and the sites of martyrdom.

Thuan always remembered with pleasure the three years he spent at the Urbanian University, a pontifical institute founded by Pope Urban VIII in 1627. When Thuan attended the university it was known as the *Collegium Urbanum de Propaganda Fide*. Unlike the seminarians who both studied and lived there, Thuan lived at Collegio San Pietro.

He studied very hard and read as much as possible. After experiencing the limited resources available in the libraries of Vietnam, Thuan marveled at the wealth of the Roman libraries. However, Rome offered Thuan much more than architectural treasures and books; it gave him the opportunity to meet interesting people.

In Rome Thuan came to know people who would later play major roles in his life. He met the future Cardinal Gantin, who would become the Prefect of the Congregation of Bishops in 1984, and who also lived at Collegio San Pietro. The circle of Bishop Thuc's friends and acquaintances in Rome was quite large, and thanks to his introductions, Thuan found himself at home in most of the agencies of the Vatican Curia.

It was in Rome that Thuan became a believer in the essential role of the laity within the Church. He met many outstanding laypersons including De Habicht, a leader at the Pontifical Council for the Laity who worked at Palazzo San Callisto. He felt a profound admiration for others, including Jean Larnaud, the director of the Catholic Center at UNESCO; La Pirra, who had an instrumental role in the drafting of the Preamble of the Italian Constitution after World War II; Veronese, a politician and intellectual; and Amintore Fanfani, the leader of the Christian Democratic Party. Thuan felt privileged to know each of these men personally, and their spirituality inspired Thuan to believe that the Church had not done enough to promote the essential role of the laity.

———————◆ι◆ι◆———————

FROM ROME THUAN COULD EASILY reach most European countries and he decided where he wanted to go during his vacation. In the summer of 1957 Thuan went to Dublin and spent time with Frank Duff, the founder of the Legion of Mary. To further his devotion to Mary, while in Dublin Thuan read the works of Cardinal Leo Suenens of Brussels. Suenens's writings helped him to understand better the Catholic charismatic movement, which always gave Mary a special place.

His conversations with Duff inspired Thuan with the desire to one day visit Fatima, where the Virgin Mary had appeared to three children and asked them to spread her message of repentance, penance, and the recitation of the rosary to save the world from wars, plagues, and from the evil of Communism. First, however, Thuan went to southern France to visit Lourdes.

In August 1957 Thuan took the train to Lourdes. Just as he had in the jungle of La Vang, Thuan felt the physical presence of the Blessed Virgin Mary as soon as he came near the site. Instead of rushing to the grotto where Mary, the Immaculate Conception, had appeared to Bernadette Soubirous, Thuan walked around the site, taking in the beauty of the cloudless sky, the pine trees on the surrounding hills, the mountains, and the basilica where thousands of candles burned day and night.

Thuan arrived in Lourdes on an ordinary day. There was no crowd. Small groups of pilgrims came and went. A few children ran, laughing, up and down the marble steps of the basilica. The grotto, to the left of the basilica, was almost deserted.

Thuan knelt down a short distance from the grotto. He felt so happy that no prayer came to his mind. He looked up at the life-size statue of the Blessed Virgin Mary, placed on the spot where she had appeared to Bernadette. In one of the eighteen visits of the Lady, Bernadette had asked her to reveal her name. The Virgin Mary had replied: "I am the Immaculate Conception."

Overcome by standing on the site where Mary had announced one of the greatest mysteries of God's creation to a young and innocent girl, Thuan bowed his head. Bernadette had suffered persecution, humiliation, and jail for the love of her "beautiful lady," and she dedicated her life to spreading Mary's simple message, "I am the Immaculate Conception."

Thuan often meditated on this mystery, as he did on the title "Mother of God" and on the mystery of the Incarnation. They contained such splendor and glory, such an intricate involvement of the Holy Trinity with the person whose likeness stood before him now: his heavenly Mother.

Thuan prayed at the grotto and he heard in his heart the very words the Blessed Virgin Mary had spoken to Bernadette: *"I do not promise you joy and consolation on this earth, but rather trials and suffering."* He suddenly realized that these words applied to him as well. The more he prayed, the more distinctly he heard the message. Without fully realizing what he was saying, Thuan murmured, "For your Son's name and yours, Mary, I accept trials and suffering."

As this thought sank in, Thuan did not feel any bitterness. He knew he had distinctly heard a call for martyrdom and had accepted it, but it gave him no inkling of what his trials and suffering would be.

He moved closer to the grotto and gazed on the statue of the Immaculate Conception. For a second, he imagined superimposed on the calm face of the statue an expression of immense pain that he had also observed in the *Pietà* in Rome. He touched the stone where the Virgin Mary had stood during the apparitions and thought, "I did not plan for this, but I will go on to Fatima now...and I promise to return here every summer for as long as I am in Europe."

Thuan did not want to leave the grotto. He stayed nearby and prayed far into the night. The next day he went to the railway station and bought a ticket to Fatima. His trip became the first of many pilgrimages to Lourdes and Fatima.

Countless people prayed for miraculous cures at Lourdes, but Thuan did not seem to experience the healing of any ills. On the contrary, he left Lourdes believing he would suffer tremendously in the future. At Fatima, the Blessed Virgin Mary had exhorted people to pray, repent, and do penance to avert war and the spread of Communism. But Thuan did not experience any relief from his concerns for Vietnam while in Fatima.

Nevertheless, he prayed for his country that was once again on the brink of civil war, and for his uncles as they tried to stop the mounting campaign of kidnappings and assassinations orchestrated by Communist guerrillas. Thuan looked at the image of Our Lady of Fatima and believed that it must be very close to the beauty of Mary's real face. Wherever he lived in the future, he always gave the image of Our Lady of Fatima a place of honor in his home.

During the next summer of 1958, Thuan returned to the grotto of Lourdes and again fervently accepted whatever "trials and suffering" might come to him in the future. Years later, events confirmed Thuan's premonition. The "trials and suffering" he had been promised at Lourdes took shape in the tragedies which shattered his family, in the lies about his uncles which were a thousand times repeated and amplified after their deaths, in the fall of South Vietnam, and in his thirteen years of captivity. Like Saint Bernadette, Thuan accepted without bitterness the Immaculate Conception's invitation to embrace suffering.

———◆◈◆———

Pope Pius XII died on October 9, 1958 and Thuan shared the grief of the crowds in Rome and leaders of the Church. Pius XII had been such an inspiration to Vietnamese Catholics during World War II, and he had stood steadfastly against Communism. He was truly the Supreme Shepherd for the suffering people of Vietnam.

The sorrowful atmosphere became joyful with the election of John XXIII on October 28, and his coronation on November 4. Thuan loved recounting in detail for friends and family those momentous events he had witnessed in Rome.

Amid the changes around him, Thuan continued his studies and labored over his doctoral dissertation, its subject born of the concern he had always felt for young people and his pastoral work, which had made him aware of the great need for spirituality in the armed forces worldwide.

His dissertation, "Organization of military chaplains around the world," looked at the structure of military chaplaincies, pastoral care for young soldiers, counseling for military spouses, and services for the children of military personnel. The more Thuan read and wrote about the subject, the more he viewed the ministry of military chaplaincy as an extremely important one. He prepared himself to take an active role in that ministry once he returned to Vietnam.

That would never happen, however. Instead, Thuan would be assigned to teach at the minor seminary of Hue, and then become its rector. He would go on to assume increasingly important leadership roles in the Archdiocese of Hue and become its vicar general.

After Diem's overthrow, the United States poured more and more troops into Vietnam. It was then that Thuan, as the bishop of Nha Trang, was finally asked to help train and motivate the American chaplains in Vietnam. His work in Rome prepared him particularly well for this task. He enjoyed giving lectures and sermons on how to support the spiritual life of Catholics in the American Armed Forces.

Eventually, Thuan's involvement with the U.S. military chaplains became yet another excuse for his arrest and imprisonment by the Communist authorities.

————◆◦◆◦◆————

IN ROME THUAN SUCCESSFULLY defended his dissertation and obtained his doctorate in canon law in the summer of 1959. He planned to spend a few months traveling through Europe after completing his studies, but he received the news that his aunt, Hoang, was dying of cancer. He had to return to Vietnam as quickly as possible.

CHAPTER THIRTEEN

Going Home

So teach us to count our days
that we may gain a wise heart.

Psalm 90:12

There is a Vietnamese saying: "Birth is a pilgrimage, death
a return home." For this reason the deceased are buried
facing the mountains in my country, as if, like Jesus at the
ascension, they will go up to heaven from those peaks.

Testimony of Hope,
F. X. Nguyen Van Thuan

HIEP HAD BEEN IN SAIGON for months caring for her
sister, Hoang, whose cancer had already reached an
advanced stage when doctors discovered it. At that
time in Vietnam few doctors had even heard of oncology, and the
treatment available was the most basic. If the family had any hope
for Hoang's recovery it came from their faith in prayer and the
promise that a French cancer specialist would go to Saigon specifically to help her. Tragically, the oncologist died in a car accident the
day before he was to leave for Saigon. Hoang, her brothers, and her
sister prayed for a miracle. The miracle did come, but not as they
had imagined.

President Diem and Nhu visited Hoang at Saint Paul's Hospital almost every evening, and they prayed the rosary together. Diem
and Nhu rarely missed this evening prayer with their sisters, and
when Bishop Thuc was in Saigon for one reason or another, he

would also go to the hospital for their evening prayer. The Sisters of Charity at Saint Paul's were awed not only by the faithful presence of the Ngo Dinh family, but also by the tight security surrounding the president. Diem was a simple man and he often invited the Sisters to join the family in their prayers.

Hoang had been terrified of dying, but as the family prayed with her, she slowly began to lose her fear of death and ultimately welcomed it. As Hoang's fear dissipated, she began to laugh again and to show interest in the small daily events, a true miracle.

Hoang's brothers and sister also gained from her illness and journey toward death a better understanding of how to trust in God's loving providence. They were able to accept Hoang's death with great humility and without bitterness or reservation.

Thuan left Rome hoping to be able to see Hoang before she died. In his haste, he neglected to receive the diphtheria, malaria, and tetanus vaccinations required when traveling to a tropical nation. Unfortunately, in Bombay, India, Thuan nearly missed his connecting flight because the airport's health officers questioned him for over an hour about his failure to receive the required shots. He pleaded with them until they finally allowed him to continue.

Thuan had never been particularly close to his Aunt Hoang, but during the flight from Bombay to Saigon he found himself praying for her and crying. He suddenly felt how tightly knit his family was—that they were a small group of kindred minds sharing the same faith in God. He realized that Aunt Hoang had fully participated in the realization of Ngo Dinh Kha's dream for Vietnam. She was not only Diem's sister, but also a political ally.

Thuan sensed that he would not arrive in time to see Hoang and he blamed himself for the delay in Bombay, just as he had blamed himself for being absent when Khoi and Huan had been arrested and executed. And by the time he reached Saigon, Hoang was already dead. Thuan's only consolation was the strength his parents and uncles seemed to draw from his presence. His mother tried to hide her tears from him, while the men of the family wept more openly.

Hoang's death forced Thuan to consider the certainty of his own death. He meditated on his mortality and Christ's promise of eternal life. In his conversations with Thuc and Diem, he discerned that they had long ago found the answers to the many questions he was now facing. He was impressed with how much stronger their spirituality had grown during the course of Hoang's agony.

After Hoang's funeral, Thuan received word that Urrutia, now an archbishop, wished to meet with him to discuss his new assignment. Thuan had returned to Vietnam with more knowledge and a greater wisdom, filled with a renewed hope springing from the vibrant vision of the Church in Rome. While Thuan grieved for his aunt, he prepared himself for his meeting with Urrutia and his future. It was obvious that the bishop would expect much more of him now that he had completed his studies. He wanted to live up to those expectations.

Thuan arrived at the bishop's residence and Urrutia greeted him warmly and invited him to stay for dinner. Then the bishop and Thuan strolled outside along the paths of the sizable grounds. The bishop had the gait of a young man, his eyes were bright and clear, and his laughter hearty. Thuan had always admired Urrutia, who had been his teacher, mentor, spiritual counselor, model, and leader for more than two decades.

The bishop stopped unexpectedly and said, "I am happy to hear that there are plans underway to replace all the foreign bishops in Vietnam with Vietnamese bishops." Thuan had heard rumors to that effect, but Urrutia's words brought home the implications. For the face of the Church of Vietnam to change, missionaries such as Urrutia would have to leave. For a moment, Thuan made no response. There was no trace of bitterness in the bishop's voice. Thuan had never known Urrutia to pretend; if he said he was happy, he really must be happy.

Once again, Thuan felt that he was about to witness the end of an era. The time of missionary leadership was about to close, and the Church in Vietnam would have its own native bishops. Thuan asked, "When the time comes, what will you do?"

There was mirth in Urrutia's blue-gray eyes when he answered, "I will certainly not be unemployed." Then he resumed a serious expression as he said, "You and I are priests. We go where the Church wants us to go. Yet, if I had it my way, I would stay in Vietnam and serve as a parish priest, or as a chaplain in a leprosarium, or as the caretaker of a shrine."

Thuan exclaimed, "A shrine? What kind of a shrine?"

A smile played on Urrutia's lips, "Yes, a shrine, perhaps the Shrine of Our Lady of La Vang." Thuan was moved beyond words. La Vang was in the mountains of Quang Tri, far from every trace of civilization. Then the bishop surprised him further by saying, "In La Vang I would be closer to Mary, whom I began loving as a child."

The bishop looked at Thuan and commented, "You would also like to be in a place like that, wouldn't you?" Thuan's reply did not take Urrutia by surprise. "I have always wanted to be a parish priest like the Curé of Ars, working somewhere in the country. Yes, of course, a place like La Vang would be a very appealing assignment."

The bishop nodded, and then stopped walking and looked directly at Thuan. "Soon I will be leaving for La Vang, but you will not be coming with me," he said. "The Church needs you elsewhere and in other capacities. Erase your dream of becoming a country pastor from your mind. That is not going to happen."

Thuan felt a little foolish and kept his eyes on the ground. Urrutia said, "Once I taught at An Ninh Seminary, then I became its rector, then vicar general of the archdiocese, and before long—may God forgive my inadequacies—I was appointed bishop of Hue. I am going to assign the same path to you." Thuan shook his head, but Urrutia said firmly, "I did not send you to Rome for nothing. The Church in Vietnam will need many new leaders, and you will be one of them. Do not let false modesty get in the way of good judgment. You must prepare yourself for a leadership role. And that requires work and prayer…and cooperation with your bishop."

Against the background of a glorious sunset, the white bearded older man looked like an Old Testament prophet. Thuan was visibly shaken.

Urrutia continued, "As a first step, you will teach at the minor seminary for a while. Then, who knows? Someday, in the foreseeable future, you will become its rector."

Urrutia began walking again, and Thuan remained by his side. The grass, the smell of ripe fruit from the orchard, the darkening sky seemed to convey Thuan's contradictory emotions: a sense of joy and anxiety at the same time. When he looked at the bishop, he saw him smile. Urrutia said, "I promised you a good dinner. You will tell me about your studies in Rome, all the books you have read, and the people you have met. I want to know where you are now in your spirituality."

Thuan nodded with gratitude. Somehow, the bishop's words and paternal attitude brought back his peace of mind.

CHAPTER FOURTEEN

In the Shadow of Power

Among family members their leader is worthy of honor, but those who fear the LORD are worthy of honor in his eyes.

Sirach 10:20

When you assume the responsibilities of leadership, remember that even after you have achieved success in the task at hand, you should still regard yourself as a useless servant and recognize that you still have many faults and failings. And do not be surprised or annoyed when the response to your efforts is only misunderstanding and ingratitude.

The Road of Hope,
F. X. Nguyen Van Thuan

THUAN ENJOYED BEING WITH young people and he welcomed his new assignment at the minor seminary, which had been moved to the former Phu Xuan Major Seminary. After the partition of Vietnam, the minor seminarians had found refuge in Phu Xuan, while the older seminarians had gone to Saigon.

The rector of the seminary was Father Andre Nguyen Van Tich, and Thuan was pleased to work under his supervision. But Thuan also had the uneasy feeling that Tich was actively grooming him as his successor. From Thuan's first days on the seminary staff,

Tich began telling him about what had happened during his years as rector. They discussed various issues involving the welfare of seminarians, early screening of candidates to weed out of those unsuited for a vocation to the priesthood, the choice and evaluation of the teaching staff, and the general management of the seminary. Thuan could not refuse to listen, but it became clear to him that Urrutia's prediction would become a reality sooner than he expected.

A few months after Thuan's return to Vietnam, the Communist organization, the National Liberation Front of South Vietnam, began fighting against South Vietnam in the south. With the birth of the NLF, known in the United States as the Viet Cong, civil war erupted. While Thuan's family gathered in Hue for the anniversary of Ngo Dinh Kha's death and their annual family council, the Battle of Ap Bac was launched.

Thuan went to Pham thi Than's house only for lunch and dinner on Kha's anniversary. He did not participate in the family's meetings, but he could feel the frustration and concern in the air. His mother, who attended all the meetings, said, "If the Communists can mount battalion-level action, the war will escalate. We will need more foreign aid and our independence will erode."

Nhu was Diem's advisor on national security, and he painted a darker picture, "We have had a few years of relative peace, but now we are at war. Behind the NLF stand the armed forces of North Vietnam. The United States have supplied us with helicopters and told our generals to use them. But without proper training in their use, General Huynh Van Cao made a fool of himself and we lost a number of helicopters. Now the Americans are telling us that our army is inept and that we need advisors who are more competent. If the president resists a massive increase in advisors, the Americans will no longer support him."

Thuan had previously tried to distance himself from politics precisely because his uncles were in power. Now he was very concerned. He wanted to know Diem's views and was glad Diem asked to take a walk with him in the garden after lunch.

Only after Diem heard Thuan's latest news about his work, the Phu Xuan Seminary, Father Tich, and Bishop Urrutia did he begin to speak about the situation. "Your Uncle Nhu told me of your concern," he said. "I must tell you that we are now caught up in a fight for our very survival. I am not overly concerned about the NLF's military capabilities, despite the fact that they have Hanoi's total support. We simply have to make it impossible for their troops to assemble and launch attacks. The other front is more dangerous. The Americans want us to accept their advice and personnel. They want us to immediately adopt their form of democracy. They want us to include in our government structures elements that so far have only worked for their own personal interest. They want me to submit to their ambassador. But I am the head of state; if I submit to the will of the U.S. ambassador, South Vietnam will have lost its national sovereignty."

Thuan was startled. "But, Ambassador Durbrow has been a great friend of yours." Diem smiled weakly, "Yes, and he is still a friend. But he must fulfill his duties as the U.S. ambassador. He wants to protect American interests. If I reject his recommendations, Elbridge Durbrow may no longer be a friend."

Diem gazed at the sky for a while, then added, "I cannot allow any encroachment upon our national sovereignty. I will do what I believe is the right thing and I am ready to pay any price for that."

Tension at the family reunion and Lunar New Year celebrations ran high, and the cause went beyond concern over the war and American diplomatic pressure. The family's indivisibility seemed no longer to be possible. Thuc, Diem, Nhu, Can, Luyen, and Hiep were still very close, but there had come between them a constant irritant: Nhu's wife, Le Xuan. The irresponsible improprieties or "intentional faux pas" committed by Le Xuan, known to the family and public as Madame Nhu and to the press as "the First Lady," was making it difficult for the family to remain united. Her imprudent and thoughtless actions and words, especially her insulting remarks about the Buddhists who protested against Diem, also jeopardized Diem's political standing by making him seem anti-Buddhist himself.

Annoying incidents constantly marred the atmosphere at major family events. When the family gathered at mealtimes, Madame Nhu made sure that her children sat with President Diem. By doing so, Diem's brothers and sister could not be at the same table. Can,

Luyen, Hiep, and her husband Am did not mind sitting at another table, but this prevented them from discussing together important family or political matters. Diem fumed over the selfishness that forced their separation. Not knowing what to do, Nhu, looking guilty and helpless, sat by and did nothing. He did not have the courage to interfere with his wife's actions.

At the yearly family gathering in Hue, Madame Nhu insisted that her children sleep in the one large bedroom in her mother-in-law's home. Thus, Luyen's far more numerous children had to use a much smaller room. After this occurred at a few reunions, Luyen's wife decided she would never again attend a family gathering.

Nhu continued to feel embarrassed by his wife's behavior, but he never dared to interfere in what she was doing. While Thuan's parents also curtailed their participation in family reunions, Can and Luyen became more openly hostile to Madame Nhu. Irritated, Can would say, "You just have to look at the way she is acting when she is in Hue to guess what she must be doing in Saigon. She will be our ruin." Luyen agreed with his brother. He also believed she would eventually bring disaster on the entire family.

Thuan was concerned. Diem drew much of his strength from the family, and it was splintering. Thuan wanted to see the family united, but it was obvious that Madame Nhu undermined that unity, both personally and politically. On the other hand, Thuan acknowledged her strong will, energy, and vision, which was far ahead of her time. Torn as he was, Thuan felt so unhappy at family reunions that he, too, wanted to avoid them.

Later, Thuan wondered if the Ngo Dinh brothers would have suffered the same fate had they been able to remain more united. He would also wonder if Madame Nhu's ambitions and extravagances, as well as the anti-Buddhist cloud of suspicion that she personally had caused to hang over the family, had not played a major role in the Ngo Dinh clan's eventual downfall.

———— ◆◆◆ ————

ON NOVEMBER 11, 1960, the Airborne Brigade, under the command of Colonel Nguyen Chanh Thi, attempted a coup d'état. The rebels gained control of several strategic points in Saigon and tried to seize the Presidential Palace. Diem negotiated with the rebels, while calling on loyal troops to move into Saigon. The leaders of the rebellion fled, and the airborne troops surrendered without a fight. The coup was almost bloodless.

In many ways, the failed coup was a warning to Diem. Although Diem had reason to believe that there may have been American involvement, he did not publicly accuse the United States. It seemed to Diem that the U.S. government had begun a game of cat and mouse in Saigon, which had succeeded in revealing his own regime's vulnerability. Diem was aware of the fact that the rebels had recruited many of his own generals for the coup, but he somehow sincerely believed that if he ignored their role in the incident, he might regain their loyalty.

Soon after, U.S. Ambassador Durbrow left Saigon. America's new administration, under the leadership of President John F. Kennedy, sent Frederick Nolting to replace Durbrow as ambassador to Vietnam. He received clear instructions to cooperate with Diem.

Everything appeared to have returned to normal, but Thuan feared Diem was in mortal danger, and not so much from enemies as from himself. Diem's refusal to allow any rescue columns to crush the rebels during the attempted coup proved his reluctance to use force and revealed an essential weakness to potential enemies. It was now clear that Diem would never order South Vietnamese troops to shoot at other Vietnamese. The thought of bloodshed horrified him. Thuan saw this as "the beginning of the end." He prayed Diem would resign, and his mother pleaded with Diem to step down or at least not to run for re-election. But Diem would not give up, though he had little chance of success.

—◆◆◆—

ON NOVEMBER 24, 1960, Pope John XXIII issued the historical decree establishing a Vietnamese hierarchy and three archdioceses: Hanoi in the north, Hue in the center, and Saigon in the south. Bishop Thuc was to become Archbishop of Hue. Thuan rejoiced in his uncle's new appointment, but could not help being a little concerned that he himself would now be under Thuc's direct supervision. Thuan also grieved that Archbishop Urrutia would be leaving for his assignment at the Shrine of Our Lady of La Vang. At his farewell party, Archbishop Urrutia put his hand on Thuan's shoulder and said, "We have walked a long way together. I have enjoyed being your teacher, your mentor, and your bishop. I am now receiving what I have desired most in my life. I hope that someday you will see your most secret wish fulfilled."

Even before Archbishop Thuc settled down in Hue, the council of priests approved the retirement of Father Andre Tich and elected Thuan the new rector of Phu Xuan Seminary in December of 1960. Thuan worried that his appointment had come too soon, but Archbishop Thuc assured him that the appointment was timely and had been the result of a decision made entirely by the council of priests. No one could say Thuc had anything to do with it. Thuan put aside his fear of possible allegations of nepotism and concentrated on other matters, primarily the construction of a new minor seminary. The students of the major seminary had to return to Phu Xuan, but that could not happen until the students of the minor seminary had somewhere to go.

The construction of the new Hoan Thien Seminary took two years to complete. Thuan had major input in the initial drawings and strongly emphasized the blending of Oriental and Western features in all of the structures. Thuan spent a great deal of time going over the details as the seminary's construction progressed. A marvel of architecture, it was finally inaugurated in the summer of 1962. At the ceremony, Thuan commented, "As a seminarian I lived in An Ninh, which was a paradise of very large grounds with enough space for buildings, courtyards, gardens, orchards, and wildlife. In this urban environment, I wanted to give the seminarians a place to live and study that is not totally devoid of enchantment." In fact, the main building faced a large body of water stocked with fish of all colors that swam between the stone pathways and under the bridges.

For a while, the final touches on the new Hoan Thien Seminary occupied Thuan. But as its doors opened to receive seminarians in the fall, the Roman Catholic Church moved toward the final preparations for the Second Vatican Council, and Thuan turned his full attention to the events in Rome, praying fervently as Pope John

XXIII opened the Council on October 11, 1962. He followed with ever-increasing interest as the 2,500 Council Fathers worked to reveal the riches Christ had given his Church and find new ways to present the Church to the modern world. The Council, which ended on December 8, 1965, would be the guiding light for all of Thuan's future reflection and work.

Thuan was much busier now as rector, but he did his best to find time to talk with Thuc and Can. Because they were very close to the president, their conversations helped to keep him abreast of the political situation. On one occasion Thuc and Can explained why Diem had suddenly accepted massive aid from the United States. Diem's concern was the speedy completion of a project involving the construction of strategic hamlets for the defense of South Vietnam. Once the project was complete, Diem would ask the United States to phase out aid and withdraw most of its advisors. His uncles assured Thuan that Diem would never endanger the sovereignty of Vietnam by again allowing foreign troops onto Vietnamese soil.

As Thuan listened, he also heard what was not said: Diem was in danger of losing the support of the United States because of his resistance to control at any level. Diem bristled with anger when U.S. advisors used economic aid as a way of gaining the support of his province chiefs.

Whether or not Diem intended it as temporary, accepting U.S. aid was dangerous. It was no secret that members of the Kennedy administration were eager to test new anti-guerrilla warfare techniques and counter-insurgency programs in Vietnam. But Diem would not allow Vietnam to become a testing ground, and Thuan guessed that any adamant opposition to the arrival of U.S. combat troops in Vietnam was an attitude the United States government might not tolerate for long.

Thuan's long hours of prayer gave him the strength needed in those days: to rise in the morning, fulfill his duties, and listen to and advise the priests, seminarians, and people who came to him for counsel. Each night he went to bed thanking God for the many graces received, while his heart and head throbbed with the pain of knowing that danger was moving closer to his family every day.

CHAPTER FIFTEEN

Broken Dreams

Hear, O women, the word of the LORD,
and let your ears receive the word of his mouth;
teach to your daughters a dirge,
and each to her neighbor a lament.
"Death has come up into our windows,
it has entered our palaces."

Jeremiah 9:20–21

Wherever Jesus went there were those who were willing to live and die for him and those who were determined to kill him. Why then do you expect everyone to love you, or become discouraged when someone hates you?

The Road of Hope,
F. X. Nguyen Van Thuan

O N MAY 8, 1963, A CROWD of Buddhists surrounded the radio station in Hue to protest a recent law stipulating that religious flags should be flown below the national flag and only on religious sites. The Buddhists were celebrating the birthday of Buddha and the crowd wanted the station to broadcast a taped speech by Thich Tri Quang, a leading Buddhist monk. Can happened to hear the harmless religious theme of the speech the day before, but the speech actually aired contained inflammatory invectives against Diem's government. Before long, people in the crowd tried to rush into the station, and the station director was forced to close the doors and windows of the building and call for help. Police and military units came in to help control the crowd. While the commander of the troops and the Buddhist monks were negotiating, there was an explosion. Eight people were killed.

Foreign media immediately released reports of the "massacre" of demonstrators, mostly Buddhist, who were fired upon by soldiers and crushed beneath government tanks. However, what investigators found contradicted these reports. It was soon determined that there had been no tank or vehicle at the site, and that the explosion had been caused by a hand grenade. None of the victims had died of bullet wounds and there was proof that no member of the military or police force had shot into the crowd. Neither had the police or military been issued fragmentation hand grenades; the source of the grenade causing the explosion was unknown.

Diem formed a special commission to negotiate with the Buddhist leaders and hoped to reach an agreement on the issue of the flags. But the so-called "Buddhist affair" would not go away. Diem, who had helped to build hundreds of Buddhist pagodas during his administration, was openly accused of persecuting Buddhists and depicted as a dictator who favored Catholics in a largely Buddhist country. News media clamored that Catholics held all the key political positions in Vietnam, ignoring the fact that in South Vietnam Catholics occupied only ten percent of all government positions—a reflection of the existing ratio of Catholics in the general population. Madame Nhu's cruel remarks against Buddhist protestors added to the fray. It would take only three months for foreign newspapers to make a monster of Diem over the "Buddhist affair."

In response, the United States sent Ambassador Henry Cabot Lodge to replace Frederick Nolting. Within a few weeks, the U.S. government and some discontented Vietnamese generals allegedly began plotting Diem's overthrow.

Thuan was terrified by the plots and lies. He realized that the surprising conflict between Buddhists and Catholics would have lasting and devastating effects. The seeds had already been sown; mistrust and enmity would soon bear fruit. Though the Buddhist faction which was propped up by international media and U.S.

policy-makers would eventually fade, and the pro-Buddhist delegation sent to Vietnam to investigate the Buddhist affair later cleared Diem's government of all wrongdoing, the lies and the rancor would continue to fuel animosity between Buddhists and Catholics for years to come.

WHILE THUAN GRIEVED OVER these events in Vietnam, another event of global importance was taking place far from his native land. Pope John XXIII was dying, and his terrible agony was broadcast all over the world. Thuan, like all Catholics, turned his eyes toward Rome as he listened to the words of the pope.

In late May and early June Thuan truly "lived" Pope John's sufferings by participating in them through prayer. Every day, he prayed with his seminarians and all the Church for the pope. Thuan felt both emotionally and physically close to the man who had been elected Supreme Pontiff while he was studying in Rome. On his death bed the pope courageously offered all of his pain for the glory of God.

The highly publicized agony of the pope helped Thuan to visualize, with more acuity than ever before, Christ's suffering and death. He prayed and found solace in the knowledge of the grace others would experience because of the pope's offering.

Though he had expected it, when the pope died on June 3 Thuan was distraught. Still, John XXIII's spirituality and courage would later strengthen Thuan in his own agony. Indeed, the lessons he learned from the pope's example would make it easier for him to offer his own sufferings for the glory of God.

The swelling tide of events in Vietnam soon engulfed Thuan in a profound sadness. So many factors—the self-immolation of Buddhist monks, the rumors of a coup, the incessant condemnation of Diem by the U.S. government and media, the threat of Hanoi and the National Liberation Front, the plotting of South Vietnamese generals seemingly encouraged by American agents—contributed to Thuan's sense of despair.

Thuan felt completely helpless. He could do nothing to avert the rising momentum of events leading his country and his own family toward catastrophe. He could only stand by and watch as his uncles, Vietnamese generals, Buddhist activists, and the U.S. government made their moves. Tragically, these actions brought them all a step closer to a bloody, shattering end.

Thuan found scant solace in prayer. He looked around him for help, but the one person closest to him after his parents and Diem—Archbishop Thuc—had gone. Diem had asked Thuc to leave the country, and he reluctantly departed for Rome. The newly elected Pope Paul VI, Thuc's former classmate and good friend, kept him in Rome, away from the ineluctable tragedy. Thuc's departure left a painful void in Thuan's life.

In the meantime, everything was in place for a final push to do away with Diem, but Vietnamese generals still hesitated. As a clear signal to them and other military commanders, the U.S. government suspended economic aid to Vietnam and stopped paying the salaries of the Vietnamese Special Forces. U.S. leaders took turns publicly affirming their dissatisfaction with Diem's administration.

The coup finally occurred on November 1, the Feast of All Saints. Initially, those behind the coup had few troops; it would have been easy for the presidential guards to stage a counterattack and seize the Joint General Staff headquarters, the heart of the rebellion. But Diem decided against bloodshed and again attempted negotiation. This time the negotiations failed. All the loyal commanders were trapped and killed, and Diem was forced to flee.

At noon, Thuan was in his grandmother's home when news of the coup reached Can. A few rebel units had been seen moving into Saigon. Can told Thuan, "Don't worry. We can take care of this. Go back to your seminary and pray for us." Thuan looked at Can and saw that he was worried, but his uncle kept smiling.

Instead of going directly to the seminary, Thuan stopped to see his parents. Thuan's father shook his head and said, "What we all feared has finally happened. The U.S. government has succeeded in persuading our generals to act against the president." Thuan asked about his mother and Am indicated the chapel. Thuan rarely interrupted his mother when she was praying, but now he walked in and asked, "Have you heard the news?" She nodded and reluctantly stood up to follow Thuan to the parlor.

Hiep sat down and faced Thuan and Am. Her gestures and words were calm, but Thuan sensed her distress. "There is nothing we can do except pray for the president." Thuan asked, "Do you think that he will be all right?" Hiep was silent for a while. "Whatever must happen will happen," she said. "Whether the president comes out of this safely or not, it is in God's hands. We should pray for his safety, but we must also be ready to accept God's will."

At that moment Thuan remembered that Thuc used to refer to Thuan's grandmother as *ma sainte mere* (my saintly mother). *How fitting a title for my mother as well,* he thought. Thuan returned to the seminary with a heavy heart not only because of the coup, but also because he was so far from being able to accept whatever would happen like his mother.

After evening prayer, Thuan went back to see Can. The situation had worsened. The Presidential Palace was under siege and, one by one, top military commanders had publicly declared themselves against Diem on Radio Saigon. Colonel Nguyen Van Thieu, who had hesitated until the last moment, finally moved his division into Saigon, sealing the president's fate.

Can faced Thuan and said, "This is the end." He went to his office and began making calls to a number of military commanders. When he returned he told Thuan, "None of the military commanders will raise a finger to save the president. It seems they have all spoken with American officials. Some are still hesitant, but they will soon join the coup. They have no choice."

Thuan became so absorbed in his own thoughts he was barely aware of what Can was saying. He realized that most of the commanders loyal to Diem must have been either arrested or killed. As Thuan stood up he felt a searing pain in his head and chest. He prayed that at least Diem's life would be spared and that he would be allowed to leave Vietnam safely. But in his heart, he already knew that the rebels and the foreign leaders who had plotted with them would never allow him to live: they feared him too greatly. Diem's piercing eyes seemed to see right through the pretenses of anyone in his presence. His own generals were uneasy around him, especially those who were incompetent or corrupt, because they believed he was aware of their corruption and deception. Even though Diem proved to be a forgiving leader, as long as he was alive, there would be those who would dread his return to power.

In addition, Diem was a staunch patriot who would never accept anything less than Vietnam's total independence, clearly a roadblock to certain military strategists in the United States who believed Vietnam could be the key to their global strategy. In Diem's absence, the war with North Vietnam would escalate in scope and intensity. To match the sophisticated and expensive weaponry of the United States, Ho Chi Minh would no longer be able to afford the luxury of straddling a political fence between his main suppliers: Moscow and Beijing. China could not provide North Vietnam with the necessary weaponry and Ho Chi Minh would be pressed into to relying solely on Russia for weapons supplies, even at the risk of antagonizing the Chinese. Ultimately, this would force China and Russia into a confrontation, and that would fulfill another goal of certain American strategists.

Thuan stood in his grandmother's garden feeling as if he and his family and the entire country were sinking into shifting sands. He turned to his uncle and asked, "Are you afraid?" With a slight smile Can said, "Of what? Diem and Nhu have been ready to die for a long time and I am a sick man. If the revolutionaries don't kill me, my diabetes will. I am only afraid of what will befall Vietnam once we are gone."

◆◦◆◦◆

AT THE HEIGHT OF THE COUP on November 1, 1963, Diem and Nhu had escaped the Presidential Palace and fled to Cho Lon. On November 2, All Souls' Day, they went to Saint Francis Xavier Church in Cho Lon for Mass. Afterward they stayed for a time to pray and go to confession. After leaving the church, Diem phoned the rebel leaders in the hopes of arranging a negotiation. The generals sent an armored car and convoy to pick them up. Diem and Nhu climbed into it and were driven to headquarters of the Joint General Staff. When the convoy arrived, Diem and Nhu were in the back of the armored car, hands tied behind their backs, a bullet in the back of their heads.

At first the rebel generals announced to the public that the Ngo Dinh brothers had committed suicide, but photos of the murdered brothers circulated on the streets of Saigon, and people saw that their hands had been tied behind their backs. The generals then hastened to correct their report; they meant to say that their deaths had been an "accidental suicide," which was no more believable to the public than their first story. "Accidental death" was their final version.

Thuan went to his parents' home in a daze. He did not want to cry, but tears streamed down his face. He kept repeating to himself that it could not be possible. Yet, in some part of his being he had expected this for a long time. Diem had had the choice of leaving safely or staying on and being killed. He had chosen to stay.

Thuan went back and forth believing the reports and sometimes refusing to believe Diem was dead. Sitting with his mother, he agonized over how it was possible for a man such as Diem to die in this way. Hiep consoled him and found words that somehow brought him back to reality. Thuan witnessed his mother's incredible strength and marveled that despite her own pain, she was still there for him.

Then Hiep stood up and walked over to a desk, opened a drawer, and pulled out a paper. She guided Thuan toward the chapel and said, "It is time that you read this. I have kept it secret long enough."

Thuan paused at the door to look at the paper. He instantly recognized Diem's simple, almost childlike handwriting—letters clear and straight, o's well rounded, and the space between words perfectly equal. It was an original document containing the vows Diem had professed on January 1, 1954, at Saint Andrew's Monastery in Bruges, Belgium, making him an oblate of the Order of Saint Benedict. The document stated Diem's religious name, Odilo. Thuan's hands trembled. Naturally, Diem would choose to take that name, because Saint Odilo's feast fell on January 1. But was the choice also prophetic? Saint Odilo was the patron of refugees and seekers of asylum, and Diem had labored for nine years (1954–1962) to help to resettle nearly a million North Vietnamese refugees and improve their lot. Saint Odilo was also the person who had initiated the celebration of All Souls' Day—the day of Diem's death.

Hiep said quietly, "Your uncle dedicated his entire life to his country. There is nothing extraordinary about his dying for his country. As a monk, he dedicated his life to God. There is nothing extraordinary about his dying when God called him."

Thuan nodded and followed her into the chapel. As he prayed, he could not forgive the men who contributed to the murder of his uncles. He asked God for the grace and strength to forgive as he expected to be forgiven. But he wanted to scream out, *How could they kill a great man like Diem?* He looked up at the crucifix hanging above the altar and prayed silently, *Lord, I know that you died at the hands of men, but your death was for our salvation. For what purpose did my uncles die?*

Thuan looked at his mother. She was calm and seemed to have already reconciled herself with the death of her brothers. She was on her knees, but there was no sign of defeat in her eyes. She did not even cry.

Thuan pleaded with God for some of her great strength and faith, for her capacity to forgive, and her peace. But Thuan did not have Hiep's strength and he felt that he would have to walk a long time in the desert of anger thirsting after peace. He entered one of the darkest periods of his life.

———————◆◆◆———————

A FEW DAYS AFTER DIEM AND NHU'S assassination, Thuan's parents and grandmother were ordered to go to Saigon. They and Thuan's younger sisters boarded a military plane for the city. That same day, Can, who had gone to the American Consulate for asylum, was promised safe conduct out of Vietnam. Escorted by a member of the consulate staff, Can boarded an American plane. However, when the plane landed, he was turned over to Vietnamese generals in Saigon. He was immediately jailed pending his trial by a military court. His fate was sealed.

Thuan sometimes walked the city streets of Hue feeling as if his chest was a gaping wound. He could not help thinking that more devastating blows might be in the offing. His family's enemies were not yet satisfied. They would go on destroying the remnants of his family. He repeated to himself some lines from the Bible's book of Sirach:

> Let your weeping be bitter and your wailing fervent;
> then be comforted for your grief.
> Do not give your heart to grief;
> drive it away, and remember your own end.
> Do not forget, there is no coming back (38:17ab, 20).

Thuan felt justified in prolonging his grief and anger. After all, the murder of his uncles had not been the final act of betrayal; Can was in prison awaiting trial and, in all likelihood, would be condemned to death. Any trail would be a farce. Thich Tri Quang and the generals were not going to let Can live. They feared him and his exceptional memory for names and facts. They would not let a witness like Can survive to tell his own story one day. He and some of his loyal friends would have to die.

Thuan knew Can's death was inevitable, yet he prayed day and night for a miracle. The refrain, hope springs eternal, kept going through his mind.

Thuan was alone in Hue: Diem and Nhu were dead, Can in prison, Luyen and Archbishop Thuc in exile, and his own parents forced to Saigon. He clung to the daily Eucharist, the rosary, and his duties at the Hoan Thien Minor Seminary to keep him from falling into an even deeper depression.

With Archbishop Thuc gone, the archdiocese of Hue was without a leader. Bishop Nguyen Kim Diem of Can Tho was appointed archbishop and administrator of Hue in his place. He would hold that title until Archbishop Thuc's resignation in 1970.

The council of priests convened and elected Thuan vicar general of the archdiocese and new responsibilities were added to those of seminary rector. Thuan was relieved to have more work. He hoped that his mind would be diverted from seeing the image of Diem and Nhu's murdered bodies. Each night, exhausted from his long days of work and prayer, Thuan sought peace in sleep, but he could not sleep.

A sense of duty led him to pray for those who had contributed to Diem and Nhu's death, but he could not forgive them for what they had done to his family. He would agonize over his inability to forgive for many years. He knew that as long as his forgiveness was not complete, he would suffer spiritually.

No one suspected Thuan's intense interior struggle, however. The people that came to see him every day found him his usual gentle and smiling self. He listened intently to their problems and questions, and if someone mentioned Diem's name he showed no pain or bitterness. He simply said, "Let us pray for the repose of my uncle's soul."

CHAPTER SIXTEEN

The Rebirth of Hope

I will open rivers on the bare heights,
and fountains in the midst of the valleys;
I will make the wilderness a pool of water,
and the dry land springs of water.

Isaiah 41:18

If our lives are safe from hunger, thirst, cold, and
humiliation; if our faces are not struck by slaps and spittle; if
a crown of thorns is not inflicted upon us; if we do not carry
the cross, are not nailed to it, or do not die on it; if we are
not buried in another's tomb, then we must be transformed.

Prayers of Hope,
F. X. Nguyen Van Thuan

T HUAN GRIEVED THE DEATH of his uncles and their
loyal friends, but also the sudden loss of national
sovereignty. Diem's many years of hard work and
dedication to national independence had been cleared away by the
sweep of foreign domination. National pride disappeared overnight.

After the coup, the Vietnamese generals knew their master.
They went to the U.S. embassy and received marching orders from
Ambassador Henry Cabot Lodge. They often struggled to get
Lodge's attention, competed for his approval, and were happy if he
simply said a kind word. They were proud when Lodge tactfully
complimented them, not without some irony, on their knowledge

of the English language. Though he had no experience in government, Lodge doled out advice to the submissive generals with the
intent of turning them into good administrators, successful politicians, and military men.

Lodge was not always diplomatic, however. He scolded when
the generals made what he believed to be the wrong move. As if
they were his "pupils," he told them what they could do and what
they should not attempt to do.

South Vietnam had become completely dependent, but it was
no simple dependence. After the coup d'état of 1963, it became
ungovernable and experienced a prolonged period of instability.
Thirteen governments succeeded each other over a period of nine-
teen months, and none of them managed to stabilize the country
or improve the standard of living. New governments were created
and then dissolved by a series of coups and counter coups, always at
the mercy of any military leader who had a few units under his command and a bit of personal ambition. The strategic hamlets that had
been built with so much hope and sacrifice under Diem's administration were torn down, leaving rural areas defenseless against roaming Communist guerrilla units.

Neither Lodge nor his future replacement, Ellsworth Bunker,
would succeed in turning the generals into good administrators.
The generals surrounded them like a group of naughty children
continually quarrelling among themselves; they were never satisfied
with their share of the spoils.

The United States began pouring troops into Vietnam. The
massive presence of these troops, well-paid in comparison to the
Vietnamese, contributed to major social problems: corruption,
smuggling, drug dealing, and prostitution.

Thuan watched these events unfold and felt even more pain
over the deteriorating condition of the country than he did over his
family's situation. The quick surrender of national independence
by the Vietnamese generals humiliated and angered Thuan. His
grandfather's dream was now broken, and everything Diem had
achieved was wiped out. He was angry that so much had been lost in
such a short time.

In EARLY 1964 PHAM THI THAN passed away, fortunately not fully understanding what had happened to her sons. She had felt their absence, however, and asked for them by name, often crying herself to sleep.

Meanwhile, Can's "trial" moved ahead. False witnesses came forward to testify against him in order to create a case. The generals told Hiep that they would spare Can's life if the family paid them a huge sum of money. But the family did not have money for the ransom. Ironically, had Diem and his family been corrupt, as some accused, they might have had hidden resources to redeem Can's life. The military's search for the "treasures" belonging to Diem, Nhu, and Can turned up nothing. The alleged foreign bank accounts and properties were pure fabrication. Any money Thuan's parents had saved had been invested in the restoration of the Phu Cam Cathedral.

Hiep sat by the radio and listened to the accusations leveled against Can, taking notes as she heard various witnesses and their false accusations. She listened calmly as the court condemned Can to death.

Pope Paul VI then personally intervened on Can's behalf. In a private audience with the pope, Henry Cabot Lodge promised that Can would not be killed. But the generals and the Buddhist leader Thich Tri Quang, who had long been opposed to Diem, encouraged by Lodge's subsequent silence, condemned Can to death and had him shot on May 8, 1964, exactly one year after the tragic demonstration at the radio station in Hue.

Hiep buried Can in the holy ground of a Buddhist pagoda as he had requested before dying. Throughout the ordeal, she showed her tremendous courage by continuing to console and support the widows and orphans of those killed for their loyalty to Diem. She comforted the wives and children of those jailed for their previous association with her brother.

Soon after this, however, Hiep collapsed. At Saint Paul's Hospital, physicians discovered that most of Hiep's vital organs were seriously affected by the trauma she had endured, and the Sisters at the hospital did not believe she would survive. Her body was literally falling apart, but her mind remained alert, however, even on her worst days. To the amazement of the physicians and nurses, she slowly recovered.

Thuan visited her in Saigon often. She was not bitter, and she did not even dwell on the recent past. She spoke to Thuan about the future. She asked him about his work at the seminary and as vicar general. She wanted to hear more about the Second Vatican Council and what was happening in Rome.

The more he saw his mother's courage, the more Thuan reproached himself for his own anger and bitterness of heart. He could not tolerate injustice, and Can's death sentence had been more than he could accept. He had grown very close to Can and fondly recalled the many weekends he accompanied Archbishop Thuc and Can to Thuan An. Sometimes the entire family had joined them. Can was always happy to play host at his beach house. Thuan often sat on the sand with Can and Thuc, watching the dark sea and the lines of white foam crashing onto the shore, listening to the concert of waves, wind, and seagulls.

Now as he sat outdoors by his mother and scanned the pitiless blue sky for white clouds, he seemed to hear the voices of his uncles and siblings in the background. Those days and nights were only memories now, yet it was still so hard for Thuan to believe that Can, Diem, and Nhu were all dead, and Thuc and Luyen were in forced exile. At times Thuan wanted to scream out in his anger. The image of his mother holding Can's bloodied body after the execution haunted Thuan during the day and became a nightmare in the darkness. Thuan tried to shake it from his mind to keep himself from going insane.

There were times when Thuan thought of Madame Nhu and her children. Her effort to save Can by writing to President Lyndon B. Johnson and Pope Paul VI, asking them to intercede on his behalf, made it easier for Thuan to try and overlook her public tongue-lashings and arrogance. Still, her heartless remarks against the Buddhists who protested Diem's regime had been terrible and had made things much worse for Diem, contributing in no small part to his downfall. And Thuan could not yet totally forgive anyone who had had a part in destroying Diem, Nhu, and Can. He prayed for the day when it would be possible for him to forgive from his heart and without reservation.

Whenever he visited his parents in Saigon, Thuan saw his mother's faith and again reproached himself. *Here I am,* he would think, *a priest who has had the benefit of studies, and the graces of yearly spiritual exercises and discipline, yet she is so far ahead of me spiritually.*

◆◆◆◆◆

IF BUDDHIST ACTIVISTS BELIEVED that without President Diem they would rule the country as they wished, they were wrong. It became apparent very quickly that the rebel generals and American leaders were no longer interested in them or their political concerns. All of their demands were rejected, their demonstrations suppressed, and their pagodas continually encircled by the police force.

In response, Buddhist protesters took to the streets, using makeshift altars to barricade them from government tanks and armored cars. The generals' troops arrested their leaders, beat their demonstrators, cast their altars into the gutter, and quashed their revolt.

Buddhist monks continued to immolate themselves, now to protest the new political situation. No fewer than eighteen such suicides were committed after Diem's death, but the foreign press never mentioned these incidents. Thich Tri Quang also staged a hunger strike, but it dragged on for so long that it became a farce. Finally, with the support of local military leaders in Hue along with the stronghold of Thich Tri Quang and his followers, the Buddhists rose in an ultimate, futile gesture. Troops quickly arrived from Saigon. They stormed pagodas, rushed over barricades, and arrested all the leaders. The short and devastating efforts of these activists under Thich Tri Quang left the country badly scarred. It was June 1966.

How much the Buddhist movement was a convenient cover for the Communist cadres that infiltrated Hue is a question which would be amply answered by the future Tet Mau Than Offensive of 1968, in which many Communist leaders seized the city government of Hue in a short-term occupation. It was further evident when Communist tanks from North Vietnam pushed through Hue, when South Vietnam began to collapse in 1975, and when leaders of the movement again occupied key posts in the Communist administration of Hue.

Though Thich Tri Quang's group was not representative of the general Buddhist population, the perception of religious conflict between 1963 and 1966 was unavoidable. Catholics, believed to be Can Lao party members, were persecuted all over the country during that time. When they fought back, there was even more bloodshed. Those who profited politically from having the Catholics and Buddhists at each other's throats continued to aggravate the conflict for years. Genuine Buddhist and Catholic leaders appealed for reconciliation, but their voices fell on deaf ears for a long time. A decade-long animosity would continue to exist between the followers of Christ and the followers of Buddha, though both Christ and Buddha taught a message of universal love.

Thuan tried not to take pleasure in the disgrace suffered by Thich Tri Quang's group, which came tumbling down only three years after its rise to fame. Thuan hoped that the interreligious strife they had stirred with their virulent rhetoric would not have long-lasting effects. He prayed for a Vietnam where religious tolerance would be the norm, and interreligious relations would be founded on mutual respect and assistance.

Both before and after the fall of South Vietnam, the Communists profited from the hostility between Christians and Buddhists. Had Christians and Buddhists worked hand in hand perhaps the Communists would never have prevailed.

———————◆◦◆◦◆———————

IN SEPTEMBER 1965 THE GENERALS who had secretly buried Diem and Nhu decided to move their remains to a decent cemetery. In their haste to dispose of them after the coup, they had buried the bodies in two unmarked graves inside the compound of the Joint General Staff headquarters. Since the coup, the government had changed hands so often that they began to fear the political unrest would continue so long as the Ngo Dinh brothers did not have a peaceful resting place—perhaps their anger would continue to cause political turmoil and military coups.

One rainy night, a detachment of soldiers unearthed the two coffins and drove them to Saigon's Mac Dinh Chi Cemetery. The soldiers respectfully buried the remains of the two Ngo Dinh brothers side by side, and then left the scene as if fleeing from danger.

That same night a colonel took Thuan's parents to the new burial site. Hiep fell on her knees and prayed in the rain.

On Thuan's next visit to Saigon, Hiep brought him to the cemetery and showed him the plots with pride. "Now they can rest like your Uncle Can in the holy ground of the North Vietnam Mutuality Pagoda," so named because it belonged to refugees from the North. Somehow Thuan felt more reconciled with his uncles' deaths and he sensed the remaining anger beginning to fade from his heart. He asked God to forgive him for his prolonged anger and bitterness. At last he began to pray sincerely, "Thy will be done."

——————◆◆◆◆——————

AFTER HIEP HAD COMPLETELY RECOVERED her health, Thuan turned his whole attention to the progress of the Second Vatican Council. The fourth and last session of the Council began on September 14 and ended on December 8, 1965. The Church's "new beginning" lifted Thuan's spirit. He rejoiced to read the four constitutions, nine decrees, and three declarations the Council had produced. Thuan especially appreciated the *Pastoral Constitution on the Church in the Modern World (Gaudium et Spes)*, proclaimed by Pope Paul VI on December 7, 1965. A new surge of energy filled his being, and he recognized his period of mourning was truly over. He was ready to work again with joy and hope. How true his mother's intimation: he must look forward to the future of the Church, rather than backward to the suffering inflicted on his family and country.

By the year's end, Thuan's joy only increased. On December 7, 1965, Pope Paul VI and Orthodox Patriarch Athenagoras I expressed together their regret for past conflicts between Roman Catholics and Orthodox Christians. Obviously, the deep resentment caused by the mutual excommunication by Pope Leo IX and Patriarch Cerularius in A.D. 1054 would not be forgotten in a day, but Thuan still hoped that the Orthodox and the Catholic Churches would one day be reunited.

In 1966 Thuan found time to become more involved with Vietnam's young scouts. The Buddhist scouts were very active in Hue, and Thuan spent a great deal of time with them, working to build a strong link between the Buddhist and Catholic scouts. Thuan knew that this small effort at rapprochement would not wipe out the recent events that had opened a chasm between Catholics and Buddhists, but he was determined to make a first small step toward reconciliation.

On April 13, 1967, Thuan was appointed bishop of Nha Trang; he had not expected the appointment, nor had he sought it. Since the death of his uncles, he wanted to lead a life hidden from the public eye. He had seen the price one paid for honors and power, and he wanted none of it.

Yet, when the news of his appointment came, Thuan was moved to tears, feeling once again Pope Paul's tenderness and affection for Thuan and his family. Thuan was also grateful to God for the opportunity to serve more people. Keenly aware of the responsibilities and duties of a bishop, he implored God for the strength to do whatever the Church asked of him in the future. Thuan prayed day and night for the courage and wisdom to fulfill his new duties.

When Hiep heard the news she called to say, "A priest is a priest. The Church has honored you and given you a greater mission, but as a person, you have not changed. You are still a priest, and that is the most important thing to remember." The clear memory of the happiness Thuan had experienced on the day of his ordination, when he became *a priest forever,* flooded his heart. His mother was right. Nothing had changed.

CHAPTER SEVENTEEN

Bishop of Nha Trang

Let me hear of your steadfast love in the morning,
for in you I put my trust.
Teach me the way I should go,
for to you I lift up my soul.

Psalm 143:8

From the very beginning, Christianity was called *the way*;
Jesus called himself *the Way*. I must leave the safety of my
fortress, Lord, because those who wish to follow you are
not found there. You did not ask me to shut myself
behind some fortification, but to follow you.

Prayers of Hope,
F. X. Nguyen Van Thuan

THUAN'S JOY WAS OVERWHELMING as he welcomed his
parents back from Saigon for his Episcopal ordination. He accompanied them to the cemetery in Hue
where Kha and Khoi were buried. It was the morning of June 22,
1967, just two days before the ordination ceremony, and his parents
had not been in Hue since November of 1963.

Hiep placed a bouquet of flowers at the family's crypt and,
with bowed head, prayed silently for a long time, while Am stood
awkwardly at her side. Thuan thought she was weeping, but when
she looked up there were no tears in her eyes. She said to him, "The
dream of my father is not irreparably broken. As long as there are

people who continue to fight for our country's genuine independence, nothing is lost. But now we have another dream..." She did not finish her thoughts, but the look she gave Thuan seemed to indicate what the dream might be: Thuan himself was Hiep's hope for her family's future.

Thuan followed his parents back to their home in Phu Cam. The house had been closed since their departure from Hue. For a moment, he had wished that his parents would come back to Hue and stay there with him, but he knew Hue was no longer a safe place to live. Units of the National Liberation Front and North Vietnamese troops were roaming the area and becoming bolder in their attacks. Communist infrastructures, once effectively neutralized by Can, now expanded their activities within Hue.

Nevertheless, once again in the house where he had grown up, Thuan felt rejuvenated just by being there. Hiep asked Thuan to sit down and tell her about his dreams for the diocese of Nha Trang. Thuan complied despite his natural reluctance to speak about himself. He watched his parents while he spoke about Nha Trang's beautiful beaches, the city, and the cathedral dedicated to Christ the King. He saw their pride and happiness.

Thuan was determined to be a pastor first. As his episcopal motto he chose the title of the new constitution, *Gaudium et Spes* (Joy and Hope), because he desired to be an apostle of joy and hope. His coat of arms showed a blue background and a white star for the Virgin Mary, *Stella Maris* (Star of the Sea). Set against the blue under the star were three mountains representing *aqua et arida*, the sea and the land. The three mountains and the sea represented Nha Trang as well as Vietnam, sitting on the Pacific Ocean. In ancient times *aqua et arida* meant the entire world, and thus the words symbolized that Nha Trang and Vietnam interacted with the entire world. The coat of arms was framed with ten bamboo segments, similar to Diem's presidential coat of arms. The straight segments represented righteousness, and the empty space in the heart of the bamboo represented selflessness.

Thuan told Hiep and Am about his diocese. The first bishop of Nha Trang, Lambert de la Motte, had set foot on its shore on September 1, 1671. Now the diocese comprised an area of 20,000 square kilometers. With a total population of one million, 158 thousand, the 130,000 Catholics made up more than ten percent.

Thuan talked about his priorities for Nha Trang. His first was to direct his energy toward his pastoral duties. He was strongly convinced that the laity must play a vital role in reviving the Church. He foresaw spending most of his time training, motivating, and organizing the laity. He would be very active in restructuring parish councils and training parish council leaders. His second priority was vocations. The number of seminary vocations had decreased in the diocese and he planned to work at doubling their number.

And Thuan had dreams. First, he intended his episcopal motto—joy and hope—to be a plan of action. He wanted to bring joy and hope to the hearts of all the people of Nha Trang, to bring a message of love to Christians and non-Christians alike, to help the people of Nha Trang to become joyous and to smile again despite the devastation of their war-torn country. He would later say, "My message is a smile."

Thuan's father seemed unconvinced of the importance of such a message. Am shrugged and said, "When the Communists come to Nha Trang—and everywhere else in South Vietnam—the people will not continue smiling." Instead, Hiep nodded her approval and asked about his second dream. Thuan wished to see the Blessed Virgin Mary's presence in the midst of his people. He would work to strengthen the Diocesan Legion of Mary and bring the Marian spirituality of the Cursillo and Focolare movements to Nha Trang because he believed that all things are possible with Mary.

Thuan was touched with his mother's interest. The gift she had used to help both Kha and Diem verbalize their thoughts and clarify their ideas she now used with her son. Thuan found comfort in her presence. She had been the solid rock of the family through its recent disasters. He looked at her and gave thanks to his heavenly Mother Mary, who had made it possible for him to live under the gaze of such a saintly woman.

———◆◆◆———

HIEP WEPT AT THUAN's episcopal ordination, just as her own mother had been moved at Archbishop Thuc's in 1938. Standing beside Hiep, Am looked prouder than ever and had to exercise great effort to control his emotions. They knew that their son would do well as a bishop because of his firm convictions and dedication to the Church.

The ceremony took place in the front yard of the Hoan Thien Seminary. The seminarians and teachers were sure Thuan's presence there would now be seldom. They were sad to lose him, but filled with pride for "their" rector. Among those gathered at the seminary were Thuan's Buddhist friends, acquaintances, and guests from all over Vietnam.

Besides her deep joy, Hiep also felt that her family's honor had been restored, that once more her clan had a leader. Around her were loyal friends who had been released from prison. They had come to salute the revival of her family. She thanked God and the Church for this blessing. *Now,* she thought, *no one can say that my family is under a curse.*

Though rain had been forecasted for the ordination day, the sky was blue and cloudless. Hiep did not stay long in the receiving line. She moved from group to group, nodding her recognition and expressing her gratitude to all who had come.

Thuan watched her from a distance. From his heart he thanked God for having given his mother so much joy after so many sorrows. He twisted the episcopal ring on his finger and repeated to himself the words he had had inscribed on it: *Todo pasa.* These words of Saint Teresa of Avila, *"Todo pasa, solo Dios basta"* (everything passes, only God is enough), seemed to enfold all the terrible events of the past.

SOON AFTER THUAN'S EPISCOPAL ordination, the Vietnamese Bishops' Conference elected him president of the Committee on Social Communications and of the Committee on Development. Both committees required a great deal of his time.

Thuan tried to juggle his increased duties by working long hours. In addition, his father's words two days before his episcopal ordination continued to trouble him. The possibility of a Communist takeover of South Vietnam was all too real. As the leader of the diocese he had to do *double planning*. He would have one plan of action in the event that South Vietnam avoided Communist rule, but more important was the second plan, which took into consideration the more probable outcome of South Vietnam under a Communist regime. Thuan planned without bitterness. It seemed inevitable that the Communists would win, however many U.S. troops were sent into Vietnam.

Less than a year after Thuan became the bishop of Nha Trang, the Communists staged the devastating Tet Mau Than Offensive. Most of the cities of South Vietnam came under attack without warning: several important cities were seized and held by Communist troops for days. Hue had the unpleasant distinction of being occupied for more than a month. The great question was how the movements of so many Communist units could have gone undetected by either the South Vietnamese security network and army or the sophisticated reconnaissance equipment of the U.S. forces.

Nha Trang also came under attack and Communists troops succeeded in securing many areas within the city. A few American tanks that had positioned themselves at the end of the street where Thuan lived attempted to attack the nearby Communist posts, but instead fired shell after shell into Thuan's residence. When it was over no one offered an apology. Visitors could see the large holes left in the walls of Thuan's bedroom and parlor. Thuan did not file any complaints. He had more important concerns.

Thuan's strong conviction that the laity would play a major role in the revival of the Church in his lifetime led him to spend a great deal of time organizing lay groups. Nha Trang was the first diocese in Vietnam to reorganize parish councils. Thuan introduced a democratic approach to parish council elections, reorganized the various parish council structures, and gave intensive and repeated training to council members.

Diem had once said how foreign media and governments criticized Vietnam for not having their kind of democracy. They were ignorant of the fact that Vietnam had exercised democracy for over a thousand years, long before the birth of many Western countries. But Vietnam's democracy had been developed at the village level where it had the most impact on our people's lives. Diem had worked within that cultural environment. He believed that his work was to lift democracy from the village to the national level, and that required time.

Thuan thought, *My uncle did not have enough time to "lift democracy from the village to the national level." But I may have the time to plant the seeds of democracy at the parish level and watch them grow to the national level.* He did not have to wait long. Other dioceses soon began emulating Thuan's initiative and parish councils were renovated and democratized everywhere in South Vietnam. Council members received training to help them to fulfill their role as leaders in their communities. Thuan watched all of these positive developments and thanked God for the quick progress.

Thuan believed that parishioners had the duty to work for social justice, and he began to organize Justice and Peace committees in his diocese. Other movements began to flourish as well. In 1958 in Rome, Thuan had met Monsignor Juan Hervas, the founder of Cursillos de Christianidad, whom Thuan had greatly impressed. As soon as he was ordained bishop, Thuan went to Manila to attend Cursillos, and began organizing them in Nha Trang when he returned. Likewise, Thuan had known the Focolare Movement in Rome. Though it took him some time, by 1974 he was finally able to organize both in Nha Trang and then in Saigon four "Mariapolis" centers for priests, religious, and lay people. He had an enormous admiration for Chiara Lubich, the founder of the movement. Later, Thuan would become a permanent member of the group of bishops who met frequently to advance the cause of Focolare around the world.

In the meantime, with the rest of the world, Thuan learned that President Lyndon B. Johnson had announced he would not seek re-election. Johnson looked tired and his failure to run in the presidential race of 1968 was a clear indication of his personal defeat and perhaps an acknowledgment of the war's disaster as well. The Communists had suffered many casualties during the Tet Mau Than Offensive, but their strategic objective of breaking the will of the United States was achieved. The United States was not winning the war and eventually it would have to withdraw from Vietnam. If that happened, it was merely a question of time before the South Vietnamese generals were left to fend for themselves against the Communists, and that would mark the end for South Vietnam.

For this reason, as a spiritual provision against a Communist takeover, Thuan made an urgent priority the training of as many men as possible for the priesthood. The situation in the dioceses of North Vietnam was a strong warning. The Church there had been entirely unprepared for Communist rule and now suffered from a lack of priests. Thuan wanted to build up a large contingent of priests who would be well equipped to work within a Communist country. To accomplish this Thuan decided to expand the major and minor seminaries in his diocese and to create new ones where possible. Over the next eight years Thuan increased the number of major seminarians from 42 to 147, and minor seminarians from 200 to 500.

On the very day the Communists drew near Nha Trang in April 1975, Thuan ordained his major seminarians and could well afford to smile when Communist troops entered the city. He had managed to complete at least one of the most important spiritual preparations for the takeover. Even though the diocese would henceforth suffer Communist restrictions on the recruitment of new seminarians, Nha Trang would not suffer from a lack of priests to serve the faithful.

———◆◆◆◆———

THE WORK OF A BISHOP IS NOT limited to his own diocese or country and Thuan became involved in activities at the regional level with the bishops of Asia and at the international level in Rome.

In 1970 Thuan worked with a committee of bishops on the future Federation of Asian Bishops Conferences. He went to India to prepare for the first General Assembly of Asian Bishops to meet in Manila in November. While he was in India the Plenary Assembly asked Thuan to speak on "The Political Problems in Asia and Their Solutions" at their November meeting.

His work on the committee familiarized Thuan with the many faces and names of the members, so that at the November meeting in Manila Thuan already had many friends among the 200 bishops and archbishops gathered with Pope Paul VI for the birth of the federation.

It was a historical moment. The Church in the Philippines, Vietnam, Laos, India, Malaysia, China, Japan, Korea, and Indonesia among others, did not need an overarching structure to help their Bishops' Conferences administratively as much as it needed a forum to facilitate the exchange of ideas and experiences. The meeting provided this forum. When Thuan delivered his speech on November 24, it was widely applauded for the global vision and strategic perspectives Thuan shared. (Twenty-five years later in Manila, at the Sixth General Assembly of the FABC, Pope John Paul II celebrated the anniversary of that historic event in which Thuan had participated. On that occasion Thuan would receive the accolades of many friends who had prayed and petitioned for his release during his captivity.)

In 1971 Thuan became Consulter for the Pontifical Commission for the Laity in Rome. Thuan had always promoted the role of the laity, and he found the commission a great encouragement for the laity's future.

During his trips to Rome in his capacity as consulter, Thuan made the acquaintance of a member of the same Pontifical Commission, Karol Wojtyla, cardinal archbishop of Krakow. Wojtyla had become a cardinal in 1967, the same year Thuan became the bishop of Nha Trang. Thuan immediately noticed Wojtyla's great devotion to the Blessed Virgin Mary. A theologian and scholar, he spoke simply, succinctly, and always with a great sense of humor. Thuan also discovered that Wojtyla shared his conviction that the laity should play an increasingly important role in the Church.

As they dined together in small restaurants around the Piazza of San Callisto, Thuan could not have guessed the significant place Wojtyla would have in his own life.

THE THREE LARGE U.S. INSTALLATIONS in Thuan's diocese gave him a great deal of contact with American soldiers. The bases in Nha Trang, Cam Ranh Bay, and Thap Cham were a constant reminder to Thuan of his duty to care for the spiritual needs of all Catholics, including foreign soldiers, servicemen, and officers.

Thuan was seriously concerned with the particular problems the U.S. forces faced in the bewildering frontless war with its unclear purpose. He spent much time talking to American chaplains and became the most popular speaker for their retreats at Cam Ranh Bay. They knew he was the nephew of former President Ngo Dinh Diem. Perhaps they wondered if Thuan felt some hostility toward Americans because of what had happened to his uncle, but they never asked, and Thuan never volunteered any remarks.

Gradually, Thuan became a familiar face to the American chaplains. Terrence Cooke, General Chaplain of the United States Armed Forces and later Archbishop of New York, met with Thuan and decided that he would visit him each time he returned to Vietnam.

Cooke was always curious about Thuan's uncles and once asked if Diem and Nhu had hated the United States. Thuan assured him that neither man had hated Americans or the United States. He told Cooke what Diem had once said regarding America: "The United States is a big country. It can survive a thousand mistakes made by its leaders. South Vietnam is a small country and if we made a few mistakes, our country would no longer exist on the map. That is why we cannot make mistakes or allow the United States to make mistakes for us." Cooke's response was to offer his sincere regrets for Diem and Nhu's assassination.

On November 2, 1970, seven years after Diem and Nhu's murder, a huge crowd filled Saigon Cathedral and spilled over into Queen of Peace Square. Thousands came to the Eucharistic celebration in honor of the former president, his brothers, and their comrades-in-arms killed following the 1963 coup. In attendance were several generals and government ministers, and First Lady Nguyen Van Thieu—the wife of the general whose division had attacked the Presidential Palace in 1963.

A much larger crowd gathered later to pray at the tombs of Diem and Nhu at Mac Dinh Chi Cemetery, and another crowd attended a Buddhist service at the North Vietnam Mutuality Pagoda, whose leading monk had allowed Hiep to bury Ngo Dinh Can in the pagoda's holy ground, a testimony to the mutual respect between the Ngo Dinh brothers and the Buddhists.

Thuan drew courage from these events. He believed that one day the names of his uncles would be entirely vindicated. Clearly, it would take much longer for foreign media to come to the truth about Diem and Nhu and the courageous people who had fought and died with them or spent years in prison because of their loyalty to the Ngo Dinh brothers.

———————◆◆◆———————

IN SEPTEMBER 1971 THUAN celebrated the three hundredth anniversary of the arrival of the French bishop, Lambert de la Motte, in Nha Trang. In a moving tribute to Lambert and the missionary work over three hundred years before, Thuan extolled the role of foreign missionaries and spoke with barely contained emotion of the martyrs who had suffered and died for their faith in the various provinces of the diocese. On that occasion, the joyful tone of Thuan's pastoral letter was in sharp contrast with his earlier letters condemning widespread social corruption.

Whatever their topic, Thuan's pastoral letters were always well written because he spent a long time shaping them and because he wrote what he truly felt in his heart. He possessed the art of putting complex ideas into simple language and so succeeded in making both the general population as well as the socially elite appreciate his observations and remonstrations.

———————◆◆◆———————

HO CHI MINH HAD DIED IN 1969 of heart failure, but his Communist forces had not weakened. On Good Friday, March 31, 1972, the North Vietnamese launched another offensive. The fact that Communist units could once again penetrate South Vietnamese and U.S. defenses and capture large areas of key South Vietnamese cities prompted American leaders to seek peace at all costs.

All the urgent diplomatic efforts of Secretary of State Henry Kissinger were wasted on the Communist negotiators. They believed, and with reason, that they could afford to wait. Time was on their side. Eager for a resolution, Kissinger continued to make concessions, and when the Communists refused, he offered more. Ultimately, the survival of South Vietnam became impossible.

Nguyen Van Thieu, a former general who had led the coup of 1963, won the presidential election held in 1965 in South Vietnam. He tried to extract guarantees from President Richard Nixon and Kissinger that the United States would not abandon Vietnam completely. Public assurances to that effect were given, but Thieu judged these insufficient against future offensives by North Vietnam. Ultimately it was Nixon's private assurances—containing more compelling language—that convinced Thieu to sign the Paris Peace Agreements in February of 1973.

The Agreements contained provisions for a cease-fire and established a deadline for the withdrawal of all U.S. troops from Vietnam. There was no mention of even a partial withdrawal of Communist troops from South Vietnam. In fact, the Agreements left part of Quang Tri, the northernmost province of South Vietnam captured by the Communists in the Good Friday Offensive of 1972, entirely in their hands. The Agreements also confirmed the occupation of very large portions of South Vietnamese territory by Communist troops.

In the talks which led to the Agreement, the Communist leaders of North Vietnam sought the withdrawal of U.S. troops, the demoralization of the people of South Vietnam, and guarantees that the United States would not return even if North Vietnam launched an all-out offensive against South Vietnam. The United States was provided a safe and honorable withdrawal of its troops from Vietnam, and a "decent interval" between such a withdrawal and the inevitable collapse of South Vietnam.

The voice of South Vietnam remained unheard and it gained nothing from the Agreements. At the time, President Nguyen Van Thieu's only concern was Nixon's private pledge that U.S. troops would return to fight if North Vietnam launched an all-out offensive. Tragically, Thieu did not understand that the strong anti-war feelings in the United States and the Watergate scandal destroyed any possibility of such a return. If Thieu did not grasp this reality, the leaders of North Vietnam did.

Implementing the Paris Peace Agreements to the letter, the last U.S. units left Vietnam on March 29, 1973. Even the most naïve South Vietnamese understood that they would not return, and what they knew, the North Vietnamese also knew. Without fear of American intervention, North Vietnam would soon launch a general offensive to subdue South Vietnam. Exactly when this would happen remained the only question.

Thuan watched South Vietnam's agony and recalled Diem's advice never to rely on a much stronger ally. The leaders after Diem's overthrow had relied too heavily on U.S. support. They had gambled and lost. Now President Thieu told reporters how much he regretted his part in the coup that deposed Diem. Many Vietnamese began to state publicly that things would have been different if Diem were alive.

American casualties numbered 56,227 dead and 303,605 wounded. South Vietnam suffered higher casualties: 188,000 dead and 430,000 wounded. Allied troops from Korea, Australia, New Zealand, and Thailand lost 5,221 men. The soldiers and guerrillas of the National Liberation Front and North Vietnam killed in action totaled 920,000. The number of casualties on both sides of the conflict horrified Thuan. He constantly asked himself how so many people could die in so fruitless a cause.

Once again, Thuan shuddered at the ugly face of war. His desire now was to be an apostle of peace and to contribute to the healing of wounds; his wish was immediately granted. As soon as the Paris Peace Accords were signed, Thuan was asked to head one of the largest humanitarian programs ever conceived, planned, and implemented by the Church in Vietnam. The Vatican, entire networks of the Catholic Church's charitable and development assistance organizations, and the bishops of Vietnam provided Thuan with the means to heal the wounds of war and raise peace from its ashes.

CHAPTER EIGHTEEN

The Mission of Love

Give graciously to all the living;
do not withhold kindness even from the dead.
Do not avoid those who weep,
but mourn with those who mourn.

Sirach 7:33–34

Charity knows no boundaries; if it has boundaries,
it is no longer charity.

The Road of Hope,
F. X. Nguyen Van Thuan

I N A HANDWRITTEN LETTER addressed to Cardinal Jean
Villot, then Vatican Secretary of State, Pope Paul VI created the Pontifical Council *Cor Unum* on July 15, 1971.
The principal goal of the council was to promote and coordinate
Catholic humanitarian efforts aimed at alleviating the suffering of
the poor, the downtrodden, victims of natural and man-made disasters, and assisting Third World countries in their development.

Cor Unum became involved in South Vietnam through the creation by the Vietnamese Bishops' Conference and bishops from
other countries of an agency known as the Cooperation for the Re-
construction of Vietnam (COREV).

The Vietnamese bishops decided that Thuan, as president of
the Committee on Development, should be the driving force behind
COREV and appointed him executive vice president of the new
agency. Thuan accepted his appointment without realizing the in-

credible scope of the work involved. It was an enormous task, almost impossible considering that Thuan still had to administer a
diocese.

Family history seemed to be repeating itself. Just as Diem had
managed the refugee crisis in 1954, now Thuan was managing an
agency with the daunting mission of giving aid to the more than
four million persons displaced by twenty-eight years of war. To com-
plicate matters, not long after the Paris Peace Accords, it became
clear that the cease-fire at the heart of the agreements could not be
maintained even for a single day. The contested areas of South Vietnam kept expanding and this produced an overwhelming sense of
insecurity in the countryside. People from rural areas began to move
en masse into urban and suburban areas in their desperation to find
safety at any cost.

The needs of refugees were so great that Thuan kept asking
himself how he could possibly supply the necessary help to resettle,
feed, and shelter the refugees, and provide the seeds and farming
tools needed to restart their lives. How could he help them to build
schools and make available even the most basic educational materials for their children? How could he ever raise enough money to
provide all the required relief, rehabilitation, and development activities? Above all Thuan worried about how he would manage to
accomplish all of this on a part-time basis.

Thuan spent every day of the next two years working to the
point of exhaustion. Thousands of requests for assistance projects
flooded his desk weekly. He had to screen the requests, research the
circumstances in order to make recommendations to the grant committee, and then monitor and evaluate the projects. At a bi-monthly
meeting Thuan made a general presentation of all the requests received and spoke specifically on the merits of each request and, in
those few cases, the reasons why some had been rejected.

Thuan set up COREV headquarters in Saigon and began traveling back and forth between there and Nha Trang. As far as fi-
nances were concerned, the bishops had given him full authority,
but he never made a decision without consulting the full committee
of bishops. Despite the challenges, the COREV villages he initiated
were successful according to the directors of *Misereor* and Caritas

Germany, *Secours Catholique de France,* Catholic Relief Services of the United States, and *Secours International* of Belgium among others.

Despite his weariness, Thuan acted as though he had the energy of five men. Aside from the mountains of paper work and meetings, Thuan also visited each project site to observe its progress and to evaluate its success or failure. He also took visitors and donors to the COREV villages scattered throughout South Vietnam. During the day he traveled around South Vietnam to see those who were building the houses, digging the wells, and planting the seeds COREV had provided. At night he returned to his bare room and slept on his hard bed with a straw mattress.

At times Thuan look up at the heavens and asked Diem to help him. The more successful COREV became, the more the Communists considered Thuan a threat.

——◆◆◆——

ON MARCH 11, 1975, Communist tanks rolled into Ban Me Thuot, the capital of the central highlands. The commander of the region, General Nguyen Van Phu, panicked and ordered his troops to evacuate. It was the beginning of a great debacle: the "Spring Offensive."

Lacking a plan, soldiers traveled alongside refugees via Highway 7 in a chaotic exodus. The highways had not been repaired or even used in years and the bridges that were not destroyed during the war had not been maintained. The situation quickly degenerated into a nightmare. Military trucks and cars were left behind while refugees and soldiers trudged down to the coastal plains on foot several hundred miles eastward. They waded across streams and rivers and marched through thick jungle. Hungry and exhausted, the mass of human misery kept moving under constant threat from guerrilla mortar and artillery fire. The refugees progressed at a snail's pace as they carried thousands of wounded on makeshift stretchers and stopped to bury the dead along the way. Finally, they ran out of food.

Thuan received reports of the refugees' plight and immediately took action by renting planes to drop tons of medicine, rice, bread, and milk to the refugees. He had no doubt that his intervention would incur the wrath of the Communists, but Thuan heard in his mind the voices of his grandfather and uncles saying, "We have to do what is right, and we are willing to pay the price." Although their actions had jeopardized their personal safety, this had never stopped them, and Thuan would follow their example.

Actually, Thuan had not made the decision to supply aid on his own. He had consulted the apostolic delegate and other bishops, and they had all concurred with his idea. Nevertheless, Thuan would ultimately bear full responsibility for the decision.

CHAPTER NINETEEN

The Fall of South Vietnam

Your men shall fall by the sword,
and your warriors in battle.
And her gates shall lament and mourn;
ravaged, she shall sit upon the ground.

Isaiah 3:25–26

The typhoon that sweeps through the trees breaks the dry
and rotten branches, but it cannot uproot the cross that is
planted deep in the earth.

The Road of Hope,
F. X. Nguyen Van Thuan

WHEN PRESIDENT NIXON resigned on August 8, 1974, President Nguyen Van Thieu came to the realization that he had relied too heavily on Nixon's private promises at the peace talks. The resignation opened a floodgate for Communist activity, and now there was no one to answer Thieu's plea for help.

On January 1, 1975, the city of Phuoc Long, located sixty miles north of Saigon, fell to the Communists. It was the first time Communist tanks had come that close to Saigon. Thieu protested the act of aggression and South Vietnamese radio stations praised the heroism of those who had defended Phuoc Long. Still, the South Vietnamese government made no effort to recapture the city.

The subsequent southward march of North Vietnamese divisions was relentless. Quang Tri was lost on March 19; the troops approached Hue. Thuan had been expecting the worst for a long time. He was about to witness the final act of the war.

The Communists entered Hue for the second time in seven years. The first time the city fell to the enemy, during the Tet Mau Than Offensive in January 1968, it had been recaptured in a bloody battle. But afterward people said that Hue had lost its soul in the fight. People had believed that the Communists would act generously with them because the city had been the most "revolutionary" in South Vietnam. Instead, the Communists massacred thousands, and the city fell. After that, a heavy air of sadness and despair had settled over Hue. Thuan wondered what would happen to Hue this time.

Thuan grieved for his country. Communism never benefited any country, but Vietnam's situation was even worse. For more than a millennium the Vietnamese had resisted all kinds of domination. Whenever they did not succeed they suffered greatly because they refused to submit to tyranny, preferring death to capitulation. Now that the most repressive regime possible was about to be imposed on the entire country, Thuan wept.

Undoubtedly, the greed, corruption, and injustice of the South Vietnamese government had certainly contributed to its demise. Thuan had seen enough examples of this in the eleven years following the coup: the pusillanimity of its military and civilian "leaders," the blatant corruption in the government at all levels, the insatiable greed of officials, and the extreme poverty of the people. Perhaps the country was undergoing a necessary process of purification, however painful it proved.

As the Communist tanks neared Nha Trang, Thuan received permission from the apostolic delegate, Henri Lemaitre, to ordain all of the seminarians who were prepared to receive Holy Orders. As Thuan ordained the young men, he could hear the American helicopters that were evacuating the remaining U.S. personnel nearby. A few hours later, the first Communist units entered the city of Nha Trang.

Thuan was about to begin his life under a Communist regime. In the past, he had never hidden his opposition to the lies and errors of Communism and some of his pastoral letters contained strong condemnations of Marxism. The fact that Communist troops were swarming into his diocese did not change his opposition to Communist philosophy and practice. He knew he would have to pay for his convictions. But on that day, after the ordination of his new priests, Thuan did not feel any fear of the future. His only feeling was that of exhilaration. He had managed to put the final touch on his preparation for the diocese's life under Communism.

On April 3 the largest U.S. base in the world, Cam Ranh Bay, fell to the Communists. On April 18 the Communists captured Phan Rang, President Thieu's native province. With the country rapidly collapsing around him, President Nguyen Van Thieu re-signed on April 21 and went into exile in Taiwan. General Duong Van Minh, who had headed the junta that overthrew President Diem, became president for a few days, but he surrendered to the Communists when their tanks crashed through the gates of the Presidential Palace.

Thuan was ashamed of the disgraceful capitulation of the men who had once been so sure of U.S. support. Again, he regretted that Diem was not there to help the country. He could only breathe a sigh of relief when his parents and two of his sisters, Tuyet and Tien, made it onto a flight out of Saigon. They went to Australia and joined Ham Tieu and Thu Hong, two other sisters who had already settled there.

Then on April 23, while South Vietnam lay in ruins, Thuan received news that he had been appointed coadjutor archbishop of Saigon, now renamed Ho Chi Minh City by its conquerors.

Pope Paul VI's decision to elevate Thuan to archbishop of Saigon and thus place him in the position of being the future successor of Archbishop Nguyen Van Binh, would have dire conse-quences. But Thuan was, as always, a good foot soldier; he went where he was asked to go. Without much thought of what might happen to him personally, Thuan prepared to leave for Saigon and assume his responsibilities there. In the meantime, Bishop Nguyen Van Hoa took over the diocese of Nha Trang. Thuan turned over the keys and important documents of the chancery and planned to leave as soon as the highway between Nha Trang and Saigon reopened.

Thuan packed a small suitcase and left for his new assignment on May 8, 1975. As he drove toward Saigon he saw traces of recent battles everywhere: charred tanks, trucks, and jeeps; half-burned buildings; homeless people carrying all their belongings on their shoulders and wandering aimlessly near towns and villages. Overcome by the misery Thuan turned his eyes to the sea, beautiful as ever. War had marred Vietnam's landscape, but it could not touch the sea—a symbol of the country's soul. He sighed and prayed for his country. In his mind he repeated, *My country is forever beautiful.*

With this reminder to himself, Thuan experienced a sense of peace and he thanked God for his new assignment. He was ready to face the consequences of his past words and deeds. He was ready to pay for the honor of being a member of the Ngo Dinh family and of serving God and the Church.

As he drove toward Saigon, Thuan's mind traveled over his past. He thought of his childhood in Phu Cam and the years at An Ninh Seminary, where he had found such peace and joy. He remembered the struggle he had at Phu Xuan Major Seminary as he contemplated becoming a religious rather than diocesan priest. He recalled the day of his ordination, his first assignment, and his near-fatal illness. He reflected on his miraculous healing and how someone had told him God never wastes a miracle. He prayed that the miracle had not been a waste. After his recovery he had gone to Rome and returned to teach, to become seminary rector, and a bishop. Now, unexpectedly, he was an archbishop.

It occurred to Thuan that whenever something good happened in his life, something bad always seemed to follow. Right after his ordination he had become so ill that he literally had one foot in the grave. After his uncles became the most powerful men in the country they were killed. When he became a bishop South Vietnam fell to the Communists. Now that he was an archbishop he couldn't help wondering what would happen next. He smiled and decided not to worry. He would leave the future to God. Thuan prayed and felt ready for the gathering storm ahead.

PART THREE

THE
STORMY
YEARS

I was at ease, and he broke me in two;
he seized me by the neck and dashed me to
*   pieces;*
he set me up as his target;
his archers surround me.

JOB 16:12

In Saigon on August 15, 1975,
the Feast of the Assumption,
I was arrested…so began a new and
special stage of my long adventure.

Testimony of Hope,
F. X. NGUYEN VAN THUAN

CHAPTER TWENTY

The Ordeal Begins

You cast me into the deep,
into the heart of the seas,
and the flood surrounded me;
all your waves and your billows
passed over me.

Jonah 2:3

You must lose in order to gain, die in order to live, and
abandon everything in order to meet the Lord.

The Road of Hope,
F. X. Nguyen Van Thuan

THUAN ARRIVED IN SAIGON and immediately met with
Archbishop Nguyen Van Binh. He had to decide
where to take up residence and chose to stay at the
archdiocesan major seminary. When asked why he did not choose
to stay at the villa that served as COREV headquarters, he replied
that the major seminary was a part of the archdiocese, and he ought
to live in a building that belonged to it.

Thuan settled in and waited. It was only a matter of time before the Communist authorities made a move against him, but
Thuan felt free of worries. He prayed and took long walks on the
seminary grounds in the morning and evening.

By August Thuan began to receive "friendly" visits from several Catholic "intellectuals" who had become recent supporters of
the Communist regime. The purpose of the visits was to ask Thuan

to return to Nha Trang quietly and as soon as possible. Thuan sympathized with their delicate position, caught as they were between the Church and the Communists, but he calmly insisted, "Nha Trang has a new bishop and I am no longer needed there. I have been assigned to Saigon and I cannot leave unless I am told to leave by the Holy See."

People pleaded with him to consider wisely what he was doing. Unless he left Saigon he would almost certainly be arrested by the Communist authorities, who feared having another member of the Ngo Dinh clan in a position of power in Saigon. Others wrote to say that if he did not leave he would incur the full wrath of the authorities "who will make your life a hell."

———————◆◦◆◦◆◦————————

EARLY ON AUGUST 13 THUAN was informed that Communist authorities had invited all the priests in Saigon to assemble at the old Parliament Building (which had once housed the deputies and senators of South Vietnam) on August 15 at 3:00 P.M. Obviously the meeting would not be a purely social gathering. Thuan smiled when he thought about the date of the meeting. August 15, the feast of the Assumption, was one of his favorite celebrations since his childhood. If the authorities attempted to do anything against him on that day, he would consider it sent to him personally by the Blessed Virgin Mary.

At 1:00 P.M. on August 15 a small group of secret police entered the seminary, handed him an invitation issued by the authorities, and asked that he sign the receipt of delivery. He was told to be at Independence Palace (formerly the Presidential Palace) at exactly 3:00 P.M. It was clear to him that all of the priests were being assembled at the Parliament Building so that they would not know what was happening to him at the palace.

At the same time, secret police also went to the chancery to see Archbishop Nguyen Van Binh. He too was to meet with government officials at Independence Palace at 3:00 P.M. After the secret police left Binh went directly to the major seminary to see Thuan. They calmly discussed together what might be in store for them and left for the meeting at 2:00.

As they drove up to Independence Palace, the guards told them to leave their car just inside the gate and to walk to the main entrance. A group of photographers were there and they surrounded Binh and Thuan, snapping pictures as they walked through the park leading to the palace door. Apparently the authorities wanted evidence that the bishops were not handcuffed or injured.

Inside the palace, guards immediately separated Thuan and Binh. Thuan was taken to a small room where several government officials were waiting. One man spoke to Thuan while the others listened. The official rebuked Thuan for inciting trouble and accused him of being a lackey for the imperialists and a pliant tool of the Vatican. The official told Thuan that the Communist government would never—and he emphasized never—allow him to assume the responsibilities of coadjutor archbishop of Ho Chi Minh City. He scrutinized Thuan's face as he said, "It is evident that your appointment to Ho Chi Minh City is a Vatican plot!" He questioned Thuan, "Is it true that being coadjutor means that you have the right to automatically replace Archbishop Binh if he is incapacitated or dies?" Thuan shrugged, "Yes, but Archbishop Binh is quite healthy. He is not going to die or become incapacitated any time soon." Thuan's response did not seem to satisfy his interrogator.

Thuan asked why he had been called a "fomenter of troubles" and a "lackey for the imperialists." The interrogator retorted angrily, "In this city and elsewhere reactionary Catholics are saying that the Catholic Church needs a leader like you. Why are they saying this? Why does the Catholic Church need a strong leader? To fight against whom? Against what? Against patriots? Against the revolution? That is why I called you a fomenter of troubles!" He paused briefly before shouting, "It is plain to everyone that you are a reactionary. We fought for twenty years because of your uncle Diem. Our enemy was *My-Diem* (U.S.A.-Diem). He was a lackey for imperialism. You headed COREV and begged money from every country in the world. Are you surprised to be called a lackey?"

Thuan responded calmly, "My Uncle Diem was a patriot who died because he refused to be anyone's lackey. And as for COREV, it has been the work of all the bishops in Vietnam and, as you said, it received donations from many countries around the world, including developing countries. I do not see how COREV can be accused of collaborating with imperialists."

But the official was not listening. "Admit that your appointment as coadjutor archbishop of Ho Chi Minh City is a plot designed by the Vatican and the imperialists," he demanded.

Thuan looked at the man, but made no reply. The official grew angrier and screamed in his face, "Did you hear me? I told you to admit that your appointment as coadjutor archbishop of Ho Chi Minh City is a plot designed by the Vatican and the imperialists!"

Thuan shook his head in disagreement. "I will not admit anything of the kind because it is not true. My appointment to Ho Chi Minh City is not a plot of the Vatican, or imperialists, or anyone else."

Not having made any progress, the officials turned their backs on Thuan and talked among themselves in low voices. A few moments later the leader of the group faced Thuan and said, "You are under arrest. Follow the security agents standing outside the door. They will take care of you."

Thuan nodded politely and then stepped outside the room. He followed the secret police back outside and through the park to a white sedan. He got into the car with four men and they drove through the gate; a jeep and a military truck with a squad of armed soldiers led the way. Thuan was amused by the precautions. Apparently the authorities feared someone might try to help him escape.

Thuan sat between Nguyen Tu Ha, an official of the Ministry of the Interior from Hanoi, and another man who was the Chief of Youth Service from Nha Trang. An armed guard occupied the seat beside the driver. As Thuan looked at the government officials escorting him he smiled and thought: *This is too great an honor.* He was not amused for long, however. He closed his eyes and tried to pray in the crowded car.

Thuan had anticipated that the Communists might arrest him. Now he began to consider how long he might be held captive. He hardly expected sympathy or leniency from the officials who had just insulted him. They were men filled with hatred and cruelty. But because he had prepared himself for this moment for months, he did not feel afraid.

He opened his eyes just as the small convoy rushed past Ho Noi and Xuan Loc, Catholic settlements north of Saigon. Thuan was struck by the strange absence of other vehicles on the highway. Then he noticed that there was not a single person outside on the streets. Thuan later learned that the parishioners had been ordered to an all-day "training course" at a number of meeting halls in the settlements to prevent any interference with his arrest.

Meanwhile, at the Parliament Building Communist officials droned on about unimportant matters, and the priests who had been there for a few hours were showing signs of boredom. Everything changed at precisely 4:00 p.m. A Communist official announced that Archbishop Thuan had been arrested and had already arrived in Nha Trang via helicopter. No one knew that the officials were lying: there was no helicopter and the convoy transporting Thuan was still moving along Highway 1.

Back at Independence Palace in Saigon, Archbishop Binh waited in a room alone. He thought that Archbishop Thuan was still being interrogated and was praying for him. Then, at the same time that the priests were informed about Thuan, officials told Binh the same story.

The interrogator had told Thuan that he was being sent back to Nha Trang, a 250-mile drive from Ho Chi Minh City along a highway in poor condition. Thuan was praying when he suddenly realized he did not really know what would happen once they reached Nha Trang. Perhaps there was no definite plan, but Thuan did not want to ask any questions. He did not want his captors to think he was worried. He did not have a penny in his pocket or the slightest clue what his future would be. He sat back and thought very calmly, *I have been arrested on the Feast of the Assumption, on the day the Church celebrates the glorious ascent of the Blessed Virgin Mary to heaven. She, who shows me the way to eternal life, will tell me what to do with my remaining days on earth.*

◆ ◆ ◆

THE CONVOY SPED ALONG in the dark, bright headlights flooding the road ahead. Thuan shut his eyes and tried to continue praying as he considered the possibilities he might face. He would not be able to stay at the bishop's residence in Nha Trang; Bishop Hoa lived there now, and Thuan did not wish to be a burden. Then again, the choice was not his. He would have to live wherever the Communist officials decided. There had been no mention of prison, but Thuan knew that was also a possibility.

Thuan took his rosary—now his only earthly possession—out of his pocket and prayed. He prayed for the Church in Vietnam, and for Archbishop Nguyen Van Binh and Bishop Hoa. He prayed for the men escorting him and the officials who had ordered his arrest. He prayed for all Vietnam and for the Universal Church.

The convoy stopped at a roadside eatery and his captors offered him some food, which he accepted with gratitude. His stomach was growling and he had not wanted the men sitting beside him to hear it. They were on the road again in less than half an hour.

They arrived in Nha Trang around midnight. The car stopped in front of Public Security Headquarters and the officials went inside. Thuan, left outside alone, began to walk around. Public Security Headquarters was near the sea and Thuan walked toward the beach. No one bothered to keep a watch on him and no one called after him. He felt the luxury of walking on sand, listening to the thunderous waves. He realized the exhilaration of this freedom was literally momentary.

Soon a soldier ran toward him and shouted, "Time to get back." Thuan answered, "Of course," and followed the soldier back to the convoy thinking that they must have reached some kind of decision concerning his immediate destination.

In the car Nguyen Tu Ha told Thuan, "Tonight, you will sleep like a cadre, on a small uncomfortable bed." Thuan chuckled, "I've always done that." They drove to the headquarters of the Dien Khanh district. There Thuan's captors and he shared a room crammed with canvas beds. Thuan again took his rosary out to pray but, overwhelmed by fatigue, he fell asleep immediately.

In the morning, Nguyen Tu Ha was more decisive. He took the convoy to Cay Vong parish and stopped at the rectory. He had communicated earlier with Bishop Hoa, who came to Cay Vong at 10:00 A.M. Ha informed Hoa and the pastor of Cay Vong that Thuan was under house arrest. He must not communicate with parishioners and would have to celebrate Mass privately.

As the official spelled out the conditions of his semi-captivity, Thuan realized he must abide by them or cause trouble for Bishop Hoa and the diocese. He nodded his agreement. Then he was left alone with the pastor. Thuan turned to him and said, "I will have plenty of time on my hands." The old priest smiled, "I'm sure you will find something to do."

Thuan had been to the parish many times, because it was only a few miles from the city of Nha Trang. The familiarity of the place lifted Thuan's morale. Yes, he would soon find something useful to do in that small parish. He thought how it was a shame that he was not allowed to undertake any pastoral work. Not to be a pastor—the thought horrified him. He would no longer be free to do God's work, but for how long? Thuan had no idea.

During the long days ahead, Thuan prayed with the breviary given him by the pastor. He prayed the rosary in the evening and during his first days, delighted in the sense that his solitude seemed to allow his prayers to God and the Blessed Virgin to arise more easily.

But during the long sleepless nights, Thuan experienced doubt and pain. Was he no longer to do God's work? How could he endure such a "useless" life? He was angry with the injustice of his arrest. Why had the Communists targeted him and none of the other bishops? Was it because he had been born into a certain family? Neither he, nor his parents, nor his siblings had ever taken advantage of their relationship with Diem during his presidency. Burying three uncles—that was all they had received for being members of the Ngo Dinh family. Were they punishing him for being related to Diem, Nhu, and Can? Or was it because he headed the charitable work of COREV? Because he begged foreigners for the money that enabled people to dig wells, build houses, and clear land for the poor who came to live in COREV villages? Because he had had tons of food and medicine dropped down to refugees and soldiers? He tried to overcome the bitterness in his heart, to reconcile himself to the situation, but in the darkness of the night the bitterness only grew.

Thuan was beginning a spiritual journey that would lead him to renounce the little he had not already surrendered to God. He would go through a spiritual desert and years of suffering before he would become a voice of hope heard over all five continents. He would undergo a radical change, and the next thirteen years of captivity would purify his senses and mind and help him to see all his failures and weaknesses, his mistakes and sins. By the end of his trial, a new man would emerge.

Thuan was interrogated regularly and he had to answer the same questions. He was ordered to write his life story again and again, and he was questioned on the minute discrepancies in the versions he submitted.

Despite his prayerfulness, the emptiness of his limited freedom at Cay Vong began to frighten Thuan during the first few weeks. Isolated from all human contact, he struggled with the problem of how to reach out to God's people as a pastor while under house arrest.

Once, while contemplating Saint Paul's example and how Paul's imprisonment had only served to enrich his teachings, Thuan considered ways to minister and the method of communication he might use. He suddenly envisioned the possibility of writing letters to the faithful. An avalanche of ideas came to his mind: a myriad of simple thoughts coalesced into a code of Christian conduct, which could help a Christian progress from indifference to attention to God's call, to purification, sanctification, and, ultimately, total surrender to God.

As he went on imagining the benefits that someone might draw from such a text, Thuan began to see some hope. He would write a small book summarizing his knowledge and experience, his hopes and aspirations, the fruit of his prayers and meditations. That would be his pastoral activity. This was the genesis of *The Road of Hope*.

CHAPTER TWENTY-ONE

The Road of Hope

For you, LORD, are my hope,
my trust, O LORD, from my youth.
Upon you I have leaned from my birth;
it was you who took me from my mother's womb.
My praise is continually of you.

Psalm 71:5–6

Be prepared to reject wealth and position—even to give
up your own life—in order to preserve your ideals, your
integrity, and your faith. You must never behave
otherwise, for to do so means to lose everything.

The Road of Hope,
F. X. Nguyen Van Thuan

THUAN REMEMBERED DIEM telling him, "When we were
poor, I rarely wrote on paper. I learned to write Chinese characters on banana leaves and in the dirt."
Under house arrest, Thuan only had a pencil and a few sheets of
paper, certainly not enough for what he intended.

As he pondered this problem, he glanced at the wall and noticed a calendar—a typical block calendar with a cardboard backing
and daily sheets. There was his solution. Thuan would write his
thoughts on the calendar's small sheets. But he would need more
calendars. In Nha Trang he had seen vendors and hawkers selling
waste paper, including old, unused calendars. The next morning,

Thuan cautiously signaled a young boy named Quang who was passing the house on his way home from Mass. Thuan asked him to tell his mother that he needed a few unused calendars. The intelligent boy understood immediately. He said, "I think that she will have to go and see a vendor of waste paper."

Thuan nodded. He thought a moment about Quang and his family. The authorities would not be pleased to learn that Thuan was trying to write a book, which he intended to smuggle out for printing. Was he making the young boy and his family accomplices? Was he inadvertently placing them in danger? He had to be certain Quang's mother understood the possible repercussions. He explained, "What I want to do is write a book, a small book. Every day I will write a few thoughts on the sheets of a calendar. I want you to tell this to your mother. Ask her if she would permit you to take the sheets home and copy what I have written into a notebook."

The boy smiled. "Sure, I can do that, and my sister can help, too. She writes better than I do." Thuan said, "You must understand that it is dangerous." The boy laughed. "Dangerous?" His voice sounded slightly incredulous. Thuan answered, "Tell your mother what I have just told you. She will see that it is dangerous. She will tell you whether you should help me or not." The boy looked at him and said with assurance, "We will help you." Thuan was moved, but he persisted in his warning, "The authorities may not like it because I am not supposed to communicate with people, and what I will write is for all people in Vietnam."

Quang's eyes widened, "Wow! You want to print your book? We can't print it."

Thuan nodded. "When the manuscript is complete, I will tell you to whom you may give it, and he will take care of the printing."

The boy was clearly happy to be participating in a secret plot. As he was leaving, Thuan reminded him again, "Tell your mother everything I just told you."

The boy nodded: "I understand. But she will help too, I know she will."

Quang came back with the calendars a few days later. He said his mother had told him, "There's no danger. Who would be interested in what I am doing?"

Thuan was grateful that Quang's family was willing to collaborate with him without the slightest misgivings. He was also grateful for the opportunity to be able to do something for God's people, because many holy men and women have discovered the road to conversion through reading good books. While Saint Ignatius recuperated from wounds received in battle, he read three books that brought about his conversion: *The Imitation of Christ, The Life of Jesus,* and *Lives of Saints.*

Thuan spent a few days focusing on the content and structure of his book, thinking about the typical writing style of many spiritual authors. He recalled one of Blaise Pascal's typical maxims: "No other religion besides Christianity has recognized that man is highest of creatures and, at the same time, the most miserable." Thuan smiled to himself as he thought, *This is not the kind of stuff I want to write.*

Then turning over in his mind a few sentences he remembered from *The Imitation of Christ,* he found the impetus to launch his own reflections. Particular inspiration came from the words of the chapter titled "Endure All Grievous Things for Eternal Life": "Neither should you covet the pleasant days of this life, but be glad to suffer some tribulation for God. Esteem it your greatest gain to be thought of as nothing amongst men."

Thuan decided his book would be called *The Road of Hope,* and he began with a short sentence: "I have traveled along life's road and have experienced joys and sorrows, but I have always been overflowing with hope, because I have God and his Mother Mary by my side."

Throughout the book he would travel on the road of hope with his reader, a constant and faithful companion from the moment of departure to the journey's end. Except for two instances, he would reflect only on quotes from the Gospel—the only book he had been permitted to keep. He would only give advice that he himself lived.

Thuan continued to have a clear image of Saint Paul writing from his own prison cell, and he pictured Saint Paul by his side urging him to sharpen his thoughts, to keep his words simple and his sentences brief. Also like Saint Paul, Thuan had to keep an eye out for "official visitors." When an official from the Public Security Services showed up, Thuan hid his writing materials and pretended to be bored. In reality, he had never been so excited.

Every evening Quang stopped by the rectory to take away what Thuan had written that day. The boy hurried home and, with his sister's help, copied Thuan's thoughts into a thick notebook.

A few months later Thuan completed the final summary chapter, "A Life of Hope." Quang smuggled the notebook to one of Thuan's friends and within a short time printed copies of Thuan's messages from captivity were being passed from hand to hand in all Vietnamese Catholic communities throughout the country.

No name appeared in the book, but no one in Vietnam—including the Communists—had any doubt about the author's identity. Communist officials were even more furious when they discovered that the book had been sent to France and the United States and was already being translated.

On March 19, 1976, the Feast of Saint Joseph, seven months after his arrival, a police convoy drove into Cay Vong. Thuan was taken from the rectory and shoved into a car. His worst nightmare was about to begin.

◆◆◆◆

THE POLICE BROUGHT THUAN to the Phu Khanh Prison Camp, and he was confined to a painfully narrow cell without windows. The prison camp was large, but Thuan did not see a single inmate during his nine months of captivity there. He guessed that there must be hundreds of prisoners in the facility.

The moment Thuan met the wardens of Phu Khanh he knew he was in, as he later phrased it, "deep trouble." The men were all very strong, hardened, and cruel, mistreating Thuan at the slightest "provocation." They showed no respect or kindness and seemed to take particular pleasure in humiliating and abusing him. However, it was not long before Thuan was placed in total isolation, where he did not have contact with even the wardens.

All Thuan saw day and night was the four filthy walls of his damp cell. At times the walls seemed to close in on him and the cell to become ever narrower. An electric light bulb dangled from the ceiling at the end of a short, frayed cord, and it shed a hazy, yellowish tinge on his bleak surroundings.

Thuan slept on a hard surface covered with a straw mat, almost as he was accustomed to sleeping at home. However, because of the extreme humidity, the mat was covered with mold and wild mushrooms grew on it and on the floor.

On the first night Thuan was delighted to hear through the walls the sound of waves. The prison camp, located near Nha Trang Airport, was not far from the ocean, and the familiar sound encouraged him. It reminded him of his days at Hoi An Beach where he had enjoyed long horseback rides with Khoi and Diem. It stirred up memories of Cua Tung Beach near the An Ninh Minor Seminary and of family outings at Thuan An Beach. Somehow being near the water strengthened him. *I will be all right,* he thought, *they are not going to frighten me.*

At first the perpetual isolation at Phu Khanh did not trouble Thuan, but it was not long before he actually began looking forward to the regular interrogation sessions. At least while he was being interrogated he saw someone sitting in front of him and heard a human voice. He even came to appreciate the curt and abusive language of the guard who, twice daily, pushed a tray of food into his cell. Even the harsh comments and insults were a welcome sound.

But gradually the isolation began to produce the desired effect. Thuan began to dread the emptiness and silence around him for days on end. Bereft of any sign of human presence nearby, he yearned for sounds—of people shouting, shoes or bare feet approaching his cell, a hammer hitting a nail or a saw biting into hard wood—anything but silence.

His captors also used darkness to torment him. Without warning or reason the dim light bulb in his cell would be turned off, sometimes for days at a time, and Thuan did not know when it was day or night as he sat in the empty, silent darkness. He felt as if he no longer existed in the world of the living.

As a child Thuan had never experienced fear of the dark, but now the unremitting darkness and absolute silence terrified him.

The guard who brought him food no longer spoke—no more curses or insults, just a hand reaching through the space under the door to remove one meal tray and replace it with another.

Thuan ached to hear human voices, to see human faces. He was forbidden to make any noise or to speak out or call on the guards. A few times a day, and only once during the night, he was permitted to use the latrine located near his cell. And that offered him no respite from his suffering. The gagging stench made Thuan physically sick each time he went there. Other than that, he never left the cramped space of his cell.

Thuan's cell was as hot as an oven and, because the latrine was nearby, it began to reek with a nauseous smell in the summer heat. Suffocating from humidity and lack of air, Thuan would lie down on the dirt floor and put his nose near the crack of space under the door to try to get some fresher air. Instead, there was only the horrid odor of the latrine.

At first Thuan consoled himself with the thought that at least he could still pray. But even prayer became more difficult and elusive. His entire body ached from the dampness and he was always starved and thirsty. His mind wandered uncontrollably. It was nearly impossible to move in the small cell, but Thuan realized that if he did not force himself to walk, he would not survive. So he began pacing back and forth until the stifling summer heat caused him to perspire profusely so that his clothes felt glued to his skin. After only a few minutes he would be forced to lie down on the floor, put his nose near the crack under the door, and try to breathe.

Thuan's captors were trying to break him, and they were about to succeed. Thuan's mind seemed to play tricks on him and his almost perfect memory began to falter when he tried to recite even the most familiar prayers. When he could not remember the words of certain prayers, Thuan panicked. He tried to recite the Our Father and the Hail Mary aloud and was shocked that he could not.

Thuan began to feel that he was on the brink of insanity, and knowing he was losing his mind made him physically sick. He no longer felt hungry or sleepy. He vomited frequently and suffered constant dizziness and pain all over his body. His attempts at prayer were reduced to brief greetings and messages of thanksgivings, but he was afraid that he would become incapable even of this. His mind became blank for longer periods of time.

Thuan started to suspect that the guards were poisoning his food and became extremely careful about what he ate of the meager meals. But then he found himself going back and forth between this suspicion and wondering if he was becoming paranoid. He believed that he was falling apart both mentally and physically.

Summer faded into autumn, and one evening the guard brought a large meal and a gourd of fresh water. The food was very salty, but seemed safe, and Thuan ravenously finished the entire meal and drank all the water. Later that night the guard did not return to let Thuan out to use the latrine. As soon as the guard unlocked his cell in the morning, he rushed to the latrine, but by refusing to relieve himself in his cell, he had become extremely sick. For the next few days Thuan would not touch any food or water, fearing the same torture would be repeated. He grew weaker from hunger and thirst as the guards continued playing this game with him. If he chose to eat and drink what they brought, he suffered terribly all night long. If he chose to refuse to eat and drink what they brought, he suffered extreme hunger and thirst. Although inhumanely hungry and thirsty, Thuan would not fall for the same trap. A starved, dehydrated prisoner who was not able to resist food and water then suffered the indignity of having to relieve himself in the cell and the humiliation of being berated for dirtying the cell like an animal. Such continual degradation made it easier for the interrogators to break a prisoner. Thuan was determined to resist as long as he could.

COMMUNIST OFFICIALS FROM HANOI came regularly to Phu Khanh to interrogate, threaten, and torture Thuan. Nguyen Tu Ha, who had brought Thuan from Ho Chi Minh back to Nha Trang, was in charge of Thuan's case and, therefore, always came with the delegation of interrogators. Each time they came, the officials demanded that Thuan sign a confession admitting that he had plotted with the Vatican and the imperialists against the Communist revolution. When Thuan denied the existence of such a plot, they demanded that he confess to working with the CIA, citing his contacts with several Americans and foreigners. He denied knowing any CIA agents, though he admitted to having had contact with foreigners, but firmly described the nature of their conversations as harmless.

When the interrogators failed to make him change his statements or sign the confession, they disparaged him for being Diem's nephew. Thuan angered them each time by saying that he was honored to be Diem's nephew and that Diem was a patriot who had fought for Vietnam's independence as hard as any other revolutionary.

Exhausted, emaciated, and unsteady on his feet, Thuan faced his interrogators and somehow felt stimulated by the mental challenge. Thanks to the men who came to break him, Thuan's mind was strengthened, and, ironically, his tormentors saved him by providing him with the human contact he so desperately needed.

Still, Thuan knew he had to remain vigilant. His long isolation and physical weakness made him vulnerable to the traps his interrogators set to trip him. He had to be very careful. When their questions seemed to sharpen his mind, and Thuan managed to side-step their traps with concise answers, the officials were surprised by Thuan's resilience. They had received prison reports describing him as a broken man who sat in a corner of his cell all day and moaned incoherently. To the contrary, they found him physically diminished, but still a formidable opponent.

Between these regular interrogation sessions, Thuan remained in solitary confinement. When the guards led him through the long corridors to the interrogation room, the cell doors of the other inmates were always closed. No one was allowed to see Thuan, and he was allowed to see no one.

The isolation began to affect Thuan in another way as well. He now wondered why God allowed him to waste so much time in prison. He could be doing so much for God's kingdom. He did not really question God's will, but he regretted the endless days and nights in a lonely cell that kept him from serving God's people.

When Thuan felt stronger, he prayed one rosary after another to make up for the times he could not pray. One day, while he prayed and lamented the fact that he could not serve his people, he felt these words race through his mind: *There is God's work, and then there is God.* He suddenly realized that even if he could not do God's work, he could still love God, and that loving God was more important than loving God's work. It was a moment of transforming revelation. Thuan pictured Jesus crucified and understood that when Jesus was most helpless, his arms and legs nailed to the cross and life draining out of his body, it was then that he accomplished the most for humanity. At his weakest moment, Jesus redeemed the world.

Thuan had finally grasped the truth that God was showing him. In all the years he had toiled in the Lord's vineyard, he believed *he* was doing God's work. But it was God who was doing the work, and Thuan was his instrument. Thuan had complained about not being able to do God's work when he should have been leaving the work in God's hands. Thuan had only to dedicate himself to loving God, not God's work. Loving God was the most important thing in his life, and no one could take that away from him. No prison cell could ever isolate him from God.

Then Thuan thought of his friends: Saint Thérèse of Lisieux in her Carmelite cell, Theophane Venard in his cage, Francis Xavier on a deserted beach near China. He knew then that he could offer all his pain and suffering to God and to the Blessed Virgin Mary as tokens of his love. Now his prison cell seemed transformed: there, in that damp, filthy hole where he had been almost completely broken, he saw another aspect of the face of Christ. Pain gave way to joy and suffering became a source of hope. A line from Charles Péguy's poem, "The Threshold of the Mystery of the Second Virtue," unexpectedly came to his mind:

"For Faith only sees what is, and Hope sees what will be. Charity only loves what is, and Hope loves what will be."

Thuan could envision love, and hope for whatever would be in the future even when he could not do God's work, or spread the faith, or distribute goods to the poor and needy. Thuan clasped this new knowledge like a treasure to his heart.

━━━◆◆◆━━━

ON NOVEMBER 29, 1976, the Monday following the First Sunday of Advent, Thuan was taken from his cell and loaded onto a

truck with other inmates. None of the prisoners dared to talk because of the presence of guards, but they greeted each other with a
smile. This was the first time Thuan had contact with his fellow inmates. He recognized some of them. There were Catholics and Buddhists among them, and some had once served in the regime of
South Vietnam. They were being punished now for their years of
collaboration with "imperialists."

The truck traveled National Highway 1, moving south on the
same stretch of paved road from Nha Trang to Saigon that Thuan
had used each month while he worked for COREV. The highway was
no longer littered with the debris of war as it had been in early May
1975 when Thuan had driven south to Saigon. Still, it looked like part
of an occupied country. There was an air of sadness. The people walking along both sides of the highway looked despondent and anxious.
No one smiled. At one point Thuan caught a glimpse of the ocean on
his left. He contemplated its beauty and felt God's peace within him.

A guard informed them of their destination: they were going
to a transit camp in Thu Duc, ten miles north of Saigon, and in two
days would board a ship that would take them to North Vietnam.

After the realization that his impatience to do God's work was
wrong, Thuan had begun to serenely embrace whatever happened
to him. He intended to surrender himself to God's will without reservation, but he had no delusions. He was a novice in this phase of
his spiritual journey. He had to pray for the strength to persevere in
selfless abandonment to God, whatever the future might hold.

On December 1, 1976, the prisoners were chained together in
pairs, loaded onto another truck, and driven to Tan Cang or "New
Port" in Saigon. Thuan had never been chained, but he thought of
the martyrs of Rome and of Vietnam who had suffered the same treatment before him. The clanking of the chains whenever he moved was
a novelty. Thuan listen to the sound, feeling oddly content that he
had one more experience of prison life. He tried not to make any
jerking movements for fear of injuring the man chained to him.

When the prisoners were pushed off the truck onto the dock it
was nearly dark. An old cargo ship that appeared to have been used
to transport coal was anchored nearby. The prisoners marched to the
ship and then climbed up the gangway and assembled on the deck.

Thuan estimated it to be around 10:00 or 11:00 P.M. when he and his companions were finally forced down into the hold of the ship. There had to be more than 1,500 people already crammed into the hold. Under the light of a single oil lamp he saw the emaciated faces around him. There was a look of defeat and anguish in the prisoners' eyes; they seemed beyond despair.

The cargo of human misery cried out to Thuan and his heart filled with compassion. He began speaking to the prisoners nearest him. The man chained to him was a Buddhist. Many were Catholics. Thuan spoke compassionately, showing them that he cared for them, their families, and their futures. At first the prisoners did not react; they were so exhausted that most of them fell asleep. But Thuan went on talking in a soothing voice of the need for all of them to have hope for the future, and of solidarity among themselves as prisoners. How many listened to him? Thuan did not know; perhaps not many on that first night. Still, Thuan literally had a captive audience, and a new pastoral work was opening to him. In 1954 he had been a chaplain of the provincial prisons of Hue. Now he was an inmate, sharing God's words with his fellow-sufferers.

The next morning, a little sunlight penetrated the hold. A few of the prisoners discovered one man trying to hang himself with a steel wire. They wrestled him down to the floor, took the wire from him, and called on Thuan to reason with the man.

At first the desperate man stared into space. He did not see or much less hear Thuan. Nevertheless, Thuan kept talking. With unlimited patience, he tried to find the words that would strike a responsive chord in the man's heart. Suddenly the man began to sob, saying he did not want to live anymore, that he preferred to die. Thuan continued to comfort and encourage the man until his sobs subsided. At last, he told Thuan, "I am all right. I am no longer afraid. They can do what they want to me. I am no longer afraid."

Thuan was exhausted after counseling the man, but he kept comforting his fellow prisoners. Gradually, the attentive circle around him grew larger and he had to speak louder, but with great caution for fear that the guards would come down to investigate. This fear proved unnecessary because the prisoners were left alone for the entire trip, except for brief contact with the guards twice a day when they distributed the almost uneatable food.

That night Thuan noticed it was much colder. He wondered if the drop in temperature was due to the ship having reached northern waters. There were no blankets, so the prisoners shivered all night. Thuan sat with his eyes closed and prayed for his companions in misfortune. He truly felt himself one with them. He had learned many of their histories. Most of them were being unjustly punished; others were guilty of real crimes. But Thuan saw no differences among them anymore: Buddhists or Catholics, military officers or civilians, innocents or criminals; in a certain way, they were now all under his care. He prayed that God would give them all the courage and strength to survive captivity.

The next day, December 3, Thuan continued to pray for his fellow prisoners as he silently celebrated the feast of Francis Xavier. His patron saint had also traveled north over the same channels of the South China Sea.

Miraculously, Thuan felt no resentment when he thought about the chains he wore, his starvation, and the possibility of his dying in prison. He prayed to the Blessed Virgin Mary, "Mother, if I am to die in North Vietnam far from all the people who have known and loved me, help me to die content. Help me to die without any trace of bitterness."

By the last six days of the journey, Thuan had befriended most of the prisoners and saw that they drew strength from him and his words. He thanked God and prayed that he would continue to have enough strength to share.

The ship docked in Haiphong on December 10, 1976. Thuan felt strangely excited to be in North Vietnam, a region of his country that had been a great unknown for him during the war years. He thanked God for allowing him to be in a part of his native country that he had been able to visit only in his dreams.

CHAPTER TWENTY-TWO

Inside North Vietnam

Out of the depths I cry to you, O LORD.
LORD, hear my voice!
My soul waits for the LORD
more than those who watch for the morning.

Psalm 130:1, 6

Within prison, I myself lived the suffering of the Church.
I would notice time pass, day after day, without seeing
its end.

Testimony of Hope,
F. X. Nguyen Van Thuan

THUAN AND HIS COMPANIONS were immediately transported to the Vinh Quang Prison Camp in the mountains of Vinh Phu. The camp was near the Tam Dao Mountains and Hung Kings Temple—the legendary founders of Vietnam. From the camp, on a clear day, one could see the Tam Dao Mountains, almost 4,000 feet above sea level. In Vinh Phu province, where the Trung Sisters had established their capital in Me Linh after challenging the Chinese, Thuan felt closer to Vietnam's ancient past.

The prisoners were told that they would be doing farmwork. Thuan smiled at the thought. His grandfather and uncles had become farmers after the French stripped Kha of all ranks and honors. It had not killed them.

Thuan's fellow prisoners did not want Thuan doing this kind of work and they tried to spare him the heavier tasks. But Thuan felt happy working in the field or carrying green manure to the vegetable gardens. On rainy days Thuan worked as an apprentice carpenter. *Imagine, I am becoming a carpenter, like Jesus no less!* he thought.

With some of the guards looking the other way, Thuan managed to have a family member send him wine as medicine for a "stomach aliment," together with bits of bread hidden inside a flashlight. He was then able to celebrate Mass and give the Eucharist to the Catholics imprisoned with him, but he had to be extremely careful. The guards kept a vigilant eye on him at all times. He also had to be prudent with the precious supplies—a few drops of wine cupped in his hand, and some tiny crumbs of bread sufficed.

Now, with daily Eucharist, Thuan always felt joy. He also began to feel more ambitious. He wanted to carve a cross from the wood found in the area of the Hung Kings Temple, and as a carpenter's apprentice he had access to the tools he needed.

One day a guard noticed Thuan carving two small pieces of wood. "What are you doing there?" the guard barked. Thuan could not tell a direct lie, so he answered, "I am making a cross." The guard was stunned by his honesty and exclaimed, "But that's illegal!" Thuan replied confidently, "I know that it's illegal, but I really need a cross. I am a priest and I need to have a cross with me at all times."

The guard stared at Thuan in shocked silence. Then he said, "But you can't wear a cross. It is illegal!" Thuan nodded, "I know. So I will keep the cross hidden in a bar of soap. I am permitted to carry a bar of soap in the camp, am I not?" The guard seemed to relax a little and gave a short laugh. "Yes. That's permitted." Then, looking around, he said in a low voice, "If you want to make a cross, it's okay with me, but do it quickly." With this "illegal permission," Thuan carved the cross that he wore as his pectoral cross until his death.

Although the food at Vinh Quang Camp was not too bad, Thuan developed a terrible case of dysentery, which almost killed him. There was practically no health care or medicines in the camp, but fellow prisoners and guards tried to help; despite the warden's calls for a physician, it was three weeks before a doctor finally came to the camp with some medicine. Thuan recovered slowly from his dysentery but was back to work within a week.

Thuan was popular at the Vinh Quang Prison Camp, but this did not work to his benefit. Communist authorities watched him from a distance and eventually decided he needed to be kept under tighter surveillance. On February 5, 1977, two months after being brought to Vinh Quang, Thuan was taken to the Thanh Liet Prison Camp in the suburbs of Hanoi. Thanh Liet had been used as a detention center for American POWs and there were signs of their presence everywhere. It filled Thuan with pain when he thought of the young men who had carved their names on the walls. He thought about how much they had suffered being so far from their families and native land, and of the terror they had faced at the hands of their interrogators who did not speak their language.

At Thanh Liet Prison Thuan shared a cell with a colonel of the National Liberation Front who had been convicted of corruption. A strange friendship developed between the archbishop and the colonel.

At first things did not go well between them. When the colonel walked into the cell, Thuan recognized him for what he was: an informant. He had been planted there to spy and report on Thuan's every word and move in exchange for an early release from prison. Thuan studied the colonel as if observing a dangerous animal. Everything about the man conveyed anger. The colonel also studied Thuan. For days they watched each other closely like a pair of boxers in the ring at the beginning of a match.

When they started talking, however, Thuan was relieved to find that his cellmate was a native of Hue—his accent left no doubt about that. Not only was he from Hue, Colonel Thuyen had also been a classmate of some of Thuan's childhood friends. According to his own account, Thuyen had studied at the Polytechnic School in Hue before joining the Viet Minh in 1945 and slowly rising through the ranks. After the war he became disgruntled and was accused of accepting bribes.

Thuan had nothing to hide, so he began speaking more openly with Thuyen about his past. He refrained, however, from commenting on the reasons for his arrest and the poor treatment he had received in captivity.

One day Thuan began talking about the last few days before his arrest in Ho Chi Minh City. He was stunned when Thuyen put a finger to his lips. Thuan laughed; Thuyen did not. "I am here to report on you," he confessed. "I was brought from Hoa Binh camp to this cell three days before your transfer here. Do not trust me, because I work for them. I have to work for them because I want to be released from prison as soon as possible. So, I will report on you, my new friend."

Thuan shrugged. "As a matter of fact, I don't have anything to hide, so you can report on me as much as you wish."

Then Thuyen advised him, "Do not trust anyone, especially your cellmate. Do not trust yourself, especially your memory. You have been asked to write your life story many times. I know that you have made the mistake of not copying down your initial declaration. Take my advice, the next time they ask you to write your life story, make a copy and hide it well. Go back to your cell and memorize every word you put down. Then the next time, and the time after that, when they ask for your story, you will write exactly the same thing, without changing a comma. Then they will stop asking you."

When Thuan knew the prison guards a little better, he asked one for a favor. He needed a long piece of steel wire and pliers to make a chain for his pectoral cross. Just like the guard in Vinh Quang, this one objected, "But that's illegal!" "I know that it's illegal," Thuan insisted, "but I really need a chain so I can wear the cross. All bishops must wear a cross." "It's illegal to wear a cross," replied the guard who was becoming alarmed. Thuan again insisted, "Yes, I know. But I need a chain for my cross so I can wear it. I promise to keep it hidden until I can wear it legally." The guard finally gave him the wire and pliers, and apparently neither the guard nor Colonel Thuyen reported his "illegal activity."

Colonel Thuyen was able to obtain early release for good behavior. Although Thuyen did actually report on him, Thuan never knew how much he told. Thuyen and Thuan were sad as the time came for them to part. Thuyen said he was returning to Quang Tri.

"My house is quite near the shrine of La Vang. Maybe sometimes I will go there and pray for you."

Thuan could not help laughing. "But you're not even a Christian." Colonel Thuyen shrugged as he said, "I know, but for you, my friend, I will go to the shrine and tell the Lady Mary that you need help and that she should hurry and send you some."

Then Thuan remarked sadly, "Thank you, but you actually can't pray at the sanctuary; it was completely destroyed by American bombs in 1972."

Thuyen replied doggedly, "Then I will pray for you on the ruins of the shrine."

◆◆◆◆◆

AFTER FIFTEEN MONTHS IN THANH LIET CAMP, international pressure in Thuan's favor had mounted and the Communist authorities decided to send him where they could keep a better eye on him, and where he could not make any friends.

On May 13, 1978, Thuan was taken to Giang Xa in the Hoai Duc District. The government chose Giang Xa because the village was only twelve miles from Hanoi, which made it far more convenient for the public security representatives to "visit" him at any time, with or without prior notice.

Thuan was taken to the rectory in Giang Xa and a guard was assigned to watch him day and night. The last pastor of the village had been dead for ten years. The church and rectory were in a sad state of disrepair. When it rained, the roofs leaked like sieves. The parishioners did not care. Actually, they no longer practiced their faith and anti-Church sentiment, which government propaganda fueled methodically, was rampant.

Thuan had permission to celebrate Mass privately and, as a preventive measure, only at 4:00 A.M. He could walk about the village as long as he communicated with no one. At first such conditions were unnecessary because none of the villagers came near Thuan.

The villagers had been forewarned by Communist cadres to stay away from the "bloodthirsty traitor." Their story was that Thuan had been captured in Nha Trang when the revolutionary forces arrived. The enemy had fled without a fight except for a band of men that hid in a cave under the bishop's house. They had fired on the revolutionaries for hours, killing and wounding many of the Communist troops. Finally they ran out of ammunition and came out of the cave wearing their camouflage uniforms. Supposedly, Thuan was the last to surrender. "We should have killed him on the spot," they told the people, "but our government was practicing a policy of national reconciliation. For this reason he has been well treated. He will live with you here, but you must be careful. He is a dangerous and bloodthirsty man."

Thuan had no idea what the Communist cadres had told the villagers. He only knew that when he walked into the village the people shunned him.

On the second day after his arrival in Giang Xa, Thuan walked around the church and recognized something familiar in the curved ends of the roof. An old man was passing by and Thuan stopped him to say, "I don't remember where, but I've certainly seen a roof like this before." The old man scratched his head and glanced at him suspiciously, but he finally replied, "This church was modeled on that of the shrine of Our Lady of La Vang. The old priest who built this church had made a pilgrimage to La Vang and sketched a few of the shrine's features in a notebook. He came back here and tried to build a church that looked a little like the shrine."

Thuan smiled as he bowed his head in thanksgiving. The shrine of Our Lady of La Vang had been leveled by American bombing raids. Now he was living next to a church that was the shrine in miniature.

A few days later a man who had just returned from visiting an elderly uncle in South Vietnam stood in front of the church speaking with a friend. Thuan chanced to walk by and overheard some of their conversation. He stopped and asked the man who had traveled back to Giang Xa, "Excuse me, but did I hear you say that you just returned from South Vietnam?" The man nodded and Thuan asked further, "And that you went there to see a man named Can?" The man nodded again and said uneasily, "Yes, he is my uncle." Thuan asked, "Does your uncle have a brother named Than?" The man asked Thuan, "How do you know Than is also my uncle?" "While you were talking," Thuan answered, "I heard you mention enough details that I was able to recognize who you were discussing. I know Than very well. Actually, he is also my uncle by marriage."

The two villagers stood there looking at each other as Thuan added, "Not only is he my uncle, but when I was bishop of Nha Trang he volunteered to serve as my housekeeper. He stayed with me for ten years, until the country was reunited in 1975."

He had not made the connection at first, but as they continued speaking Thuan realized Than, his uncle and faithful housekeeper, had been born in Giang Xa. He was living in his uncle's native village.

The two men quickly told other villagers and before long a small group of people had gathered around Thuan. One elderly man said, "Than went south to serve the family of the Duke of Phuoc Mon, Minister Nguyen Huu Bai. How is it that he became your housekeeper?"

Thuan was not conscious of the tears streaming down his face. He sat down on the grass and began to tell the villagers about the deep friendship between his grandfather, Ngo Dinh Kha, and Nguyen Huu Bai. Thuan told them that his grandfather was a military commander under Emperor Dong Khanh and had come to Giang Xa to fight a major battle against the Chinese Black Flag bandits. Kha and his troops were victorious. The day after the victory he received news that his mother was very sick, and he decided to resign and go home to care for her.

Fortunately, on that very same day, Kha met a former classmate, Nguyen Huu Bai. He asked to have Bai replace him as head of his troops. Bai stayed on in Giang Xa for a while and married one of the village women. Later the couple moved to Hue, and Than went to serve in their household. Than married one of Thuan's aunts in Hue.

One woman spoke up to confirm, "We are all familiar with the battle fought right here against the Black Flags. Some say many of the bandits are buried all around this place."

The man who had just returned from South Vietnam stood close to Thuan and said, "So, in a way, we are all related. Those people from Hanoi came here to tell us lies about you, and we were stupid enough to believe them." Then he told Thuan what the cadres had said about him. Thuan was astonished. He knew that the cadres had little respect for the truth, but never thought they could be so imaginative.

As the men and women gathered even closer, they said to Thuan, "We must keep this to ourselves. Your guard should not know that some of us are related to you."

Long after all the villagers were gone, Thuan still sat there on the grass. The leaders in Hanoi could not have known that by sending him to Giang Xa, they had enabled Thuan to solve one of the greatest puzzles of his life that had troubled him for years.

He went over the pieces again in his mind. His mother had told him the story of the battle against the Black Flags fought by his grandfather somewhere in North Vietnam, how he had resigned his command after his own mother became seriously ill, and how he had petitioned for Bai to replace him as commander. This actually began Bai's long career as a mandarin.

According to his grandfather's detractors, Kha had indeed waged that battle, but in Central Vietnam and against supporters of Emperor Ham Nghi. They claimed that by fighting Nghi's supporters, Kha had fought against patriots.

Now Thuan had the facts: Kha had really fought at Giang Xa; his enemies had been Black Flag bandits from China. It was in Giang Xa that Nguyen Huu Bai had taken over his grandfather's troops; it was here that Bai had met his wife.

Thuan bowed his head and prayed with a heart full of gratitude. Giang Xa was no longer a place of exile for him. It was part of his life, part of his family's history.

———◆◆◆———

THUAN'S HOUSE ARREST REQUIRED that he be carefully watched by his guard at all times. Actually, the guard did not seem to take his job too seriously. Though Thuan was not supposed to interact with any of the villagers, the guard turned the other way when he saw Thuan speaking with someone. The villagers remained cautious, and Thuan approved of their prudence. But from the day they had learned the truth about Thuan, there was a kind of complicity among them. He was family. He was accepted.

Under the benevolent eyes of the villagers, Thuan thrived. At first he could not receive visitors or celebrate Mass for the parishioners. Gradually, however, the guard became more lenient regarding the strict rules of his house arrest and allowed or rather ignored the visitors who came from Hue and Nha Trang to see Thuan.

Thuan enjoyed taking long walks, tending the garden, and chatting with his guard. He spent the rest of his time in prayer and writing. The relative freedom he enjoyed in Giang Xa became the most productive period of Thuan's entire captivity. He had time to think about how to make *The Road of Hope,* with its cryptic sentences and abbreviated thoughts, more easily understood by his readers. Now Thuan wanted to write additional books to expand his ideas, explain his concepts, and add examples to his statements.

His books *The Pilgrims on the Road of Hope* and *The Road of Hope in the Light of God's Word and Vatican II* were both completed in Giang Xa. The manuscripts were smuggled into South Vietnam and finally printed in 1980. During their *ad limina* visit in 1980, the bishops of Vietnam gave copies of both books to Pope John Paul II.

International pressure on Thuan's behalf obtained for him the official permission to receive a few visitors. Visits were always under the surveillance of his guard, and all foreign visitors were accompanied by representatives of the Ministry of Interior with its personnel acting as interpreters.

Thuan did not mind the presence of official government interpreters. He spoke with his usual sense of humor and managed to slip in a few messages here and there during these exchanges. For instance, when asked by a representative of Catholic Relief Services whether he was being treated well, Thuan replied, "The government always takes good care of me. A while ago, when I was very sick, a physician came to see me three weeks later." And on another occasion, "The government always shows their concern for me. As a matter of fact I am always watched attentively by a hundred pairs of eyes."

In Giang Xa Thuan became more daring and took up activities more dangerous than writing "subversive" books to be smuggled outside the country or slipping critical remarks into conversations with foreign visitors—he began pastoral work in the village. By doing so, Thuan unwittingly began dismantling a network of spies that the Communists had spent years building up.

In order to understand what a dangerous move this was, it is necessary to know that in North Vietnam the Communists had worked for years recruiting four or five Catholic families in each parish and spent a great deal of time converting the heads of these families to Marxism. Once they agreed to join the Communist Party, they enjoyed all kinds of privileges, received a salary, and exercised power over the other parishioners.

These Catholic spies became the eyes and ears of the government. Because of this network of spies many unsuspecting Catholics were arrested, convicted, and imprisoned. As for the spies themselves, once they were discovered, many were excommunicated for their hostility to the Church, the abandonment of their religious duties, and the grave harm they caused other parishioners.

Giang Xa also had its spies who watched and reported every move made by the parishioners. The worst of these spies was a couple that lived next to the church. The parishioners feared and hated them, and their cooperation with the Communists earned for them the sarcastic nickname "the saints." The superstitious among the villagers actually believed them to be devils. As the parishioners grew closer to Thuan, and the guard allowed them to participate in his morning Mass, "the saints" became a greater threat to them all.

Nguyen Tu Ha of the Ministry of Interior would drop by the village periodically and get an ear-full from "the saints." He would go to the rectory to castigate the guard for neglecting his duties and to remind Thuan of the rules: he must not to speak with or celebrate Mass for the parishioners.

But by now the guard was completely on Thuan's side. He continued to allow parishioners to visit Thuan in the rectory and to speak with him, sometimes privately, sometimes in small groups. The guard simply waited outside and kept watch for the village spies. If they approached the rectory, the guard warned, "The saints are coming!"—the signal for everyone to slip out.

Even "the saints" themselves eventually succumbed to Thuan's goodness. Occasionally, they sent Thuan a bowl of soup or boiled sweet potatoes. The guard always told Thuan, "Send their gift back

to them. They are evil. Perhaps they have put poison in the food."
But Thuan laughed him off saying, "Why don't we give them a second chance? Who knows what they will become if we are kind to
them?" Then the guard retreated to a corner of the house and, convinced that Thuan had gone crazy, would mutter, "It is insane to
deal with those evil people!"

Time proved Thuan right. One day "the saints" asked Thuan
to hear their confessions, and he was astonished by their sincerity.
He secretly contacted Cardinal Joseph Marie Trinh van Can, the
archbishop of Hanoi, and requested permission to release them
from their excommunication. In time "the saints," who became very
devout Catholics, joined the guard in keeping watch as Thuan celebrated Mass for hundreds of people who now visited him. The parishioners remarked, "We called them 'saints,' and now they truly
are saints."

Rumors of "the saints" traveled quickly and Thuan began to
receive more repentant spies into his rectory. First they came from
the neighboring parishes, then from more distant provinces. They
came to confess and to be accepted back into the Church.

Nguyen Tu Ha came for his regular inspections, but now he
only received good news: Thuan had been very quiet. He no longer
celebrated Mass for the people. No one ever came to see him.

------◆◆◆◆------

ON AUGUST 6, 1978, Thuan was filled with great sadness when
he learned of the death of Pope Paul VI. Paul VI had previously
intervened for Ngo Dinh Can, and had placed Archbishop Thuc
under his protection. He had been a dear friend and true father to
Thuan. And the pope's continued solicitude for him in his imprisonment touched Thuan deeply.

After the election and sudden death one month later of Pope
John Paul I, Thuan exulted at the election of Pope John Paul II on
October 16, 1978.

Thuan had read the novel, *Shoes of the Fisherman,* written by
Morris West in 1963. He was struck that like the hero of the novel, a
cardinal who had lived under the Communist regime was chosen to
sit on the Chair of Peter. Thuan could not repress his joy. He was

sure that the Church would see a period of growth under the leadership of the new pope. He fervently prayed for him, and wondered whether Wojtyla still remembered him.

Thuan was preoccupied with other matters as well. He had heard news of a wave of refugees described as "boat people" leaving Vietnam. Thuan could sympathize with the motives for their exodus from their homeland to escape Communism. The dramatic and tragic stories of their ordeals on the South China Sea kept Thuan awake at night. He prayed for those who escaped, for those who perished at sea, and for those who became the victims of pirates. He raised his eyes to heaven and asked, "Father, how long will the Vietnamese people have to suffer?" Sadly, there was much more suffering to endure.

The relations between Vietnam and China had become strained during the Vietnam War. North Vietnam's decision to depend solely on Russia for weaponry had alienated China. Now Cambodia was completely in China's orbit and this represented a major threat to Vietnam. Border skirmishes between Vietnam and Cambodia became increasingly more frequent during 1978. In December of that year Vietnamese Communist troops invaded Cambodia, knowing the war would likely become a quagmire for Vietnam as the Vietnamese War had been for the United States. Thuan prayed for the Vietnamese and Cambodian troops, and wondered when the Chinese would enter the scene.

On February 17, 1979, Chinese troops invaded Vietnam "to teach Hanoi a lesson." The invasion was limited in scope and duration, but the leaders in Hanoi panicked at the possibility of a much larger Chinese invasion, which could easily overwhelm Vietnam's defenses. The Vietnamese Communist leaders had counted on Russian military support, but Russia was mired in its own problems: a guerrilla war in Afghanistan. Vietnam stood completely alone.

Vietnam's leaders were also concerned about the general health of the Communist Bloc. There was more and more news about Poland's new *Solidarnoœœ* (Solidarity) movement. The labor strikes at Gdańsk's shipyards were long over and Prime Minister Wojciech Jaruzelski's declaration of martial law at least temporarily eliminated the threat of a national rebellion. Nevertheless, the

Catholic population of Poland seemed ready to confront the Communist regime at any moment. If the entire population of Polish Catholics entered the struggle alongside the new labor unions, Jaruzelski would never dare to crush them all. The world had witnessed the regime's vulnerability in Poland, and if such things could happen in Europe, then they could happen in Vietnam. The Communist Party in Hanoi was very nervous.

Despite the good reports given to Nguyen Tu Ha, Communist leaders began to worry about Thuan's activities in Giang Xa. Some suspected Thuan was responsible for the collapse of the network of spies watching the Catholic population. True, the government still received information from their informants, but the content of the reports was suspicious. It was impossible that *all* the Catholic parishes had suddenly decided to behave correctly, *everywhere*. Secret police were sent to the provinces and confirmed that the government informant network had been rendered ineffective. And it all pointed back to one quiet man being held captive in Giang Xa.

The Communist leaders in Vietnam could not afford to have on their hands a Lech Walesa or a Karol Wojtyla, continually rallying the people against Communism. And Thuan, the man in black who seemed peacefully content to water flowers around the church grounds of Giang Xa, was a potential Walesa. He had already proved himself dangerous to the regime, and it could not allow him the chance to become the standard bearer for a counter-revolution. Thuan had to be placed in solitary confinement again so that he could never repeat what he had done in Giang Xa. He had to vanish without a trace.

Early on November 5, 1982, a government van drove into Giang Xa. Thuan was quietly escorted to the back of the vehicle and, after four years in the village, disappeared.

CHAPTER TWENTY-THREE

Return to Solitary Confinement

With your faithful help rescue me
from sinking in the mire;
let me be delivered from my enemies
and from the deep waters.
Do not let the flood sweep over me,
or the deep swallow me up,
or the pit close its mouth over me.

Psalm 69:14–15

In the solitude of the desert, in the darkness of the prison,
turn to those altars throughout the world where Christ
offers himself as a sacrifice; offer yourself as a sacrifice
and commune in thought. Your heart will overflow with
courage and solace.

The Road of Hope,
F. X. Nguyen Van Thuan

THUAN SAT IN THE BACK OF THE VAN and had no idea
where he would be taken this time. The double doors
of the van were closed and latched, and dark curtains
covered the small windows on both sides.

Nguyen Tu Ha avoided eye contact when he brusquely announced, "You have taken advantage of the government's generos-
ity. We are sending you to a place where you will no longer be able
to subvert innocent people."

Sitting on the hard bench, with his head bowed, Thuan tried to figure out in what direction they were traveling. From the sound of city traffic, he was certain that the vehicle was heading toward Hanoi. The two guards sitting with him in the back did not seem very talkative or intelligent; they sat staring at the naked bulb on the van's ceiling.

Thuan had the impression that they were making it impossible for him to guess where they were headed. From time to time the driver stopped the van by the roadside, made U-turns, or took a sudden change in direction without rhyme or reason.

Thuan was relieved when they finally arrived at their destination. He had a bad cramp in one leg and had to limp behind Nguyen Tu Ha as they walked toward one building in a large complex. He looked up at the bright sky. After the rain of the previous day the sky was a soft blue with large white clouds. It would be a long time before he saw the sky or sunlight again.

Once inside Nguyen Tu Ha turned to Thuan and said, "This is our residence area." "What do you mean by 'our'?" Thuan asked. Tu Ha laughed, "I mean that all the buildings around you are apartment buildings reserved for the public security officers."

"But I am not a member of the secret police," objected Thuan. Tu Ha shrugged as if regretting that he had said anything to Thuan. "We are making an exception for you."

This second experience of solitary confinement required Thuan to learn all kinds of new rules. He would live in an apartment with an officer. During the officer's working hours he would be watched by two guards. He was not allowed to leave his small room except to go to the kitchen to cook his own meals and to use the toilet. He was not permitted to go out onto the balcony or to look out the windows.

Thuan reasoned that public security services had put him in a "safe house," so that no one would know of his existence except for those with the responsibility of guarding him. The government did not intend to interrogate him further. It just wanted him securely guarded in a place where no one would think to look for him. For the next six years he would be moved from one place to another, always living in solitary confinement. But Thuan no longer feared solitary confinement. He had surrendered himself completely to God.

Thuan established his own schedule, which included the celebration of the Eucharist at 3:00 P.M.—the hour of Jesus' agony and death on the cross. At that hour his military "host" was still at work and his guards had finished their afternoon rest. During Mass he sang in Latin, French, and Vietnamese without fear of bothering anyone. The guards thought Thuan sounded like a madman when he sang in languages they could not understand. And if he were crazy, they did not mind; that only made their work that much easier.

Thuan's guards and host were not supposed to speak with him, but he was eventually able to convince them to communicate with him. Just when he had managed to gain their trust and they began relating to him as a person, Thuan was sent to another apartment with a new host and guards. This became the pattern. Thuan was never moved far; he always stayed in the Thanh Cong area, but the dozens of identical buildings had thousands of apartments. Thuan had to smile; he was a being treated like a contagious disease. He had to be moved often because of the great danger he posed to the country's socialist paradise, which could be infected by his "counter-revolutionary" thinking.

Thuan might stay only a few weeks in an apartment, but he always succeeded in bringing about some change in the perspectives of his guards and hosts. That worried the senior officers of the public security services. They were faced with a dilemma: if Thuan stayed too long in one place, he could turn die-hard Communist cadres into petty bourgeois. But if they moved Thuan too often, it gave him access to more people who would be exposed to his subversive influence.

Officials were enraged when they received reports that Thuan was teaching members of the secret police how to sing the *Te Deum* and the *Veni Creator* in Latin. They hated it when they heard their own members arguing with each other, using Thuan's brand of logic. They decided that Thuan had done enough damage to public security services. He had to be removed, taken as far out of their universe as possible.

One day Thuan was escorted to a van and driven to the prison on Nguyen Du Street in Hanoi. He was placed once again in traditional solitary confinement. Thuan was back to the daily schedule that had become familiar to him in Thanh Liet Prison, near Nha Trang. Initially he was afraid. His memories of how he nearly lost his mind at Thanh Liet were not comforting. But by this time, he had grown accustomed to captivity. He had gone through fire and been purified. He was now able to accept what happened to him as God's will. Again, he pleaded with the prison warden to allow friends to send medicine for his "stomach ailment." Once again, the medicine—altar wine—was permitted, and he was able to celebrate daily Mass. The Eucharist continued to be Thuan's strength.

Nguyen Tu Ha came to check on Thuan from time to time. In fact, they had almost become friends. Though Tu Ha was reluctant to give Thuan any sensitive information, he talked about Pope John Paul II's first two visits to Poland in 1979 and 1983. He told Thuan about the advent of Mikhail Gorbachev in 1985, and of *glasnost*, and said he would not mind seeing a similar program in Vietnam. Thuan listened but never commented. He knew from experience how dangerous Tu Ha could be. In his mind he heard an echo of Colonel Thuyen's warning: "Trust no one. Don't even trust yourself; and especially, don't trust your memory."

Changes in other Communist countries made the Vietnamese Communist leaders ever more confused and cautious. They were afraid of both the Buddhists and Catholics in Vietnam. If the opportunity arose, years of religious repression would call down on them the just anger of the population. They saw no alternative other than continued repression.

In 1985, on the twenty-fifth anniversary of the establishment of the Vietnamese Catholic hierarchy, a petition for the canonization of Vietnamese martyrs was sent to Pope John Paul II. In the name of all his brother bishops, Cardinal Can, President of the Vietnamese Bishops' Conference, signed the petition on November 16.

Agitated by the cardinal's actions, Tu Ha told Thuan that the Vietnamese hierarchy and the Vatican were creating an intolerable tension between the Vietnamese government and the Catholic Church. Still, following Cardinal Can's lead, other petitions were sent to the Vatican from the Dominicans, the Paris Foreign Mission Society, and the Bishops' Conferences of France, the Philippines, and Spain.

Tu Ha informed Thuan that the government had once considered releasing him, but now that was impossible. The Vatican and the Church in Vietnam planned to honor people who had helped the French to dominate Vietnam. With such open hostility toward Hanoi, a counter-revolutionary like Thuan could certainly not be freed.

Thuan assured Tu Ha that the men and women to be honored with canonization were martyrs who had died courageously for their faith. And no matter how the canonization of these martyrs affected his own release, Thuan rejoiced that the heroes he had always venerated were about to become saints of the Universal Church.

———◆◈◆———

THUAN WAS AGAIN MOVED TO A PRISON with a higher security level in the area of Hoa Ma Street in Hanoi, where he remained in solitary confinement. Thuan no longer minded being alone. He wrote: "Your life, Lord, is a prayer, sincere and simple, directed to the Father." He wished his own entire life to be a prayer directed to the Father, in imitation of Jesus Christ. He began to write short Gospel prayers, which he tried to connect together to "form a life of prayer…. Like a chain of discrete gestures, of looks, of intimate words, they form a life of love." A collection of these prayers was eventually published in 2002 under the title, *Prayers of Hope, Words of Courage*.

Thuan would receive sporadic news through Tu Ha and other government officials that the process of canonization continued smoothly. On June 23, 1987, Cardinal Agostino Casaroli wrote to Cardinal Can announcing the petition's positive outcome. Pope John Paul II set the date for the canonization of the 117 Vietnamese martyrs for June 19, 1988. Apparently, when they recognized the uselessness of their opposition, officials in Hanoi put on a good face and allowed the Church to organize a limited number of celebrations to mark the historic event.

In his prison cell Thuan celebrated the Eucharist and sang the *Te Deum*. He asked the martyrs to give him the strength to follow their example to the end. He looked into his pitch-black future with neither fear nor bitterness. He felt the presence of that host of martyrs who had died for their faith in his native land and was awed to think that, in a certain way, he was one of their companions or descendants. He was ready for what seemed inevitable: to spend the rest of his life in prison.

A few months later he was moved to a larger cell where he could cook his own meals—very different from what he had previously endured. Thuan especially needed the extra walking space the new cell provided; the extremely damp conditions he had endured in many of the prisons contributed to his developing painful arthritis. As the bouts of arthritis became more frequent, Thuan decided he must walk in his cell for two hours every day to preserve the use of his legs. He was grateful that his captors had shown some flexibility in his treatment, but Thuan knew it was too late. His general health was becoming much worse.

CHAPTER TWENTY-FOUR

Light after Darkness

I will say to the north, "Give them up,"
and to the south, "Do not withhold;
bring my sons from far away..."

Isaiah 43:6

I rejoiced! Mary had freed me. Thanks be to you,
dear Mother!

Testimony of Hope,
F. X. Nguyen Van Thuan

I T HAD BEEN RAINING ALL DAY on November 21, 1988. Thuan listened to the rain on the tiled roof and felt the dampness seeping through the walls. The naked electric bulb hanging from the ceiling seemed brighter than usual. Somewhere in the building a telephone kept ringing.

Thuan had woken up early that morning because it was a special day: the feast of Mary's presentation at the temple. Every year Thuan celebrated with fervor this day commemorating Mary's presentation to God. She was chosen by God from all eternity to be the mother of the Word Incarnate. God received Mary's gift of herself as one of the greatest ever presented to him by humanity. One day the whole mystery of the redemption would be suspended upon her acceptance or rejection of God's invitation to be the mother of God. One day, upon her *fiat*, God would become man and live in her womb. For now, a tiny girl in her parents' arms, she delighted God above all creatures, and she already held in her tiny hand part of the promise of humanity's salvation.

It was also his parents' sixty-third wedding anniversary. Thirteen years had elapsed since he had last seen them in Saigon. He closed his eyes and prayed, "Mother of God, allow me to see my parents before they die. Give them the strength to endure in their hearts as I endure in my flesh."

The phone rang in the distance again. Thuan suddenly thought that the call might be about him. Without bitterness he prayed, "Mother, if I am of use to the Church in this prison, give me the grace and honor to die here. But if you think I can still serve the Church in some other way, let my captors release me."

Thuan sat down to eat the breakfast he had just cooked; he had not cooked much, and it did not take long to eat. Someone must have picked up the phone because it had finally stopped ringing. Thuan listened intently to the sound of muffled voices and hurried steps, the unpleasant yik-yik sound of rubber-soled sandals on the floor, the nervous scraping on the metal door of a key trying to fit into the keyhole in the latch. Then the door of his cell swung open and two prison guards hurried in. "Have you finished eating?"

Thuan gulped down the last spoonful of his rice porridge and said, "Yes, I have finished."

"Get ready," one of the guards commanded. "We are to take you to see a top-level government official." Thuan stood up and, avoiding any show of curiosity about this "top-level official," simply said, "I am ready."

The guards took a hard look at Thuan and they shook their heads. "Have you no better clothes?" Thuan smiled. "No. These are my best clothes. In fact, I only wear these on important feasts."

The guards did not care to ask what feast Thuan meant. One of them remarked curtly, "You can bet this will be an important day for you."

As they drove down the streets of Hanoi, the city looked grimy in the rain; perhaps the car window was grimy. Thuan enjoyed the brief glimpses of the buildings, trees, and people. For the last six years he had thirsted for this scene of normal life: people riding their bicycles, old men squatting on the sidewalk eating their noodle soup, children laughing or crying. Life bustled on both sides of the crowded street. Draped in poverty and soaked in the rain, the city was filled with an abundance of human emotions, dreams, hopes, and sorrows. Thuan drank in the scene, amazed that he had suddenly, and for however briefly, been given a glimpse of life outside the prison again.

As Thuan gazed out the window, he tried to repress waves of a foolish hope that he might be freed that very day. He told himself, *This will probably be a brief interrogation and then you will be back in your cell.* Even so, a miracle had taken place on the feast of Mary's presentation. After what seemed like endless months in a dark cell, he was now riding through the streets of the capital of the Socialist Republic of Vietnam.

The man sitting beside the driver turned around and told Thuan, "You are going to have an audience at the government guesthouse near Ha Le Lake." Thuan nodded and tried to hide his disappointment. Ha Le Lake was a mere fifteen-minute drive from the prison; he had hoped it would take much longer. The man shrugged and added, "You will be meeting with the Minister of the Interior."

Thuan's heart missed a beat. He was going to see Mai Chi Tho himself? Tho would not waste his time speaking with Thuan unless it was important. Thuan closed his eyes and pretended to fall asleep—he could pray in peace if they thought he was asleep. Thuan prayed that on the feast of the Presentation of Mary his captors would let him go. Fervently, passionately, he prayed for his freedom.

The car turned into the driveway of the guesthouse and his guards opened the car door for him. He was led through a lobby into a large, luxurious parlor. Mai Chi Tho, the feared Minister of the Interior, was sitting in an armchair. He got up to shake Thuan's hand as he walked into the room.

Thuan saw another man, ready with pad and pen, sitting on a small chair near the door. The Minister of the Interior pointed to an armchair and asked Thuan to sit down. He silently stared at Thuan for a long time. Thuan knew the routine very well; it was supposed to make one feel uncomfortable and become unnerved. But Thuan did not feel at all uneasy. Tea was served ceremoniously and as Thuan looked at Tho's impeccably ironed uniform, he thought, *I am really a mess!* Somehow the thought amused him and Tho noticed the change in his expression. He asked, "Do you know why you are here?"

Thuan shook his head and replied, "No, I don't."

Tho again lapsed into a long silence and seemed almost to forget Thuan's presence. Finally he asked: "How is your health?" Thuan thanked him for asking and said that, considering the circumstances, he was well. Tho laughed and repeated quietly, "Considering the circumstances...." He then leaned forward and asked, "How are you related to Ngo Dinh Diem?" Thuan replied simply, "I am his nephew."

Tho nodded and then looked out of the window. From where they sat, both men could enjoy a view of Ha Le Lake. He turned to Thuan and said, "You know, during the war Diem was identified with the United States. Once we used to say 'My-Diem' (U.S.A.-Diem), but that was a long time ago. Now we have no quarrel with him, his name, or his place in our history. If you read our most recent history books, you will see that we no longer abuse him or his name."

Again, Tho seemed lost in thought for a while. Then he continued, "I am a veteran revolutionary. Yet, I never had an opportunity to see Uncle Ho while he was alive. I spent all my war years in the South, so I knew of Ngo Dinh Diem. We had to fight him then, but not anymore. We should not look back at the past. We should look at the future and see what each one of us can do for the country."

He looked at Thuan and smiled. "Do you have some wish today?" Before he even realized what he was saying, Thuan replied instantly, "I wish to be free."

Tho seemed to enjoy this and asked, "You want to be freed just like that?" Thuan nodded, not knowing what else to say. Tho matter-of-factly continued, "Well, when do you want to be freed?" This time Thuan had to summon up his courage to pronounce the word, "Today."

His answer obviously startled Tho, who tensed visibly. With a sinking feeling in his stomach, Thuan thought, *I have ruined my chance of getting out.* But there was no going back now, so Thuan blurted out, "I have been in captivity for a very long time. I have been in prison under three popes: Paul VI, John Paul I, and John Paul II; and under four secretary generals of the Soviet Communist Party: Brezhnev, Chernenko, Andropov, and Gorbachev."

Tho burst into laughter. "That is true," he said and, still chuckling, repeated, "Brezhnev, Chernenko, Andropov, *and* Gorbachev…" as he turned to his secretary. His tone was imposing: "Do whatever is necessary to fulfill his desire." The young secretary quickly scribbled some notes and said, "There will be lengthy procedures, sir."

The Minister of the Interior glared at his secretary. In a voice indicating his effort to control his anger, Tho repeated, "Today."

Then he stood up and shook Thuan's hand. As Thuan left the room, he heard Mai Chi Tho chuckling. Thuan wondered if the meeting had been a dream or a joke.

Back in the car, Thuan realized that the meeting was real when the guards congratulated him and said that he would be free by noontime. They told him to go back to his cell and pack when they got back to the prison. Thuan scratched his head in concern. He did not have a suitcase. He did not even have a duffel bag. What would he use to carry his scant personal belongings?

He put that worry aside and began to pray in thanksgiving; his heart was flooded with immense joy: *Holy Mary, I have been released on the feast of your presentation at the Temple. You are the one who made them release me. You have set me free! Please, tell me what I should do now.*

He looked out of the car window. The rain had stopped. The city was now his. That very afternoon he would be able to walk on those streets, mingle with that crowd, buy food from those vendors, and even ride a bicycle. He sent a thought to his parents: *They set me free on your wedding anniversary! I will let you know soon and ask you to consider this my gift to you today.*

When he returned to the prison, Thuan wondered again how he would carry his few belongings. The guards came to help him and were shocked as they watched Thuan take a pair of trousers, tie up the pant legs, and stuff his few belongings inside. Thuan turned to the guards and smiled. "Done," he said.

The prison director was disgusted when he saw Thuan coming out of his cell with a pair of trousers turned into a "forked bag."

He grumbled, "People like you give our prison a bad name." He called for a jeep and instructed the driver, "Don't let anyone see him leaving here with that funny pair of trousers."

The director signed the release forms, hesitating at the words: *Cause for imprisonment.* He shrugged and wrote "illegal migration." Thuan looked at the form and read that he was to be taken to the archbishop's residence in Hanoi and would be required to remain within the city limits. Thuan hoped that his presence at Archbishop Can's residence would not make the members of his household more suspect in the government's eyes. Politely, Thuan shook hands with the director and the guards and climbed into the jeep. He looked up at the sky. Here and there, a few dark clouds were still hanging low, but the rest of the sky was blue. Tears came to his eyes as he prayed, *Thank you, my dear Mother Mary.*

Thuan's long ordeal had ended, and he was still alive. He had survived physically and mentally, but most importantly he had grown spiritually. He felt ready to return to God's work.

While the jeep sped through the streets of Hanoi, Thuan thought to himself, *I must control myself. Don't be too enthusiastic. The authorities have released me, but they will still be watching. I will have to do my work cautiously; my contacts will have to be limited.* But there was no way he could control the joy surging within him or the high hopes he felt for his new life. He prayed again to the Blessed Virgin Mary, *Thank you, my dear Mother.*

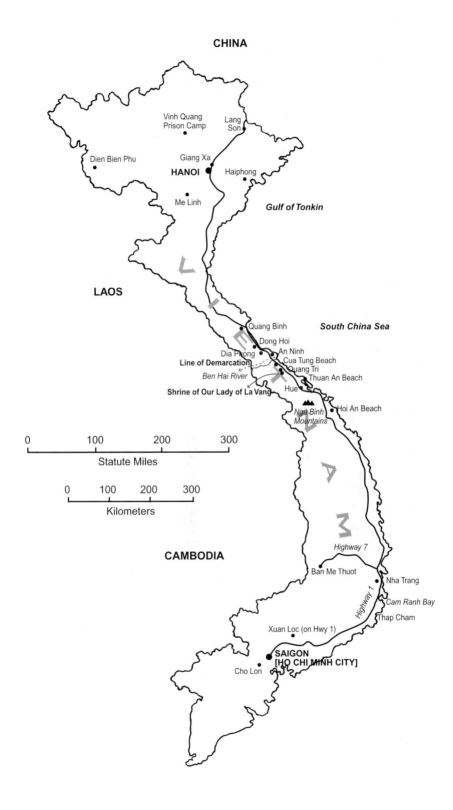

CHINA

Vinh Quang
Prison Camp

Lang
Son

Dien Bien Phu

Giang Xa

HANOI • Haiphong

Me Linh

Gulf of Tonkin

LAOS

V I E T N A M

Quang Binh

South China Sea

Dong Hoi

Dia Phong ● An Ninh

Line of Demarcation Cua Tung Beach

Ben Hai River Quang Tri

Shrine of Our Lady of La Vang Thuan An Beach

Hue

Hoi An Beach

Ngu Binh
Mountains

0	100	200	300

Statute Miles

0	100	200	300

Kilometers

CAMBODIA

Highway 7

Ban Me Thuot ● ● Nha Trang

Cam Ranh Bay

Highway 1 Thap Cham

Xuan Loc (on Hwy 1)

SAIGON
[HO CHI MINH CITY]

Cho Lon

A photo of the now famous pectoral cross Thuan carved during his imprisonment.

Archbishop Thuan (center) in Giang Xa where he remained under house arrest from 1978 to 1982. Though rarely, the authorities did allow him some visitors.

Archbishop Thuan in his simple surroundings at Giang Xa.

While still in captivity in Giang Xa, Thuan wrote Pilgrims on the Road of Hope, The Road of Hope under the Light of God's Word *and* Vatican II, and The Message of Maximilian Kolbe.

After his release from prison in 1989, Archbishop Thuan went to Australia to visit his parents. The visit was a surprise, and this photo captured the moment when Thuan met his parents for the first time in thirteen years.

Walking to the door of his parents' home in Australia.

Archbishop Thuan astonished his mother and father, who were not certain they would ever see him alive again.

Thuan's mother, Hiep, and father, Am (1990).

Thuan enjoying his first day in a free country (Australia, 1989).

Thuan visiting Australia again in 1993; here with his sister Thu Hong.

Archbishop Thuan in Rome after his first surgery in Boston.

Archbishop Thuan with his nephew Pierre at Castel Gandolfo (1990).

Archbishop Thuan and his relatives with Pope John Paul II.

Pope John Paul II and Archbishop Thuan in 1989.

Archbishop Thuan and his mother with Pope John Paul II. The photo was taken while Thuan's mother visited Rome in 1994.

Archbishop Thuan in Australia with his parents in 1990.

Archbishop Thuan in his private chapel in Rome around the time he was appointed president of the Council for Justice and Peace.

Archbishop Thuan in Australia (1990) to celebrate his father's ninetieth birthday.

Archbishop Thuan at the funeral service for his father who died June 30, 1993.

Thuan relaxing with some of his nieces and nephews in 1993. From left to right: *Francis, Lan, Hong, Thuan, Pierre, and seated on the floor, Tania and Duc.*

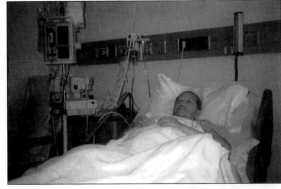

At Saint Elizabeth Seton Medical Center in Boston (2001).

After recovering from surgery, Thuan stayed at the residence of Cardinal Bernard Law.

Thuan writing thank you notes to friends after his surgery in Boston. His sister, Hong, stands at his right.

A joyful evening in Boston at the residence of Cardinal Bernard Law.

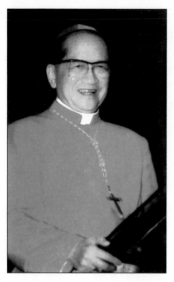

The new cardinal, February 21, 2001.

Blessing the crowd, February 2001.

▲

The new cardinal posing with members of his family, February 2001.

Thuan autographs a copy of one of his books, which have all been translated into many languages.

With Buddhist monks in California (2000).

With leaders of the Vietnamese community in California (2000).

Archbishop Thuan happily surrounded by young people, for whom he always had a special place in his heart.

Archbishop Thuan visited communities of Vietnamese Catholics all over the world.

With the Vietnamese community in Louisiana (2000).

Thuan's exceptional mother,
Elizabeth Ngo Dinh thi Hiep.

Thuan with his mother.

Thuan stops to speak with
his mother at a ceremony.

▼

Thuan concelebrating Mass with Pope John Paul II.

Cardinal Thuan and Pope John Paul II enjoying their trip to Assisi for the World Day of Prayer for Peace, January 2002.

Greeting Vietnamese representatives.

Cardinal Thuan at the Casa di Cura Pius XI with his sister Thu Hong and her three children: Pierre, Francis, and Tania, July 2002.

PART FOUR

THE TRIUMPH OF HOPE

You whom I took from the ends of the earth,
and called from its farthest corners,
saying to you, "You are my servant,
I have chosen you…"

ISAIAH 41:9

The world is changed by actions, but also by ideas.
It is ideas which direct actions.

The Road of Hope,
F. X. NGUYEN VAN THUAN

CHAPTER TWENTY-FIVE

Freedom and Exile

By the rivers of Babylon—
there we sat down and there we wept
when we remembered Zion.
On the willows there
we hung up our harps.

Psalm 137:1–2

At every moment you are carrying out God's plan
in history.

The Road of Hope,
F. X. Nguyen Van Thuan

READJUSTING TO FREEDOM SHOULD NOT BE HARD, Thuan re-peated to himself. On his first day as a free man, Thuan put on his cassock, set a beret on his head, and went outside to watch how people lived. He took a long, aimless walk along the West Lake, ventured into the maze of short narrow streets at the center of Hanoi, and instinctively cringed at the sight of a policeman.

Sometimes, in the days that followed, Thuan rode an old creaky bicycle through the streets of the capital amidst a sea of other bicycles. The people looked hungry, sick, and exhausted as they peddled along. They did not seem to notice much of their surroundings; they were too wrapped up in their own worries and misery. Thuan felt such love for them.

Each day Thuan ventured farther and farther from the archbishop's residence. The cardinal had told him not to go too far, but driven by a thirst for human faces and voices Thuan explored every street and circled around every area. He eventually ventured on toward the prison on Hoa Ma Street and found that the memories did not hurt any more.

In fact, none of the memories of his thirteen years of captivity stirred up anxiety or anger. The only thing that continued to make him anxious was the sight of a policeman. He knew that "they" could still put him back in jail at any moment. Now that he had tasted the joy of freedom, the thought of being back in a dark cell was unbearable. But then Thuan reasoned, *I may be vulnerable in the face of these irrational and arbitrary government agencies, but I am always protected by God. Nothing that happens to me can happen without God's consent.*

Full of joy and a spirit of adventure, Thuan's daily outings, his ability to celebrate the Eucharist at the Cathedral of Hanoi, and his evening conversations with the priests at the archbishop's residence seemed to him like an unending series of miracles.

Upon his release, one of Thuan's first phone calls was to his father and mother and sisters in Australia. They cried and laughed and asked, "When will we see you?" Without thinking he answered, "Very soon, I guess," but immediately regretted his words. He did not want to give them false hope. How could he be sure that the authorities would allow him travel to Australia when he was not even permitted outside Hanoi? One wrong move now and he would end up in prison again. Certainly, applying for a passport would be a wrong move.

But Thuan gathered his courage to try. He would trade many years of his life for the possibility of spending a few weeks with his parents and of seeing Rome again. Strangely, the officials who demanded that Thuan be back at the archbishop's residence by sundown each day did not argue with his going to Australia and Italy. They even facilitated or rather expedited the procedures so that he acquired a passport within a few days. With their approval he walked into the Australian Embassy one morning to apply for a visa.

THUAN WANTED HIS ARRIVAL IN SYDNEY to be a surprise for his parents. Thuan's motivation for making his trip a surprise was partly his belief that it would give his parents greater joy, but also, and more importantly, he feared that the secret police might pull him off the plane at the last minute. After years of dealing with arbitrary authority, Thuan took nothing for granted. Even the diplomats at the Australian Embassy who spoke to Thuan's sister, Ham Tieu, by phone, told her not to set her expectations too high. There was no guarantee Thuan could actually get out of Vietnam.

But everything went smoothly. Thuan knew he had reached the free world when his plane touched down at the Krung Thep (formerly Bangkok) International Airport on March 28, 1989. Thuan was to meet Ham Tieu there and she would accompany him to Sydney. He looked up at the words, Krung Thep, an abbreviation of the long name that King Rama I had bestowed on the city:

> The city of angels, the great city, residence of the Emerald Buddha, the impregnable city of Indra, grand capital of the world endowed with nine precious gems, happy city with an immense Royal Palace that resembles the heavenly abode where reigns the reincarnated god, a city given by Indra and built by Vishnu.

Thuan smiled. How free Rama had been! Free of any fear of contradiction or religious intolerance. Free to honor both the Buddha and the Hindu gods at the same time. Free to give his capital a name with many words. As he walked to the rendezvous point to meet his sister, for the first time in his life Thuan felt he knew what genuine freedom was.

He had been out of prison for only four months, but he had since enjoyed only relative freedom. He lowered his head and thanked God again, and prayed resolutely, *I love the freedom I find here, in the free world. But please make it possible for me to return to Vietnam. My work still waits for me there.*

Neither the thrill he experienced in his newfound freedom nor the excitement at being able to see his parents and the possibility of going to Rome could dispel the recurrent thought that now ironically caused Thuan to cringe: perhaps he might not be allowed to return to Vietnam.

———◆◆◆———

In Australia Thuan was welcomed by the papal nuncio who had driven immediately to Ham Tieu's home. Ham Tieu was well known to the nuncio because she had actively organized demonstrations and wrote petitions on Thuan's behalf to the Australian Bishops' Conference and the Australian government during his imprisonment. After a few hours' rest, Thuan was ready to meet his parents. Ham Tieu called them to say that a "certain monsignor" wished to see them at 3:00 P.M. sharp. Thuan's father Am said without hesitation, "Please tell the monsignor that we will be happy to see him." Unexpected visitors were not strange; for years Am and Hiep had been welcoming cardinals, archbishops, and monsignors and had appealed to them to help Thuan. Each visit brought them a little joy, a little encouragement, and a feeling that the Church did care about Thuan.

So, by 3:00 they had donned their traditional Vietnamese dress and were ready to receive the expected "monsignor." Ham Tieu rang the doorbell and Am opened the door immediately. He stood at the door in absolute shock to see Thuan on the doorstep. True to character, however, Am simply said, "Please come in, Monsignor!" Thuan went in and was unable to move when he saw his mother. Hiep looked at him and seemed bewildered. Yet she smiled, saying over and over, "You are here. You are alive!" Her exclamation indicated how much she had already come to accept the possibility she might never see her son again.

Thuan had imagined the reunion in many different ways, but he had not once thought it would be so simple and so satisfying. He thanked God for making the moment so beautiful and gentle.

Sydney is a wonderful city and Thuan took long walks on Bondi, Manley, and Balmoral Beaches with his parents and his sisters Ham Tieu, Tuyet, Tien, and Thu Hong. They all wanted to hear about his years in captivity, while he wanted to know all about their lives in Australia.

Tuyet and Tien spoke little, but Hong and Ham Tieu told Thuan hundreds of stories about their first days in Australia. Thuan listened to them with great pleasure and rehearsed in his mind what he wanted to tell his family about his life in prison. He realized that he could not tell them the whole story. He did not want to hurt them with the details of his sufferings, but on the other hand he wanted to tell them how he had found a new spirituality during captivity that was so intimately united with the pain and humiliations he had endured.

He tried to postpone telling his story by asking them about the life of the Vietnamese living overseas. As they spoke Thuan grasped for the first time just how large the worldwide communities of Vietnamese had become, how far they had been able to progress, and how their talents could one day be used to rebuild Vietnam. He instinctively felt pulled to travel to the United States and to France to meet with the Vietnamese communities there, but he knew the officials in Hanoi would deny such a request. Thuan's sisters challenged him to call the Vietnamese Embassy and inquire whether he could travel to other countries in Europe besides Italy, and whether he could go to the United States. As he had guessed, Hanoi's answer was an emphatic "No." Thuan had been authorized to go to Sydney to see his parents and then to Rome "to see the pope," but he was not allowed to travel elsewhere. He accepted the answer.

By now, Thuan had determined what he should say and what should be left unsaid about his experience in prison. Thuan saw that his family was interested in his narratives not only because they involved him, but also because of the wonderful lessons about life, people, spirituality, and God they contained.

One day as Thuan and his mother walked along Bondi Beach, she told him, "What you have lived and experienced in prison is not your private possession. You have to share your experiences with God's people." Thuan shook his head, "Then I will not be allowed to return to Vietnam." She considered his reply, turned to look out at the sea, and said, "Yet, those experiences do not belong to you alone. You *must* share them..."

————◆◆◆————

ROME. BEING THERE AGAIN WAS ANOTHER MIRACLE for Thuan. He met with Pope John Paul II several times and was moved to tears when the pope revealed how closely he had followed Thuan's ordeal. He saw Cardinal Agostino Casaroli, the Secretary of State, and Cardinal Agnelo Rossi, who had visited Thuan's parents in Australia in

1980. Thuan took a crash course in theology to update himself, and enjoyed meeting friends who came from all over Europe to see him.

Thuan was happily surprised by the progress that many of his Vietnamese friends had made. The years they had spent living in genuine freedom overseas had made them a different breed of Vietnamese. They were more self-assured and conscious of their own rights and the rights of others. They had learned to think strategically.

Thuan also delighted in finding himself again in the city he had known as a young priest. He wanted to visit all the places he had visited before, walk on the same streets, cross the same bridges, and feel no gap between the years.

From time to time he wondered: *Why am I here? Why am I still alive? God has preserved my life, what does he want from me now?* He felt no urgency to discover answers to these questions, however. For the moment he was happy to be alive and see that the world was so beautiful.

Thuan postponed returning to Vietnam because he was afraid to discover the government would not allow him back into the country. He had to overcome his fear and, more importantly, find out if what he feared was true. Thuan went to the Vietnamese Embassy in Rome and asked about an entry visa. No one seemed to be in a hurry to grant him the visa, but neither had they rejected his application. Thuan knew he would be free to go home to Vietnam.

Thuan said good-bye to Rome and flew back to Sydney to spend a few more days with his parents. He knew he might not have another chance. Once back in Vietnam, he would still be carefully watched; his former tormentors still had power over his life.

After a few days in Sydney Thuan tried his luck again and asked the Vietnamese government for permission to return to Vietnam via Manila. He wanted to visit Cardinal Sin, a dear friend since 1957. The government granted his request and Thuan flew to the Philippines. He enjoyed a wonderful reunion with Cardinal Sin and finally boarded a plane for Hanoi.

REGARDING THE CATHOLIC CHURCH, the Communist leaders in Vietnam became more anxious with each passing year. Archbishop Nguyen van Binh of Ho Chi Minh City was growing older and eventually time would force the issue of who would replace him. Although the government adamantly refused to allow Thuan to take up his responsibilities as coadjutor archbishop in Ho Chi Minh City, each time Archbishop Nguyen van Binh had so much as a cold, the leaders in Hanoi became nervous. If something happened to the old archbishop, there was no doubt that Thuan would automatically and immediately go to take his place. The government would have a crisis on their hands: they would either have to allow Thuan to function as the archbishop, or they would have to put the second highest-ranking man of the Church in Vietnam back into prison. Neither choice was acceptable now. Both would have negative consequences on the government that now claimed to practice *Doi Moi*—a national policy of renovation similar to the Soviet Union's *glasnost*—but that still wanted its citizens to cower before its rule.

As if in response to this crisis, Thuan would not resign his position as coadjutor archbishop voluntarily and the Vatican refused to force him to do so. The government's situation had become a real stalemate.

In many respects Thuan was still a prisoner. After his return from abroad the government imposed the same restrictions as before: he had to remain within Hanoi, and he had to be in the archbishop's residence by sundown every evening. But Thuan had learned to live with and to stretch the limits of the government's restrictions. He found that he could travel anywhere within a radius of 200 miles and still keep the curfew. Hidden in a car, he would leave Hanoi for the Phat Diem and Bui Chu dioceses where the majority of Catholics in North Vietnam lived. He was welcomed as a hero by Catholic communities that had successfully resisted government attempts to control them. He went to Yen Bay and Viet Tri, to the extreme west of the Red River Delta. He visited Lang Son, near the Chinese border in the north. And he was always home before sundown.

At first Thuan was very cautious. However, with time and repeatedly successful excursions, Thuan became more adventurous. One day he went as far south as Vinh and did not make it back to the archbishop's residence until midnight.

Thuan's trips were not a secret from government officials, but they looked the other way. They were not going to risk derailing their national policy of renovation over him. The officials finally decided to present Thuan with what they felt was a relatively accept-able proposal, more for their own benefit than for his.

Communist officials met with Thuan and informed him that he should not even think about succeeding Archbishop Nguyen van Binh in Ho Chi Minh City or of taking over any other diocese. How-ever, the government would not object to his having a position within the Bishops' Conference.

The officials indicated that Thuan could head a committee within the conference. They were even open to the idea of Thuan becoming an executive of the conference—perhaps vice president or secretary general. Thuan was pleased at the possibility of finally being able to work within the episcopate, but he knew that this de-pended entirely on whether or not the Communist officials kept their word.

Even as they discussed their proposal with Thuan, the chang-ing fortunes of Communism worldwide dismayed and confused the officials in Vietnam. Though Vietnam had officially adopted a reno-vation policy, the Communist leaders in Hanoi could not initiate too many social and economic reforms without endangering their own regime. They were determined not to allow any political changes for fear that they might not be able to preserve the status quo.

From prison Thuan had heard echoes of the final death throes of the Communist Bloc. Mikhail Gorbachev's democratic re-forms in the Soviet Union and the mass demonstrations staged by East Germans against their government were strong indications of the crumbling governments.

While Thuan was still in Rome, East Germans had demanded the right to emigrate from their "Marxist paradise." Nothing could stop the wave of frequent defections to the West. In May 1989 the Hungarian government decided to open its border with Austria; and the move opened a floodgate. East Germans streamed across Czechoslovakia and Hungary into Austria.

After Thuan's return to Vietnam, troubles flared up in Com-munist China that ended in the bloody massacre of students in

Tiananmen Square in Beijing on June 4, 1989. Chinese authorities had effectively repressed pro-democratic aspirations, but their actions had long-term repercussions in Vietnam. The Vietnamese people saw that even the most security conscious of Communist regimes were vulnerable. The leaders in Hanoi feared a similar incident to Tiananmen Square could happen in Vietnam. They saw signs of their military personnel becoming restless, cadres losing faith in Communism, and the people feeling less threatened by the secret police.

On November 9 the Berlin Wall fell and travel restrictions were lifted. Tens of thousands of East Germans rushed into West Berlin, while others started breaking down the Wall—the symbol of the division between the Free World and the Communist Bloc.

Communist leaders in Hanoi sat down to map out the measures they would employ to insure the survival of the Communist regime in Vietnam. One of these measures was the decision to revoke their offer to Thuan, and to prevent him from ever taking a leadership role in the Church. The Communist leaders decided that Thuan would either have to "play dead" or be forced into permanent exile.

Despite the government's new tactics, the Vietnamese bishops had expected to elect Thuan president or secretary general of the Bishops' Conference at their next meeting scheduled for December 1989. Toward the end of the year, however, Thuan became very ill and had to go to Ho Chi Minh City for the medical attention that was not available in Hanoi. His hospitalization happened to coincide with the bishops' meeting in Ho Chi Minh City.

Nguyen Tu Ha traveled from the Ministry of the Interior in Hanoi to see Thuan at the hospital. He warned Thuan that he must refuse any position the bishops might offer: he must not accept the presidency, or the office of secretary general, or the presidency of any committee or subcommittee. Thuan told Ha that he himself had no control over the conference's appointments and that if he were elected to a position, it would be impossible for him to decline.

Ha then went to the bishops' meeting and informed the assembly that the government would not tolerate Thuan's election to any leadership position within the Bishops' Conference. The bishops tried to negotiate, but Ha and other officials refused to budge. They promised the bishops that the government would be very flexible with the Church in Vietnam *if* Thuan remained inactive. Then Ha told the bishops it would be useless to elect Thuan to any position or function, because the government had many ways of preventing him from fulfilling his duties. The implied threat convinced the bishops to comply with the government's demand.

Meanwhile, at the hospital, Thuan was undergoing prostate surgery. The procedure was unsuccessful and soon a serious infection set in that endangered Thuan's life. Through the intervention of the Medical Community of Saint Egidio in Rome, Thuan received authorization from the Vietnamese government to be flown to Italy to receive necessary medical attention. Thuan later joked, "That was the only time I traveled first class."

In Rome Thuan underwent another surgery. It was successful and, after a few weeks of convalescence, he returned to Vietnam, where he found the Vietnamese authorities in a state of panic over the sudden collapse of the Communist Bloc. All pretenses of democracy and freedom vanished as the regime fought for its survival; it had no time for subtleties or compromises.

Consequently, Thuan's passport was confiscated at the airport. He protested, but to no avail. He was now a man with no official identification, without which it was almost impossible to travel in Vietnam. He returned to the archbishop's residence under his previous restrictions, and Thuan risked traveling to various dioceses around Hanoi as before.

By early 1991 the government's opposition to Thuan had become intolerable. Cardinal Pham Dinh Tung sent a letter to Pope John Paul II asking for Thuan's appointment as coadjutor archbishop of Hanoi. The Vatican approached the Vietnamese authorities to discuss the matter. The Communist leaders were irate.

Thuan was summoned to meet with Colonel Nguyen Hong Lam of the Ministry of Interior. Head of Vietnam's counter-intelligence services and the third highest-ranking official at the Ministry of Interior, Lam was also in charge of religious affairs at the Ministry. At the meeting Lam accused Thuan of playing games with the government. "The Vatican cannot appoint you without first consulting us!" Lam said angrily. "This time the leaders in Rome have gone too far. For years both they and you have been told that we will not tolerate your being archbishop of Ho Chi Minh City. Now, all of a sudden, the Vatican wants you to be the future archbishop of Hanoi. This is a plot! An even greater scheme than the one designed by the Vatican and the imperialists in 1975!"

Thuan listened calmly to the long tirade of confusing accusations and insults. Then he quietly said, "This is a misunderstanding. The Holy See 'recommended,' it did not 'appoint' me. The bishops of Vietnam proposed to the Holy See that I become the coadjutor archbishop of Hanoi. They did so because they want to plan for the long-term future. They know that I would not be allowed to function in any leadership position at the present moment. That was why they 'appointed me for the future.' The Holy See understands the wisdom of this move and that is why it *recommends* that the government of the Socialist Republic of Vietnam approve the proposal."

"You always speak with a gentle voice," Lam replied, "but you have caused unending problems for us. At present we have more pressing problems to deal with." Lam turned his back to Thuan. When he faced Thuan again, he suddenly changed his approach. "Why don't you go to see your parents?" Lam said kindly. "Stay with them for a while and then come back when things have cooled down."

Thuan sensed danger and shook his head. "I have already seen my parents."

"Well then, why don't you go to Rome for a while?" Lam insisted.

The conversation continued until finally Thuan said, "All right. I will think about it."

It was obvious to Thuan that the authorities did not want him to go for just a few months; they wanted to get rid of him once and for all. They intended to send him into permanent exile. He needed to discuss the matter seriously with the Holy See. He needed to know what Church leaders thought about him being given a "one-way ticket" out of Vietnam.

Several times he tried calling Rome, but the ever-watchful Communist authorities always interrupted any calls to Rome. In the end he had to phone Australia and ask that his messages be transmitted to the Vatican. When Thuan received his answer from Rome, it was concise and to the point: "Get out."

Vatican officials knew it was very dangerous for Thuan to stay in Hanoi now that the government had made it abundantly clear that he had become a *persona non grata*. He had to leave even if there was no foreseeable possibility of returning in the future. Though Thuan had seen this coming for a long while, nevertheless, the reality of forced exile was extremely painful for him.

In December 1991, as he boarded the plane for Rome, Thuan hoped that international pressure and the Vatican's entreaties would one day convince the Communist government to allow him to return, at least from time to time, to his beloved land.

———————◆❉◆———————

In March 1992 Thuan sent a letter from Rome to Communist officials in Hanoi asking to be allowed to return to Vietnam. In order to settle the matter, Hanoi sent a delegation led by Vu Quang, the Chairman of the Religious Committee. The committee arrived in Rome in April and the Holy See extended its hospitality to the delegation and housed them at the Hotel Columbus, a few steps from Saint Peter's Square.

The delegation met with Monsignor Claudio Celli, Undersecretary for Affairs of State. Vu Quang began by commenting on Archbishop Thuan's great intelligence and effectiveness in his work. "We wonder," he said, "why the Holy See does not give him an opportunity to do something for the Church here in the Vatican."

Celli smiled courteously and responded, "He is indeed intelligent and effective, as you said, so we cannot help wondering why the government of Vietnam does not allow him to serve his country in Vietnam?"

The discussion of Thuan went nowhere and ultimately Monsignor Celli and the Vietnamese delegation decided to spend their time together discussing other pending issues.

On April 16, 1992, Thuan received a call from Vu Quang inviting him to the Hotel Columbus the next morning. Thuan accepted. On April 17 Thuan had a pleasant breakfast with Vu Quang and the other members of the delegation. Thuan was surprised to see them opening a bottle of champagne. Then Vu Quang raised his glass and offered a toast in honor of Thuan's birthday, which they had remembered. They wanted Thuan to know that the government of Vietnam wished him well in the future. Thuan smiled, but knew that this was the Communists' way of telling him he could never hope to return to Vietnam.

The delegation returned to Hanoi. After meeting with Thuan, Church leaders began to discuss his work at the Vatican. No one believed his return to Vietnam was any longer a possibility.

CHAPTER TWENTY-SIX

The Man with a Gentle Smile

Do not fear, for I have redeemed you;
I have called you by name, you are mine.

Isaiah 43:1

Even if you carried out some colossal tasks, but did not
obey, you would not be pleasing God. God values your
heart; he has no need of your works. After all, he created
the whole universe without your help.

The Road of Hope,
F. X. Nguyen Van Thuan

T HUAN LIVED IN A SMALL ROOM at the Bui Chu House,
located at 45 Via della Pinetta Sachetti, and resumed
life in Rome as if he had never gone away.

As he walked the streets of Rome, he no longer looked over
his shoulder to check if he was being followed as he had done in
Hanoi. Thuan belonged to a very small minority of people who had
lived long years in captivity and who strongly felt the joy of true freedom. The rest of the population took freedom for granted.

For his first two years in exile Thuan focused on ministering
to the Vietnamese diaspora, and at times he worked with the Secretariat of State of the Vatican and the Congregation for Evangelization as a Pontifical Visitor, going to dioceses and seminaries in
Africa and Asia.

Thuan's father, Nguyen Van Am, passed away in June of 1993.
Thuan took the first plane to Sydney. There he found his sisters

Ham Tieu, Tuyet, Tien, and Thu Hong, and his younger brother Tuyen huddled around their mother. Once again Hiep showed extreme courage. At the funeral Mass celebrated by Thuan and two other bishops, she read some words without shedding any tears. In accord with Asian tradition, after the Mass Thuan prostrated himself three times before his father's casket, thanking him for giving him life, and for having always guided him with a strong hand.

After the funeral, Thuan sat for hours recalling his father's life of sacrifice and his sincere forgiveness of all who had intentionally hurt him or his family. The rise of Hiep's family to fame and power meant that Am had had to live in his wife's shadow, but he had not minded. He had worshiped Hiep, and she had worshiped him. When tragedy had struck his wife's family, Am was always there beside her to help pick up the pieces. He never complained.

Thuan remembered his father's stringent logic when he or his siblings had tried to find excuses for their mistakes. Am never raised his voice, yet his remonstrations were not easily forgotten. Thuan had never told his father he loved him while he was living. He had always wanted to say it, but Asian culture, and his own shyness, had made it impossible. Now he could finally say, "Rest in God's hands, rest in peace, Father. I love you."

Thuan stayed on in Australia after the funeral. One day as he was writing at his desk, Ham Tieu came to him and suddenly suggested, "Don't you think Mom could travel a little now? She would really enjoy seeing Europe and North America." Thuan dropped his pen. He turned and asked, "Do you think she is really up to that? She is ninety, or don't you remember?" But Ham Tieu convinced Thuan to speak to their mother.

When Thuan asked Hiep, she said, "It is too early to talk about such things. But eventually I would like to see Rome and Lourdes, and I would like to meet with Vietnamese communities in the United States to thank them for their support."

Thuan challenged her by asking, "For what support?"

His mother looked at him and smiled; she knew that he, too, had forgiven all the people who had hurt him and his family. "Many people have shown their loyalty to your uncle Diem," she insisted, "and many others are proud of you."

He nodded. How could he not be thankful to the Vietnamese communities where at least some had been loyal to Diem to the end and had shown their friendship and support for him and his family? He looked at the piles of condolence cards, letters, and printed e-mail messages on the desk. He had been trying to send thank-you notes to all who had thought of him and his family over the years. *Aren't these enough to justify our forgiveness of all past hurts?* Thuan asked himself. He felt more at peace with himself than ever before.

———————◆◆◆◆◆———————

BACK IN ROME THE AMOUNT OF THUAN'S writing increased, and he needed more space. He was given two more rooms so that he could spread out his work. He spent long hours with the translators and publishers of his books. *The Road of Hope* has been translated into more than a dozen languages, and Thuan's other books are all quite successful.

Thuan did not spend all of his time writing, however. He started to visit Vietnamese communities in many countries. The young people in these communities came to him for guidance and leadership. They wanted him to speak at their retreats and meetings. Large gatherings of Vietnamese Catholics, everywhere in the world, had to have Thuan as their keynote speaker or their gatherings were not considered successful.

Before long, as more and more people read Thuan's books, French, German, Italian, and Hispanic communities also invited him to speak at retreats and general assemblies. Thuan traveled to many countries to speak to priests, religious, and lay persons who appreciated Thuan's perspectives on life and faith. They respected his words, because he spoke from rich experience and as a witness of hope. His personal experience gave weight to what he said, and he drew larger and larger crowds. Young people flocked to meetings whenever he spoke. Thuan saw the good that might come from stories related to his long ordeal, but he refrained from speaking too openly or too much about the treatment he had received from his tormentors and wardens. He still nourished the hope that he would one day be allowed to return to work in Vietnam, and he did not want to jeopardize the possibility because of what he said.

Unfortunately, the prospect of returning to Vietnam became dimmer with time. After the Holy See's repeated attempts to negotiate with Hanoi for Thuan's return to Vietnam met with no success, in April 1994 Pope John Paul II decided to appoint Thuan vice president of the Pontifical Council for Justice and Peace.

This council, established by Pope Paul VI on January 6, 1967, by the Decree *Catholicam Christi Ecclesiam*, was initially an experimental organization that was restructured and made permanent by his Decree *Justiciam et Pacem* on December 10, 1976. Under Pope John Paul II the commission was made a council. Its purpose is to enrich and disseminate the social doctrine of the Church, especially where it concerns human labor. It also works on issues involving justice and peace, the progress of nations, and violations of human rights; it promotes human rights, especially the right to religious freedom.

The program of the council could also be seen as a summary of Thuan's past efforts and aspirations. Thuan was humbled when he learned that he was to work within a pontifical structure. He had become an important member of the Roman Curia overnight.

——◆◗◆◖◆——

IN 1994 THUAN FLEW TO PARIS to welcome his mother to France and accompany her to Lourdes. Hiep had traveled with her daughter Ham Tieu and her granddaughter Tania, who was fourteen at the time.

In Paris Thuan celebrated Mass at the Paris Foreign Mission Society with the superior of the community, Father Etcharrel. After Mass they visited the exhibits at the Room of the Martyrs where they all bowed their heads and prayed for a return of religious tolerance in Vietnam.

Thuan's mother was eager to get to Lourdes. She said she wanted to thank Our Lady of Lourdes for all the blessings received by her family, especially by Thuan. This made Thuan realize that while he thought so often about the great tragedies his family had endured, his mother thought only of the blessings. This put Thuan to shame. Surrounded by her two children, her granddaughter, and

Father Van, a Vietnamese priest, Hiep traveled by train to Lourdes and marveled at the landscape along the way.

Hiep's resilience surprised Thuan. She was ninety years old, but she knelt for hours in front of the grotto at Lourdes. Thuan knelt by her side, feeling that the many wonderful moments of his life were a thanksgiving both to the one who was kneeling beside him and the One to whom they prayed.

In Lourdes Thuan was once again struck by the memory of his first "encounter" with the Immaculate Conception. He still felt strong emotion when he again read the inscription at the precise spot where the Madonna had appeared to Bernadette: "I am the Immaculate Conception." *Are there many mysteries greater than this? At the moment of her conception, Mary entered God's plan of Redemption.*

Again he recalled the Virgin Mary's words to Saint Bernadette: "I do not promise you joy and consolation on this earth, but rather trials and suffering." He thought without any bitterness, *Yes, Mother, you have kept your promise.* He only wondered if he had shown himself to be as faithful as Bernadette to that promise. The young Bernadette had returned to the Lady no matter how people treated her. Threats, humiliations, and prison—she suffered all of these indignities without complaint. Her consuming desire was to see, at the appointed times, Mary, the Immaculate Conception. *She was just a child,* Thuan thought with admiration. *She was just a child when she suffered these things, and I suffered them as an adult.*

They traveled to Rome and Thuan was delighted to see how his mother enjoyed being there. She and Thuan's sister were received by Pope John Paul II at Castel Gandolfo, and, as the pope blessed her, Thuan saw tears in her eyes. Thuan lived these days in a daze. He was grateful that his mother had finally accepted something from him in return for all she had done. He saw how happy she was just being in Rome because he was by her side.

At the end of her month-long visit, Thuan was sad to say good-bye to his mother. Before parting, Hiep looked at him for a moment and said, "It is clear that God wants you here and not in Vietnam. This is where you will live and where you will do God's work. I will always be with you." Accordingly, on November 24, 1994,

Thuan officially resigned his position as coadjutor archbishop of Ho Chi Minh City. It was a decisive moment for Thuan. He would remain in Rome and serve in the Roman Curia for the rest of his life.

Still, sometimes he wondered about the plans of Divine Providence. *After so many ordeals, here I am in Rome, but why? What did God intend for me by bringing me to the Vatican and the free world?* Apparently such questions did not enter the pope's mind. Wojtyla's appointment of Thuan to the Council for Justice and Peace seemed a logical and appropriate result of his long ordeal in Vietnam. As John Paul II had told Thuan, "You are from a country of war and you were a captive for thirteen years. Now you can share your experiences with people in many countries where there are suffering and injustice, so that we can promote justice and peace and help people to understand their rights."

Thuan received his answer. War and peace, justice and injustice in the world would be Thuan's work and preoccupation. Thuan did not rush into the complex world of politics and social justice. He had much to learn from the Vatican's Secretariat of State and the President of the Pontifical Council for Justice and Peace, Cardinal Roger Etchegaray. A native of the French Basque regions, a poet and consummate diplomat, Etchegaray had been shepherd of a large Vietnamese community while archbishop of Marseilles. Etchegaray had developed a great love for the Vietnamese people and relished Vietnamese food and culture. In his apartment at San Callisto, located just above his office, Etchegaray surprised guests by treating them to delicious Vietnamese dishes. Thuan was quite fond of Etchegaray, and their working relationship could not have been better.

Thuan also developed a wonderful working relationship with Monsignor Diarmuid Martin from Ireland, undersecretary of the Council. Martin began working at the Vatican in 1977, and he was adept at handling the difficult situations that arose at the United Nations or in the world.

Thuan was a quiet man. He went about his work seriously, studied his dossiers conscientiously, and spent long hours at his desk. Cardinal Etchegaray was not a micro-manager and he left most of the work in the hands of his able colleagues, grateful to be able to do so with confidence. Aside from Etchegaray's role as president of the Council for Justice and Peace, he was also the president of the Pontifical Council *Cor Unum*, which Thuan had known so well through COREV.

As vice president of a pontifical council, Thuan was eligible for housing in the Vatican and he received an apartment at San Callisto. At first it did not look like much, but as Thuan went over the plans for needed renovation and worked with the carpenters and bricklayers, it became a lovely place. He spent time decorating his little chapel with exquisite taste, but his small bedroom looked no better than the ones he had had in Vietnam. It was as bare and uncomfortable as a cell, and he preferred it that way. He continued living like a poor man.

Thuan entertained guests almost every day after work. He enjoyed meeting old friends and new acquaintances. He even enjoyed talking with reporters, though some misquoted him.

Thuan was a patient learner and he studied everything. He learned the ways of the Vatican. He made friends from all over the world. Most of the bishops and prelates who came to the Vatican or were in Rome from various countries dropped by and relaxed in his company. Thuan always appreciated these visits; his curiosity about how the Church was faring around the world seemed insatiable.

It was almost unavoidable that after a conversation with Thuan, visitors would conclude by inviting him to visit their country or diocese to speak at a retreat or at an important event. These requests became so numerous that Thuan had to make judicious choices on how to best spend his time.

Gradually he learned the ins and outs of the issues pertaining to human rights, world trade, globalization, developing countries, and the continued consequences of the fall of the Soviet Union and Communism in Eastern Europe.

Thuan also kept a careful eye on the situation of his native country. Relations between Vietnam's government and the Church had not improved. One initiative after another proposed by the Vatican's Secretariat of State had failed.

Thuan regretted that the real opportunities of the mid-'80s for Vietnam's economic recovery had completely faded by the late '90s due to the incompetent bureaucracy, absence of law, and corruption on every level.

Thuan's spirituality continued to guide him, and he spent a great deal of time praying and preparing his speeches with loving care. He hoped that whenever he was called upon to speak, especially to young people, his words would help his listeners to find a shortcut to God's love and to hope.

CHAPTER TWENTY-SEVEN

President of the Council for Justice and Peace

He shall command peace to the nations;
his dominion shall be from sea to sea.

Zechariah 9:10

So many of your writings, so many of your speeches, so
many of your programs and important projects, which
have achieved success, have been born from the secret
recesses of your mind and heart. It is in the silent depths
of your being that you discover the fundamentals:
sacrifice, patience, reflection, and love.

The Road of Hope,
F. X. Nguyen Van Thuan

ON FEBRUARY 2, 1997, the Feast of the Presentation,
Thuan put the final touches on *Five Loaves and Two
Fish*. In it, for the first time since leaving Vietnam,
Thuan committed to paper some of the poignant memories of his
long ordeal in his homeland and recounted, in seven meditations
and prayers, some of his experiences.

The short yet powerful book was soon translated into a dozen
languages. Thuan was now comfortable telling stories about his thirteen years of captivity. He no longer felt it might be a form of pride.
He had witnessed how much the story of his own suffering and his

overcoming despair with prayer and the Eucharist had helped people of all walks of life, especially the young.

Thuan wrote *Five Loaves and Two Fish* with a great economy of words: simple, straightforward, with no irony or bitterness. His depiction of Communist guards and wardens was always charitable and kind; it was to become a characteristic approach. As far as possible he always tried to show his guards and Communist officials at their best; he stressed their humanity and compassion rather than their indifference or cruelty. Even when he had to reveal the brutality of the guards and Communist officials, Thuan excused their behavior, which he believed was not the fruit of personal evil, but mechanical obedience to an indifferent and cruel bureaucracy.

Thuan's stories contain traces of his pervading sense of humor. He never dramatized his experiences and shunned every form of self-aggrandizing. The stories Thuan told in *Five Loaves and Two Fish* were an invitation to deeper reflection.

In many countries the short book has been acclaimed as one of the most significant Catholic inspirational works of the twentieth century.

ON NOVEMBER 15, 1994, Pope John Paul II chose Cardinal Etchegaray to head the newly organized Central Committee for the Jubilee of the Holy Year 2000. Due to the scope of work to be done for the jubilee, the cardinal resigned the presidency at the Pontifical Councils *Cor Unum* and Justice and Peace.

In March 1996 Bishop Paul Cordes, vice president of the Pontifical Council for the Laity, replaced Cardinal Etchegaray as president of *Cor Unum*. Two years later, on June 24, 1998, Archbishop Thuan was appointed president of the Council for Justice and Peace.

As Thuan assumed the presidency, Bishop Diarmuid Martin became secretary, and Monsignor Giampaolo Crepaldi became the council's undersecretary. Later Bishop Martin headed the Mission of the Holy See near the United Nations in Geneva.

The journey from a prison cell to prominent role in the Vatican had taken ten years. Thuan looked back with some curious nostalgia at the landscape of his past and of his unknown future. Pope John Paul II had asked him to head the sensitive agency, and Thuan asked God to help him in his new role.

On July 1, 1998, just a few days after his appointment, Thuan addressed the World Congress on Pastoral Ministry for Human Rights at the Vatican. He took the opportunity to thank his friend and predecessor, Cardinal Etchegaray, for his leadership and efforts during his fourteen years at the head of the council. Then Thuan spoke about his surprise at his own appointment: "How did I come to this council of sages—me, a former prisoner from a country that has suffered over thirty years of war?"

He explained what he saw as the responsibilities of the Church and specifically of the Council for Justice and Peace, "The world in which we live has become a village. The Church cannot remain indifferent to war, concentration camps, massacres, racism, injustice, and discrimination toward ethnic minorities. She fights against discrimination against women, child labor, and restrictions on religious freedom. She works with all her strength to promote the civilization of life and love."

Thuan continued to work on an issue that the Council for Justice and Peace had been tackling vigorously: the international debt of developing countries. Thuan and his chief assistants viewed the debts as one of the greatest impediments to the growth and development of these countries. They contended that debt relief was one method that the industrialized world could adopt to help resolve the problem of underdevelopment. The Council also promoted debt relief for countries suffering from natural disasters.

On November 18, 1998, Thuan appealed for debt relief in favor of the countries in Central America devastated by Hurricane Mitch. Thuan thanked several countries who had "put forward new proposals regarding writing off the foreign debt of these countries." He called upon all countries "to urgently apply practical measures for the timely and definitive solution to the foreign debt" in Central America.

But Thuan also reminded leaders in Central America of their responsibilities: "An appeal is made to everyone—to leaders of the countries which were hit, and to donor countries—to commit themselves not simply to rebuilding former situations, but rather to building a more just and participatory society, with sustainable agricultural projects and social infrastructures, which better correspond to the just human aspirations of peoples."

Thuan spoke with the intensity of one who had personally experienced the devastation left in the aftermath of natural disasters, because of the frequent typhoons and floods that afflict Central Vietnam.

Early in 1999 Pope John Paul II approached Thuan and asked him to coordinate a vast effort to write and present for his approval a catechism or *Compendium of the Social Doctrine of the Church*. Though the pope originally thought the project could be completed in eighteen months and published during the Jubilee Year 2000, it was an enormous undertaking and still remains to be completed.

With the effective assistance of Bishop Martin, Monsignor Crepaldi, and experts who came from all over the world, Thuan developed the plan and central themes of the *Compendium*. Experts who had written any significant works or essays dealing with the various aspects of Catholic social doctrine were asked to send them to the Vatican. Once these were assembled, they were studied, cross-referenced, and used as materials for discussion on the contents of the *Compendium*.

Four writers drew up the first draft in four different languages. The interaction among the writers was miraculously good and the drafting process smooth. By the fall of 1999 Thuan entrusted Monsignor Crepaldi with drafting the first Italian text.

At the European Synod on October 7, 1999, Thuan announced that he would consult bishops from around the world concerning the contents of the *Compendium*, and that the work would be ready by May of 2000. Thuan called the future *Compendium* "a privileged instrument of dialogue with a new society" and "a means of evangelization."

By March 2000 Monsignor Crepaldi had finished and presented his first text, which was submitted for discussion and further comments. A second version was completed by May 2000 and was again submitted for scrutiny. But contributions from other agencies of the Roman Curia and bishops from around the world made it impossible to complete a final text during the Jubilee Year 2000.

Thuan and Monsignor Crepaldi continued to work on the text, constantly encouraged by the importance Pope John Paul II attached to its completion and dissemination. Thuan had long ceased regretting the missed publication date of the jubilee year. He knew that the continuous flow of commentaries and suggested additions showed how much the document interested bishops and experts around the world and would ultimately enrich the final version.

<hr/>

AS STORIES OF HIS ORDEAL SPREAD, Thuan had become a household name in many countries, and wherever he traveled he drew a crowd. His books were read not only by Catholics, but by people of different faiths.

On June 9, 1999, French Ambassador Jean Gueguinou bestowed on Thuan the insignia of Commander of the Order of National Merit at Villa Bonaparte. In his acceptance speech, Thuan took the opportunity to describe his cultural heritage of stone, paper, and breath. He described how attached he had been to the values that had inspired his parents, grandparents, and more distant forebears. He also explained how he appreciated the pre-Christian values in Confucianism and in the veneration of ancestors. He professed his great love for the traditional culture of his country.

Thuan had come to the height of his mental powers and he expressed himself more originally and with greater ease. At the same time he began to apply himself to discovering the most effective expression for his spirituality.

The beatification of Dom Colomba Marmion by Pope John Paul II was a further sign for Thuan to find new ways to communicate his own spirituality to others. Thuan had always loved Dom Marmion's writings and knew that millions of readers had benefited from his spirituality. Thuan wanted to emulate the great Benedictine abbot.

On December 5, 1999, Thuan was astonished when John Paul II asked him to preach the yearly Lenten Spiritual Exercises for him and the Roman Curia. No bishop from Asia had ever been offered the honor. Thuan hesitated as he considered his inadequacies, but Pope John Paul II reassured him and asked if he had a theme in mind. Thuan suggested that he speak about hope. The pope approved and asked Thuan to present his own testimony.

CHAPTER TWENTY-EIGHT

The Dream Goes On

One thing I ask of the LORD,
that will I seek after:
to live in the house of the LORD
all the days of my life.

Psalm 27:4

Action alone cannot transform the world.
It is thought that transforms the world,
because it is thought that guides action.

The Road of Hope,
F. X. Nguyen Van Thuan

THE YEAR 2000 PROMISED TO BE a magnificent Jubilee. Like all the leaders of the Curia, Thuan had been preparing for it feverishly since 1997. Yet, like the pope and other Church leaders, including Cardinal Etchegaray, Thuan knew all the celebrations would be useless if men, women, and children throughout the world did not see improvement in their material, social, and spiritual lives. If peace and reconciliation did not return to war-ravaged countries, if abject poverty continued to be the lot of entire nations, if social justice remained an inaccessible dream, then the Jubilee Year and its celebrations would make no sense.

As the Great Jubilee approached, Thuan thanked God for having allowed him to be in Rome, at the center of the celebrations, to witness the fervor of the Universal Church as she entered the Third Millennium.

On Christmas night 1999 Thuan attended the ceremony of the opening of the Holy Door at Saint Peter's Basilica. He watched Pope John Paul II being helped to his knees and then as he crossed the threshold of the central door. Thuan thought of the words in the Bull of Indiction of the Great Jubilee of the Year 2000, *Incarnationis Mysterium:* "Crossing its threshold, he will show to the Church and to the world the Holy Gospel, the wellspring of life and hope for the coming Third Millennium."

Thuan was witnessing history in the making; he was a part of that history. He looked around at people from all over the world and from all walks of life who filled Saint Peter's Square. They were all there with the Holy Father for one of the most memorable moments in their lifetime. Thuan felt overwhelmed with the great miracle God had granted him by sparing his life and plucking him out of Vietnam so that he could be a part of that ceremony.

From January 3–12, 2000, Thuan attended the Seventh Plenary Assembly of Asian Bishops in Samphran, Thailand. There, at the Baan Phu Waan Center, Thuan met with five cardinals, ninety bishops, seventy priests and religious, and thirty-five lay people to celebrate the Third Millennium and to discuss the future of the Church in Asia with the theme: "A Renewed Church in Asia: A Mission of Love and Service."

Thuan did not see this gathering as simply an opportunity to meet old friends, speak with the Vietnamese bishops, and be steeped in an Asian atmosphere. It was an important historical moment. Thuan rejoiced in the progress that the Church in Asia had made since the first Plenary Assembly of 1970.

He enjoyed the warm accolades of the participants who were glad to see the Asian Archbishops Hamao and Thuan heading two important Pontifical Councils in the Vatican. But he drew much greater joy from the fact that the Church in Asia continued to record a high number of vocations and conversions, that a new breed of Asian theologians was contributing to the wealth of contemporary theological thought, and that the stability of the Asian family continued to be a model for families around the world.

In Thailand Thuan worked day and night on the sermons he would preach to the Roman Curia. Though he had finished the drafts of some of the twenty-two meditations of the spiritual exercises, he hesitated to put a definitive stamp on any of them. One evening, as he worked late into the night, Thuan looked up at his desk calendar. The beginning of the spiritual exercises was not far off. Suddenly, Thuan was flooded with a complete understanding of what he would say. It was clear that Thuan had only to write as fast as he could the words that tumbled from his mind. Thuan wrote until he was completely exhausted, but he was ready.

The members of the Curia had spent three years preparing their minds and hearts for the Jubilee. But once inside the Chapel of the Mother of the Redeemer, as they gathered for their spiritual exercises, they cast aside all other preoccupations and listened to Thuan. His was an audience open and attentive to his words.

Thuan opened the series of retreat meditations with simplicity and closed them without fanfare. He bared his soul to Pope John Paul II and the Roman curia. In his talks Thuan included stories about himself, a man who, only a few years earlier, had been held captive in Communist prisons; a man who was nothing without God's grace, and God's grace had been powerfully with him. He heard the echo of John Paul II's words, "Do not be afraid" as he stood before his audience stripped of all pride and pretense. Thuan spoke to them from his heart and shared the treasures God had placed there.

The spiritual exercises ended on March 19, 2000, the feast of St. Joseph. Thuan noted that it was also the twenty-fourth anniversary of the beginning of his captivity. On March 19, 1976, he had been taken to the Phu Khanh Prison Camp and placed in solitary confinement. He remarked that his successor, Bishop Nguyen Van Hoa, had chosen March 19, 2000, to consecrate the new church in Cay Vong.

At the conclusion of the Spiritual Exercises, John Paul II said, "With simplicity and the breath of divine inspiration, he [Thuan] has guided us in deepening our vocation of witnessing to evangelical hope at the beginning of the Third Millennium. A witness of the cross in his long years of imprisonment in Vietnam, he has frequently recounted the realities and episodes from his sufferings in prison, thus reinforcing in us the consoling certainty that when everything crumbles around us, and perhaps even within us, Christ remains our unfailing support."

John Paul II encouraged Thuan to publish his series of meditations, as they might "help many people." Published on June 8, 2000, in Italian, *Testimony of Hope* was soon translated into more than a dozen languages.

As THUAN CONTINUED ATTEMPTING to better understand and express his own spirituality, he chanced upon an article on John Paul II's spirituality from a press release on the pope's address to the Eighth International Mariological Colloquium (October 13, 2000). There was nothing startlingly new there. Yet, the article helped Thuan to see how closely his own spiritual growth paralleled the pope's.

Thuan's devotion to the Blessed Virgin Mary had begun as a child. As he grew, his reading of Louis Marie Grignon de Montfort's writings clarified the meaning of "true devotion to Mary." Now Thuan read with tender emotion the pope's use of the very words he had so often quoted from de Montfort:

"Then I understood that I could not exclude the Lord's Mother from my life without neglecting the will of God-Trinity, who willed to begin and fulfill the great mysteries of the history of salvation with the responsible and faithful collaboration of the humble handmaid of Nazareth."

Thuan appreciated more the natural attraction that Pope John Paul II had always exerted on him as a teacher and a leader. He also better understood the pope's strength in the face of adversity. John Paul II had entrusted his life and work to Mary, and from her he had drawn the indomitable courage he had shown throughout his pontificate. This man, whom Thuan admired and loved as a friend, was about to surprise him with another personal sign of his trust.

CHAPTER TWENTY-NINE

The New Cardinal

Your hands have made and fashioned me;
give me understanding that I may learn your
commandments.

Psalm 119:73

If you lead a life of faith, you will see events with the eyes
of Jesus and you will perceive their eternal dimensions.

The Road of Hope,
F. X. Nguyen Van Thuan

THUAN ALWAYS LIVED HIS LIFE "filled to the brim with love." Every moment of every day counted. To wait for certain honors or positions to come one's way was a waste of time, because every moment offered an opportunity to accomplish God's will, to do God's work, and to love God more. Thuan did not waste time seeking positions; he worked diligently, efficiently, and calmly.

As in any human organization, the Vatican abounds with rumors, but Thuan always succeeded in avoiding the gossip mongers. Thus, on Friday, January 19, 2001, he was genuinely surprised when Pope John Paul II called to personally congratulate him on his elevation to the College of Cardinals. Thuan's first thought was that Vietnam would have two cardinals—Cardinal Pham Dinh Tung, the archbishop of Hanoi, had joined the College in 1994.

Later that same day the pope's words were confirmed by mail. Thuan left his office and went back to his apartment to pray in his private chapel. In the quiet of the chapel Thuan reflected on his priesthood and wondered if he would be able to continue his work as before.

Now his life would be even more firmly bound to Rome. He would have to participate in more Pontifical Councils and Congregations; there would be more meetings and events to attend. He would have to reduce his heavy travel schedule to the remote places of the world.

On January 21, 2001, from his window overlooking Saint Peter's Square, Pope John Paul II declared to the crowd gathered below: "I have the joy to announce that on February 21, the Feast of the Chair of St. Peter, I will hold a consistory in which, breaking yet again the numerical limit set by Pope Paul VI, I will nominate thirty-seven new cardinals.... Here are their names...." The pope went on to name the new cardinals one by one; Thuan's name was second on the list.

Afterward, Thuan's telephone rang continuously with congratulatory calls, but with his usual humility he refused to be impressed by his own appointment. When one friend exclaimed, "You must be so happy to have been chosen by the Pope for this honor!" Thuan instantly replied, "But I was already happy!"

Thuan prepared himself for yet another transition. For the first time he truly grasped the Lord's words *Omnia mea tua sunt:* All those who are mine, are yours. Thuan entrusted all those he loved and cared for to God, and felt that God was entrusting to him the care of all his people. He shared in a most intimate way the pope's dreams and concerns for all of God's people.

Thuan felt keenly how much he still needed to see and think more globally. He resolved from that moment to consider everything from the perspective of humanity's history and that of the Church. Above all else, Thuan desired to make greater progress in his spiritual life. He still faced challenges in what he saw as a need to purify his soul—and he knew these would remain with him until death.

As he faced the transition that was bound to occur when he became a Cardinal, Thuan paused to look back over his past, his priesthood, his studies in Rome, the call to suffer that he had felt at the grotto of Lourdes, the tragic events in his family, his episcopal ordination.... He recalled, with vivid detail, South Vietnam's fall and his arrest and captivity. He had long ceased to shudder at the memory of being locked in his cell and the struggle to survive and remain sane. He felt no bitterness when he thought about his exile. He was grateful for the years he had spent working in the Council for Justice and Peace.

What words could he offer to God, who had sent him from East Asia to Rome, and who had gradually elevated him to the place where he now stood? He could say nothing beyond: "Thank you, Father." In the evening quiet of his apartment, Thuan gazed up at the statue of the Blessed Virgin Mary and slowly prayed the *Salve Regina,* the prayer he had so often sung aloud within the confines of his prison cell.

◆◈◆

AT THE CHURCH OF SAINT MARTHA, as Thuan prepared for the consistory of February 21, 2001, he received news from his physicians. Recent tests showed that he had serious gastrointestinal complications that would require surgery.

Thuan laughed and said, "I have never received a good gift without a bad one." He felt very tired from the preparations for the ceremony of his incardination and the arrival of visitors, friends, and family members from all over the world. But Thuan kept smiling and showing his gratitude to the hundreds of well-wishers.

On the day of his incardination, Thuan knelt before Pope John Paul II and, with great emotion, received the red zucchetto and the biretta from him. The pope said: "To the glory of God Almighty, receive the red biretta as a sign of the dignity of a cardinal, as a reminder that you must be ready to act with renewed vigor, up to the point of shedding your own blood, for the growth of the Christian faith."

Thuan repeated silently, "To the point of shedding my own blood for the growth of the Christian faith...." In his heart, he felt he had responded to that call years before.

He had become a cardinal, a member of the College of Cardinals, whose task was to advise the pope on the exercise of his universal mission as the Successor of Peter. He would be the pope's helper, councilor, and his friend. With the other cardinals, he would be the pope's eyes, ears, and voice around the world. Yet, Thuan did not feel that he had "advanced in rank"; he had merely been given a few more responsibilities. From now on he would live and work full time in direct service to the Successor of Peter.

Not long after the Consistory, Thuan traveled to Sydney to be with his mother. Someone asked her, in Thuan's presence, if she was proud of her son's elevation. "I have always been proud of him," Hiep replied. "To be a cardinal, or an archbishop, or a priest means nearly the same thing. He has to serve God to the best of his ability. If by his elevation to the College of Cardinals the name of God is further glorified, then of course I am happy."

Hiep also teased Thuan. "A long time ago you said that only a miracle would make the leaders in Hanoi change their minds and allow you to return to Vietnam. Now I hear them declaring publicly that you can visit Vietnam any time you wish. Does that mean your miracle has taken place?"

Thuan shook his head. Indeed, government officials had conceded that Thuan could return to Vietnam, but like any other overseas Vietnamese, his visa application could be denied. Thuan did not believe the government would ever actually approve his entry visa, but he accepted this without resentment. Besides, he had no time to go to Vietnam at the moment.

In April of 2001 Thuan flew to Boston three days before Easter. He spent the Easter Triduum in prayer and, on April 17, his seventy-third birthday, Thuan underwent a six-hour surgical procedure at Boston's Saint Elizabeth's Hospital. Unfortunately, the procedure was not entirely successful. He spent two months convalescing in Boston before returning to Rome.

Thuan was not well, but he did not cut back on his work or travels. Then, as he earnestly resumed his work at the Vatican, the events of September 11, 2001, shook the world. Thuan was distraught by the haunting images he had seen of the collapse of the Twin Towers in New York. He spent hours praying over the event in his private chapel.

Thuan had often witnessed the ugliness of terrorism in Vietnam and the vulnerability of society to terrorist attacks. He knew how little one could do to shield oneself against the havoc perpetrated by determined and crazed terrorists. Still, the subsequent "war on terrorism" filled Thuan with misgivings. The fall of Afghanistan's Taliban regime did not take as long as Thuan had initially thought, and he thanked God that the military action had been brief. But the end of the war existed somewhere beyond the horizon, and the talk of other target nations distressed him. Thuan believed any war has the potential to expand and escalate; any violence calls for more violence.

On December 11 Thuan presented Pope John Paul II's message for the Thirty-Fourth World Day of Peace (January 1, 2002): "There Is No Peace without Justice; There Is No Justice without Forgiveness." From the beginning of his message the Holy Father wished to emphasize the element of hope: The shadows of evil are never sufficient to obscure the light of divine providence; on the contrary, they enhance it, and, therefore, the Church looks with unshakable faith toward the new year of 2002, despite the terrible actions of September 11.

In the speech Thuan related that John Paul II was moved to personal testimony, recalling the "inhuman sufferings" caused by the totalitarianisms of the past century, and expressing his deep conviction that the way to restore order in the world is through justice and peace.

Thuan found himself in complete accord with the pope's heartfelt sentiments.

EPILOGUE

Whoever observes the wind will not sow;
and whoever regards the clouds will not reap.

Ecclesiastes 11:4

When you live with your faith, you borrow Christ's eyes,
and discover in each event a dimension of eternity.

The Road of Hope,
F. X. Nguyen Van Thuan

AFTER HIS SURGERY IN BOSTON, Cardinal Thuan struggled with serious health problems for over a year, but he faced his future without fear or anxiety because he believed that it was of little importance whether God allowed him many or few years to do God's work. What mattered was to welcome whatever happened to him as God's will.

There was no trace of sadness or bitterness in Thuan because of his illness; neither was there any added urgency. He was so attuned to God's will that he did not feel the need to rush to finish anything or to leave a tidy, gift-wrapped "legacy." He continued to live one day at a time, exactly as he lived his thirteen years of captivity. He had long traveled the road that leads to the ultimate face-to-face encounter with God, counting every step made, and thanking God for the great gift of life. Thuan found joy in every passing moment as he walked toward the plenitude of the promise of eternal life.

The only thing that saddened him was the widening scandal of priests who had sinned and committed terrible sexual crimes against children. But he firmly believed that the scandal *had* to be made public, saying, "A public scandal is far better than sweeping sins and crimes under the rug." Thuan believed that, despite the pain involved, the scandal would lead to the purification and then the sanctification and healing of the Church. He believed that just as in other times of scandal, the Church would find in the present one a great opportunity for renewal.

Even in his last months, Thuan continued to be an innovator and his spirituality continued to expand in many directions. Thuan wanted his "political spirituality," the most difficult part of his spirituality to grasp, to become part of the core of his message. He believed that when God is present in political decisions and when God's will underpins a nation's political efforts, the result will be great benefits for a nation and its citizens.

In a homily Thuan gave in Milan at a commemorative service on the anniversary of former Italian Prime Minister Amintore Fanfani's death, Thuan offered what he called "The Beatitudes for Political Leaders":

Blessed is the political leader who understands his role in the world.

Blessed is the political leader who personally exemplifies credibility.

Blessed is the political leader who works for the common good and not for his personal interests.

Blessed is the political leader who is true to himself, his faith, and his electoral promises.

Blessed is the political leader who works for unity and makes Jesus the fulcrum of its defense.

Blessed is the political leader who works for radical change, refuses to call that which is evil, good, and uses the Gospel as a guide.

Blessed is the political leader who listens to the people before, during, and after elections, and who always listens to God in prayer.

Blessed is the political leader who has no fear of the truth or the mass media, because at the time of judgment he will answer to God alone and not the crowds or the media.

Thuan's life-teachings continue. His writings, which began simply as a stone thrown into the middle of a calm lake, have created ripples that continue to move out, expanding around the world. Through his many books, translated into numerous languages, Thuan has touched the minds and hearts of so many people. Thuan's name has found its way into the homilies of priests and bishops around the world, as well as onto thousands of websites.

The man who once lived behind bars in solitary confinement became a miracle of undefeated hope. A revered teacher of God's word and a simple yet demanding model for young people, Thuan endured sufferings in a way that inspires an enthusiasm to follow his example. The miracle of hope is being accomplished even now.

It is difficult to end a story that still continues through Thuan's rich legacy, but it is fitting to conclude this short and humble tribute to Thuan's life by quoting his own words:

> You have told me: walk with giant steps,
> go all over the world,
> proclaim the Good News,
> dry the tears of sorrow,
> reassure discouraged hearts,
> embrace the world with the ardor of your love,
> do away with what must be destroyed,
> leave only truth, justice, and love *(Five Loaves and Two Fish)*.

<hr />

I BEGAN WRITING THIS BIOGRAPHY when Cardinal Francis Xavier Nguyen Van Thuan was in good health. He suffered from a rare form of cancer from December 2000 to September 2002. He passed away on September 16, 2002, at 6:00 P.M. at Casa di Cura Pius XI in Rome. Chiara Lubich, the founder of the Focolare Movement, arrived shortly before his death to pray at his bedside. Though he could no longer respond, it seemed that he was conscious to the end.

He did not feel pain during the last few days of his life, though no painkillers were administered. He was at peace, his face serene.

On September 20, 2002, a Mass of Christian Burial was celebrated at St. Peter's Basilica by Secretary of State Cardinal Angelo Sodano, and presided over by Pope John Paul II. In his farewell homily, the pope recounted:

During the last days, when he could no longer speak, he fixed his gaze on the crucifix before him. He prayed in silence while he consummated his last sacrifice, crowning a life marked by *heroic configuration with Christ on the cross.*

Now that the Lord has tested him, as "gold in the crucible," and has accepted him "as a sacrificial burnt offering," we can truly say that "his hope was full of immortality" (cf. Wis 3:4–5). It was full of Christ, the life and resurrection of all who trust in him.

Like his life, Cardinal Van Thuan's death was indeed a testimony of hope. May his spiritual legacy, like his hope, be "full of immortality"!

He leaves us, but his example remains. Faith assures us that he is not dead but has entered into the eternal day, which knows no sunset.

GLOSSARY OF CHARACTERS

Admiral Jean Decoux—French Governor-General of French Indochina 1940–1945.

Andre Nguyen van Tich—A diocesan priest and professor at An Ninh Minor Seminary, he succeeded Fr. Jean-Baptiste Urrutia as rector.

Aunt Hoa—Daughter of Nguyen Huu Bai (Duke of Phuoc Mon), married to Ngo Dinh Khoi.

Aunt Lien—Ngo Dinh Kha's cousin, who was one of the few members of the Ngo Dinh family to survive the *van than* raid on the Catholics of Dai Phong in 1885.

Benoit Nguyen van Thai—First Vietnamese Benedictine priest in the monastery of Thien An, which Thuan visited regularly during his first year at the major seminary.

Bishop Claudio Maria Celli—As Undersecretary for Affairs of State, in 1992 met with Communist officials in Rome to discuss the possibility of Thuan's return to Vietnam.

Bishop Diarmuid Martin—Undersecretary and then Secretary of the Council for Justice and Peace. He was later made archbishop and head of the Holy See Mission near the United Nations in Geneva.

Bishop Giampaolo Crepaldi—Undersecretary of the Council for Justice and Peace, then Secretary of the Council under Thuan.

Bishop Jean-Baptiste Urrutia (1901–1979)—Member of Paris Foreign Mission Society, rector of An Ninh Minor Seminary, made bishop of Hue in 1948.

Bishop Paul Josef Cordes—Vice-President of the Pontifical Council for the Laity, and then President of the Pontifical Council *Cor Unum*.

Cardinal Agostino Casaroli (1914–1988)—Secretary of State of the Holy See 1979–1990.

Cardinal Joseph Marie Trinh van Can (1921–1990)—Archbishop of Hanoi from whom Thuan received permission to hear the confessions of the Catholics in Giang Xa, who had been excommunicated for being Communist agents.

Cardinal Paul-Joseph Pham Dinh Tung (1919–)—Bishop of Bac Ninh 1963, under house arrest 1963–1990, made Archbishop of Hanoi 1994.

Cardinal Roger Etchegaray (1922–)—President of the Pontifical Council for Justice and Peace and Pontifical Council *Cor Unum* 1984–1998.

Chiang Kai-shek (1887–1975)—(Jiang Jie-shi) Political and military leader of China who served as leader of the Nationalist Party. Led efforts to defeat Chinese Communists, and fought Japanese aggression during World War II. From 1947 to 1949, Nationalist troops under his command suffered one defeat after another and the Communists gained control of all continental China. Chiang Kai-shek withdrew to Taiwan.

Colonel Nguyen Hong Lam—High-ranking official in the Ministry of the Interior in charge of religious affairs prior to and at the time of Thuan's exile.

Colonel Thuyen—Member of the National Liberation Front, accused of corruption and sent to Thanh Liet Prison. Was held in the same cell with Thuan in 1978.

Elbridge Durbrow (1903–1997)—U. S. Ambassador to South Vietnam 1957–1961.

Elizabeth Ngo Dinh thi Hiep—Daughter of Ngo Dinh Kha and Thuan's mother.

Ellsworth Bunker (1884–1984)—U.S. Ambassador to South Vietnam 1967–1973.

Emile Grandjean—French Resident Superior in Hue, who forced Ngo Dinh Khoi to resign as governor of Quang Nam and Viceroy of the Southern provinces.

Emperor (Nguyen Anh) Gia Long (1761–1820)—the first of the Nguyen emperors of Vietnam and founder of the Nguyen Dynasty (listed below according to reign):

> Gia Long (1802–1820)
> Minh Mang (1820–1841)
> Thieu Tri (1841–1848)
> Tu Duc (1848–1883)
> Duc Duc (1883)
> Hiep Hoa (1883)

Kien Phuc (1883–1884)
Ham Nghi (1884–1885)
Dong Khanh (1885–1889)
Thanh Thai (1889–1907)
Duy Tan (1907–1916)
Khai Dinh (1916–1925)
Bao Dai (1925–1945, and as the Chief of State 1949–1955)

Emperor Bao Dai (1913–1997)—The last monarch to reign over modern Vietnam. In 1926, he became emperor at age thirteen, inheriting the nominal authority the French allowed. In 1945, the Viet Minh forced Emperor Bao Dai to abdicate. He was restored to power as Chief of State in 1949, and, in 1955, was ousted by a referendum.

Emperor Duy Tan (1894–1945)—Ascended the throne at the age of seven. The child-emperor planned an unsuccessful rebellion and was exiled on November 3, 1916.

Emperor Ham Nghi—Fourteen-year-old Ham Nghi succeeded Emperor Kien Phuc. He was forced to flee to the mountains after an attack on French positions in Hue in 1885. Ham Nghi was captured by the French in 1888 and sent into exile.

Emperor Khai Dinh—Enthroned on May 18, 1916, Khai Dinh's reign was openly criticized by revolutionary leaders, one of whom would later become known as Ho Chi Minh. Khai Dinh reigned until his death in 1925.

Emperor Minh Mang (1791–1841)—Succeeded his father, Gia Long. Suspicious of Western missionaries, he prohibited the practice of Christianity in Vietnam and initiated persecutions.

Emperor Quang Trung (1753?–1792)—Nguyen Hue, the brightest of the three brothers who rebelled against the Nguyen Dynasty, and, for a short time, established the Tay Son Dynasty. Declared himself the Quang Trung Emperor in 1788 and defeated Chinese armies sent to North Vietnam by the Qing Emperor. Emperor Quang Trung died in 1792. His son, Emperor Quang Toan, was defeated and executed by Gia Long in 1802.

Emperor Thanh Thai—Succeeded Emperor Dong Khanh. Open to Western ideas and culture, Thanh Thai encouraged French-style education, but worked toward Vietnamese autonomy. Arrested by the French and forced to abdicate in 1907, he was sent into exile. In 1945, he returned to Vietnam, but was not allowed to return to Hue. He died in Saigon on March 24, 1954.

Emperor Tu Duc (1829–1883)—The fourth of the thirteen Nguyen emperors, Tu Duc began his rule as the French became increasingly aggressive in Indochina. In his lifetime, Tu Duc witnessed the beginning of the French conquest of his country.

Father Danh—Professor of moral theology at Phu Xuan Major Seminary.

Father Dau—Taught fundamental theology and philosophy at Phu Xuan Major Seminary and became its rector after Father (later Bishop) Simon Hoa Nguyen van Hien.

Father Joseph Eugène Marie Allys (1875–1936)—Made bishop of Hue in 1908.

Father Joseph Marie Nguyen van Thich—Professor at the An Ninh Minor Seminary, taught Chinese and Chinese classics. He was also a poet who published a very popular monthly magazine, "For God" (Vi Chua).

Father Léopold Michael Cadière (1869–1955)—Member of Paris Foreign Mission Society and professor at An Ninh Minor Seminary, a respected scholar and scientist.

Father Marie-Georges Cressonnier—Member of Paris Foreign Mission Society, professor at An Ninh Minor Seminary, killed in the 1968 Viet Minh Tet Mau Than Offensive while ministering to the sick and injured.

Father Tam—Pastor of Tam Toa parish in the city of Dong Hoi where Thuan first served as an assistant pastor after his ordination.

Frederick E. Nolting, Jr. (1911–1989)—U.S. Ambassador to South Vietnam 1961–1963.

General Jacque Philippe Leclerc—French troops arrived in Saigon on October 1945 under his command to begin the re-conquest of South Vietnam.

Han Mac Tu—Significant Vietnamese Catholic poet.

Henry Cabot Lodge (1902–1985)—U.S. Ambassador to South Vietnam for two consecutive terms (1963–1964, then 1965–1967).

Ho Chi Minh (1890–1969)—(Other names: Nguyen Tat Thanh, Nguyen Ai Quoc) One of the founders of the Viet Minh (Vietnam Independence League) which was dominated by the Communists. He proclaimed the Democratic Republic of Vietnam (DRV) in August 1945, and led the war against the French (First Indochina War). Vietnam was partitioned after 1954 with Ho Chi Minh as the President in the North and Ngo Dinh Diem as the Premier, then President in the South. In 1959, Ho Chi Minh launched the Second Indochina War that ended with the fall of Saigon in April 1975.

Huynh Dinh Trong—Residential advisor under President Nguyen van Thieu.

Huynh van Cao—Lt. General in the army of the Republic of South Vietnam and commander of IV Corps in the Mekong Delta in 1963.

Le Quang Vinh—Hoa Hao general and warlord, defeated, captured, and executed under Diem.

Le van Vien—General and warlord who controlled Saigon, Cho Lon, and the national police. Defeated by Diem, Vien fled to France.

Madame Nhu (Le Xuan)—Daughter of Tran van Chuong, married to Ngo Dinh Nhu. Her sharp words during the Buddhist crisis in 1963 inflamed the international press and the Buddhists.

Mai Chi Tho—Hanoi Minister of the Interior who released Thuan from prison in 1988.

Ngo Dinh Can—Thuan's uncle who, following Diem's overthrow, was imprisoned, tried, and executed on May 8, 1964.

Ngo Dinh Diem—Thuan's uncle who was Prime Minister for a time and then President of South Vietnam. He was assassinated following the 1963 coup.

Ngo Dinh thi Giao—Thuan's aunt.

Ngo Dinh thi Hoang—Thuan's aunt.

Ngo Dinh Huan—Thuan's cousin who was killed with Ngo Dinh Khoi, his father, by the Viet Minh in 1945.

Ngo Dinh Kha—Thuan's grandfather who, under Emperor Thanh Thai, served as Grand Chamberlain, Palace Marshal, Commander of the Imperial Guards, Great Scholar Assistant to the Throne, and Imperial Tutor. His dream for the independence of Vietnam inspired all his children's lives.

Ngo Dinh Khoi—Thuan's uncle who became governor of Hoi An in Central Vietnam, and was forced by the French to resign in 1943 because of his close association with his brother, Diem.

Ngo Dinh Luyen—Thuan's uncle who was forced to remain in exile following the 1963 coup.

Ngo Dinh Nhu—Thuan's uncle who was Diem's chief presidential advisor. He escaped the Presidential Palace with Diem during the 1963 coup, and they were later assassinated together.

Ngo Dinh Thuc—Thuan's uncle who became bishop of Vinh Long, then archbishop of Hue.

Nguyen Huu Bai—Duke of Phuoc Mon and Minister under Emperor Thanh Thai, he was a close friend of Thuan's grandfather, Ngo Dinh Kha.

Nguyen Tu Ha—Official of the Ministry of the Interior from Hanoi who followed Thuan's "case" from his initial arrest to his exile.

Nguyen van Am—Thuan's father.

Nguyen van Anh Tuyet—Thuan's sister.

Nguyen van Binh—Archbishop of Saigon. Thuan was named his coadjutor in 1975.

Nguyen van Danh—Thuan's paternal great-grandfather.

Nguyen van Ham Tien—Thuan's sister.

Nguyen van Hinh—General and Army Chief of Staff under Bao Dai. He opposed Diem and was eventually exiled to France.

Nguyen van Hoa—Succeeded Thuan as bishop of the diocese of Nha Trang.

Nguyen van Niem—Thuan's oldest sister.

Nguyen van Thanh—Thuan's brother.

Nguyen van Thieu—President of South Vietnam 1967–1975.

Nguyen van Thu Hong—Thuan's sister.

Nguyen van Thuy Tien—Thuan's sister.

Nguyen van Tuyen—Thuan's brother.

Nguyen van Vong—Thuan's paternal grandfather.

Paul Tong Viet Buong—Tong thi Tai's relative, a military commander martyred under Emperor Minh Mang on October 23, 1833; beatified by Pope Leo XIII on May 27, 1900; and canonized by Pope John Paul II on June 19, 1988.

Pham thi Than—Married Ngo Dinh Kha and was Thuan's grandmother.

Pham van Dong—One of the founders of the Viet Minh movement and close friend of Ho Chi Minh.

Pham Quynh—Head of the cabinet government under Emperor Bao Dai who resigned upon the emperor's request; executed under the Viet Minh in 1945.

Prince Buu Loc—Prime Minister, who resigned on June 16, 1954 and was replaced by Diem.

Prince Cuong De—Member of the Nguyen royal house who helped to form a base for revolutionary activities in Japan.

Quang—A young boy in Cay Vong who, with his family, helped Archbishop Thuan while he was under house arrest to smuggle out brief messages to Catholics. These were later collected and published in *The Road of Hope*.

Simon Hoa Nguyen van Hien—Rector of Phu Xuan Major Seminary where he taught dogmatic theology. He became the bishop of Saigon and Dalat in 1960.

Thich Tri Quang—Monk and leader of Buddhist movement in South Vietnam that protested President Diem's government through organized public demonstrations, hunger strikes, and the self-immolations. After Diem's assassination, he used the same methods to protest against Generals Nguyen Cao Ky and Nguyen Khanh. However, this time, without the support of the international press, his protests were vain. He was rumored to be in forced residence by the Communists after 1975.

Tong thi Tai—Married to Thuan's paternal grandfather.

Tran Trong Kim—Historian who was named prime minister by Emperor Bao Dai to replace Pham Quynh; resigned two weeks later on August 5, 1945.

Tran van Ly—Set up a provisory administration to govern Central Vietnam after the French drove out Viet Minh troops from Hue.

Tran van Soai—One of the Hoa Hao warlords.

Trung Sisters—Trung Trac and Trung Nhi led a rebellion against the Chinese about A.D. 39–40, temporarily ending China's domination.

Vo Nguyen Giap—Viet Minh minister of defense who ordered the general offensive against the French in December 1946.

Vu Quang—Chairman of the Communist's Religious Committee sent to Rome with a delegation in 1992 for a meeting with Vatican officials to discuss the possibility of Thuan's return to Vietnam.

A note regarding Vietnamese names

Vietnamese personal names are usually composed of three elements. The first word is the family or clan name: Nguyen, Tran, Le, etc. The second word is usually the middle name, such as Van, Dinh, Huu, Trung, Viet, etc. Formerly, for females the second word was thi, which means "of the clan of"; for example, Tran thi Xuan means Xuan of the Tran clan. Sometimes the second word is the name of the mother's clan, for example Nguyen Tran Kiet means Kiet whose father's clan is Nguyen and whose mother's clan is Tran. More recently, however, many have dropped the thi in female names, so a girl may be named Nguyen Phuong Chi rather than Nguyen thi Phuong Chi.

Male members of the same clan or sub-clan may have different second names. In large clans, the second name is used as a discriminator for sub-clans; for example, Nguyen Bang may have three sons: Nguyen qui Than, Nguyen tuong Phach, and Nguyen khoa Lan. The male members of the three sub-clans may retain the second name for generations.

The third word in a Vietnamese name is most often the given name. More and more Vietnamese give their children a two-word given name, especially for girls; for example, Nguyen thi Minh Kha, Nguyen thi Thu Hong. Names with four words are also becoming a frequent occurrence.

It is important to know that, unlike the Chinese, the Vietnamese never call a person by their family name. Father Nguyen van Tich would be called Father Tich, Bishop Nguyen van Hien would be called Bishop Hien. So, Cardinal Nguyen van Thuan would be called Cardinal Thuan, not Cardinal Nguyen.

Christians may place their Christian name before the family name; for example, Francis Xavier Nguyen van Thuan.

ABOUT THE AUTHOR

Andre Nguyen Van Chau was born in Hue, Vietnam. After obtaining a doctorate degree in humanities at the Sorbonne, Paris, he taught literature and creative writing at various universities in Vietnam for twelve years.

In 1975, he began twenty-five years of work for migrants and refugees around the world, ten of which were spent as the head of the International Catholic Migrations Commission with headquarters in Geneva, Switzerland.

In 2002, Mr. Van Chau was inducted into the Catholic Academy of Sciences.

He and his wife, Sagrario, have four children: Andrew, Boi-Lam, Michael, and Francis-Xavier; and six grandchildren: Katelyn, Drew, Geraldine, Alix, Noah, and Isabelle.

Books by
Francis Xavier Nguyen Van Thuan

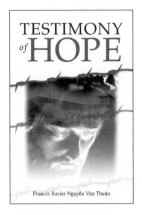

Testimony of Hope
Cardinal Francis Xavier Nguyen Van Thuan
Here is the complete text of the retreat preached by Cardinal Van Thuan to John Paul II and the Roman Curia. Enduring nine years in solitary confinement—Van Thuan faced what he describes as "the agonizing pain of isolation and abandonment." In these pages he shares the reality of hope he discovered through his pain.

paperback, 248pp. 12oz/360g
#7407-8 $15.95 ($25.95 Canada)

The Road of Hope
a gospel from prison
Cardinal Francis Xavier Nguyen Van Thuan
Faced with dire conditions aimed at breaking the human spirit, Van Thuan secretly wrote hope-filled notes to the people of his diocese. This holy man's simplicity and wisdom have inspired thousands to embrace life with a new faith.

paperback, 248pp. 12oz/360g
#6473-0 $15.95 ($25.95 Canada)

Prayers of Hope, Words of Courage
Cardinal Francis Xavier Nguyen Van Thuan
Imprisoned by a communist government for thirteen years, Cardinal Van Thuan sought meaning in the darkness of prison life. Written in the silence of his cell, these prayers and reflections resound with Christian hope and courage.

paperback, 144pp. 7oz/210g
#5938-9 $9.95 ($16.25 Canada)

Five Loaves and Two Fish
Cardinal Francis Xavier Nguyen Van Thuan
Five Loaves and Two Fish takes us on a spiritual journey with Cardinal Van Thuan as a guide, helping us to understand that God's grace gives us energy "to work and to go on, even in the most desperate moments."

paperback, 96pp. 4oz/120g
#2676-6 $8.95 ($14.50 Canada)

Pauline
BOOKS & MEDIA

www.pauline.org • USA 800-876-4463 • Canada 800-668-2078

Pauline
BOOKS & MEDIA

The Daughters of St. Paul operate book and media centers at the following addresses. Visit, call or write the one nearest you today, or find us on the World Wide Web, www.pauline.org

CALIFORNIA
3908 Sepulveda Blvd, Culver City, CA 90230   310-397-8676
5945 Balboa Avenue, San Diego, CA 92111   858-565-9181
46 Geary Street, San Francisco, CA 94108   415-781-5180

FLORIDA
145 S.W. 107th Avenue, Miami, FL 33174   305-559-6715

HAWAII
1143 Bishop Street, Honolulu, HI 96813   808-521-2731
Neighbor Islands call: 800-259-8463

ILLINOIS
172 North Michigan Avenue, Chicago, IL 60601   312-346-4228

LOUISIANA
4403 Veterans Memorial Blvd, Metairie, LA 70006   504-887-7631

MASSACHUSETTS
885 Providence Hwy, Dedham, MA 02026   781-326-5385

MISSOURI
9804 Watson Road, St. Louis, MO 63126   314-965-3512

NEW JERSEY
561 U.S. Route 1, Wick Plaza, Edison, NJ 08817   732-572-1200

NEW YORK
150 East 52nd Street, New York, NY 10022   212-754-1110
78 Fort Place, Staten Island, NY 10301   718-447-5071

PENNSYLVANIA
9171-A Roosevelt Blvd, Philadelphia, PA 19114   215-676-9494

SOUTH CAROLINA
243 King Street, Charleston, SC 29401   843-577-0175

TENNESSEE
4811 Poplar Avenue, Memphis, TN 38117   901-761-2987

TEXAS
114 Main Plaza, San Antonio, TX 78205   210-224-8101

VIRGINIA
1025 King Street, Alexandria, VA 22314   703-549-3806

CANADA
3022 Dufferin Street, Toronto, Ontario, Canada M6B 3T5
  416-781-9131
1155 Yonge Street, Toronto, Ontario, Canada M4T 1W2
416-934-3440

¡También somos su fuente para libros, videos y música en español!